ON THE RUN IN FONTAINEBLEAU

JOGGING THROUGH RETIREMENT IN FRANCE

CHRISTOPHER VANIER

ISBN 978-1-081516-39-0

Cover photo: Mylène Gallou.

Cover design: Korongo Books.

ALSO BY CHRISTOPHER VANIER

∽

Caribbean Chemistry

∽

Heart-warming and hilarious tales of Chris's youth
on the emerald island of St. Kitts

ACKNOWLEDGMENTS

A memoir depends on many people besides the author for its existence. First, I thank my fellow writers who have helped me structure my work, story by story, and optimise my language: Janet Skeslien Charles, David Curzon, Marie Houzelle, Gwyneth Hughes, Dimitri Keramitas, Barry Kirwan, and Kurt Lebakken. Next, my two reviewers, Sue Belfrage and Alan Wilkinson, who looked at the entire manuscript and made useful global suggestions. My book is self-published and I am extremely grateful to Sara Tucker (Korongo Books) for doing the proofreading and setting up my Amazon KDP contact.

So much for the literary side, but a memoir is about the lives of those around the author, in my case mainly the world of seniors. My principal memoir character is my beloved companion Mylène, present in most of my stories as a counter-voice to mine. My bothers Peter and Noel have been with me during the most tragic moments that I describe. My children Cyril and Chloé gave me useful feedback. Mylène's daughter Dorothée allowed me to feature her and her cat Pollen. My grandson, Adam, and one of Mylène's grandsons, Eliot, have played a role in my stories. Peter Cator, the lifelong companion of my sister Hazel, was indispensable. Thanks also to my lifelong Caribbean friends Rosemary and Felix, and my English Garrett family.

My sporting club RSAG is full of friends who appear in these stories. My thanks to our president, Martine Demoncy, and many others who have allowed me to use their names. On a heartfelt note, this memoir is a tribute to my friends Gérard Chabert and Georges Quélin, Claire Gallou, my mother Elsie, and my sister Hazel, who will not read this book, but whose memory will always be with me. This is the reality of a senior's life.

CONTENTS

PREFACE

Retirement often seems like falling off a cliff. What to do next?

When someone stopped working a generation or two ago, he or she was confronted by two contradictory stereotypes. Either he should be envied because he could put his feet up and be happy, free from the tyranny of bosses and time constraints, or he should be pitied for his loss of a role in the world, his approaching state of dependence, and his coming extinction.

Today, most people in France retire in their early sixties. It used to be that they faded away quickly, but now the number of over-seventies is increasing. We take care of our health and our role is evolving. This book explores my own retirement.

What happens if, in addition to the ageing transition, there is a cultural shock? Can someone like me, born and bred in the sunny Caribbean, adapt to retirement in a place where he's never lived before —a cool forest region of France like Fontainebleau? Even after working in Paris for decades, I think in English before French, and prefer warm temperatures. A new equilibrium is needed.

I am now a member of a community of retired seniors in this historic region. Together with new-found French and foreign friends of my age, we enjoy a new kind of existence: physical activity, pure air, and inspiring trees everywhere. I survive the winters.

How I got here is part of the story. Transitions are not simple.

As seniors live a great deal in their memories, my stories are also sprinkled with other times and other places, especially the Caribbean. We are not just what we seem to be, but what we *were*, and reminiscence is part of our vitality. What seems good or bad today is inevitably compared with the past.

My personal tales and essays are about this vitality. We take our time about things, but we move, mourn, marry, and we even run.

Those over seventy may seem grey-haired, wrinkled, and slow, but our lives are full of projects. No longer encumbered by studies, careers, and child-rearing, we have time to help our adult children, explore, find new homes, read, roam the web, reflect on our past, invest in our future, take on new responsibilities, travel to new countries, and look the world in the eye.

But there is a price to pay. We are not eternal. Friends and family pass away around us like trees falling in the all-enveloping forest, and we need to accept this and help others as we can.

My first book—*Caribbean Chemistry*—was about how my identity as a youth born on a tiny tropical island evolved up to the age of twenty. Growing old in Fontainebleau is no less challenging.

With so much ahead and so little time, we are always on the run.

1

NEW PASTURES

"I suppose you're at your desk and I'm dossier number seventy-five, aren't I?" she said to me in French.

Surprise—she was only number sixty—but how did she know I kept files on my contacts? It was near midnight when I phoned her. We talked until 3 a.m. and Cinderella's carriage didn't turn into a pumpkin. But why did I make that midnight phone call, and who was this woman?

FIRST, my story. Born on the tiny colonial island of St. Kitts in a warm Caribbean family with three siblings, I had left home at nineteen on a scholarship and studied in Britain, then America. While there, at the end of my engineering studies, I married a dynamic French woman, Colette. We moved to her home country so I could better assimilate her French culture. I was not sure how long we would live there. We wound up staying more than thirty-five years, loving, living, and working. We were rooted in Paris, Colette as an HR manager, and I as an IT director—demanding and satisfying careers. I stopped working when I was barely sixty (company bankruptcy) for an early retirement.

On medical grounds, Colette was also obliged to retire. We had raised two children, Chloé and Cyril, who by 2005 had both left home. The dilemma—what were we to do with our retired lives? Jogging around the Park Monceau, I hesitated between relaunching my IT career and something new. I opted for a teenage dream, becoming a writer. After all, I had once won an all-Caribbean literary prize. With Colette's encouragement, I started down this path.

I was optimistic about Colette's health despite her frequent hospital visits and home treatment. Then, in 2008, she died suddenly and my tidy world fell apart.

RETURNING FROM THE HOSPITAL, I hated everyone I passed in the street. What right had they to live when the person dearest to me had gone? I scowled at them and cursed the universe. There was nothing left for me in that wilderness. I put myself on the hate list, just after the doctors. I had trusted them blindly to find the right medicines, the right treatment for leukaemia. They had not tried a bone marrow graft, and I had not foreseen the end looming. Was it optimism, blindness, or fear?

I remembered how annoyed I had once been that my wife wouldn't walk faster when we went out together. How surprised I had been when she started asking me to help her up stairs. Her blood problems would get better, they always had. We were both in our mid-sixties, retired, and it seemed that the next third of our lives was just beginning. Only to end in despair.

My nights were filled with tears rather than sleep. Thank goodness for practical things like estate management, children, and friends. Colette's funeral brought the whole Vanier family together, an emotional commemorative event, of which there have only been a few, given the time and money constraints on an international family. I had twice been arm-in-arm with my siblings Hazel, Peter, and Noel for such events: my father's St. Kitts funeral in 1997 and Cyril's Paris wedding to Linda a few months earlier in April 2008. The family sympathy didn't stop my tears.

After the funeral, I had a tomb built for Colette in the Montmartre cemetery. I visited it every day and listened to the black crows crying overhead. Having no employment made things worse. I had no co-workers to talk to, nothing to keep my thoughts positive. I refused the antidepressants that my doctor suggested. I thought of ending my life but rejected that escape route. Instead, I used my TV to find erotic channels for several days until I became disgusted. I took refuge in my writing: I wrote about myself on a rudderless boat travelling through storms, rain spitting in my face, with no hope of finding land. It helped, but was not enough. Even banks, notaries, pension funds, and taxes became a way of trying to redefine myself. I had to adapt, to find a new world, if one existed.

I am told that if sorrow and paralysis like this persist for a year, you need extensive therapy. I didn't know the meaning of resilience, never having faced a death so close, not even that of my father when he passed away on the Caribbean island of Nevis, far from me in Paris. By the time I had flown back he was peacefully in his coffin. I had been beside Colette, holding her hand, when she died. Those dark minutes when her life force vanished still live inside me.

After two terrible months, I began using dating sites on the Internet, looking for women of my age who spoke English. I wrote long letters rather than send messages but after a few exchanges I knew I didn't want to meet most of them. With those I did meet, there was no spark. The future looked bleak. I needed someone to love.

Another month later, in New York, grabbing at every straw, I visited a friend, David, who had also lost the woman he loved and was still writing poems about her years later. I read a little-known personal requiem from one of my favourite childhood authors, C.S. Lewis, author of the Narnia tales, a theologian who renounced his God when his wife died. I began to feel I was not alone in my grief.

Soon after, I contacted someone called Mylène on the dating site.

She had been clear in dating site messages that she didn't speak or write good English, and against my preference for email our first real contact was by phone. There was no image of her. I should have been unenthusiastic. She asked me to call late, after 11 p.m., and this was why I called her at midnight.

Dossier number sixty. A week later, we met.

Mylène was a widow. She had married Jean-Jacques at age twenty in 1964, and fifteen years later they had four children. Then her husband was diagnosed with terminal cancer. The doctors were wrong about the time left. Pain and confusion became a river that flowed around her for another fifteen years until he passed away. There was no way to know what would come next. Mylène raised her children mostly alone, and after her husband's death another fifteen years went by without being able to find a new and stable partner. Her exceptional awareness was at the same time an asset and a liability. What man likes to be seen through and outmanoeuvred by his lover? Years of depression preceded our meeting.

We were both alike and not alike. The pain from the past echoed and re-echoed. Both of us had spent nine years or more at university, and both had lived in Paris for most of a lifetime; but while I was British with Caribbean roots, she was very French, in the bourgeois tradition. And although we had both had had interesting careers in French industry and were now retired, I had been an engineer and an IT manager, fighting with machines, while she had been an organisational and negotiations manager, fighting with people. We had both suffered intense emotional stress at the loss of our partners, but her husband had died slowly after a drawn-out illness, while my wife had died suddenly. Her husband had been a financial manager, my wife a personnel manager. Attraction is many things—voice, appearance, ideas, taste, smell, similarity, and dissimilarity. At first contact, Mylène and I stuck together like two magnets. When the North and South poles of two such beings are in contact, they become inseparable. If one magnet is rotated to give a North-North contact, expect divergence. She increased my perceptivity; I helped her stability.

My children were at first incredulous when they heard about Mylène. Dad? Dating sites? A new partner? At age sixty-six? Wow! At the time, my daughter was thirty-our and single, my son was twenty-nine, married. They had their own sorrow to recover from, but they seemed much more solid than I was. After all, they had jobs and homes of their own to bolster them. And perhaps the parental link is easier to sever than the husband-and-wife bond. The contradiction:

they were happy to see me happy, but felt it was impossible to replace their mother. How could Mylène and I plan a future?

I took Mylène to my favourite association, LVDN, La Vie Devant Nous, or Life Ahead of Us. It focussed on the recently retired and their problems. It tries to reconcile fresh pensioners with their past and orient them to the future. I had been close to the organisers, but it wasn't enough for us. I still rejected not only the recent past but also the term "senior". Maybe our case was too fraught, or maybe we needed to look elsewhere, not just discussion. In the years that followed, though, I would remain friends with Georges, the association president.

Mylène and I never parted. We spent our first year living together in her too-small-but-charming one-bedroom apartment facing the Eiffel Tower. Then we tried my too-large-and-untidy four-bedroom apartment near Place de Clichy. We were wonderfully happy, but it took time and creativity to come to terms with our previous lives. Things were unstable. We tried bringing our families together but it didn't work. Our own magnetism did not extend to our two sets of children, so we had to deal with them separately. Still, it was "we". But then, something other than our incompatible children began causing us problems.

In 2009, my mother Elsie was ninety-two and in a nursing home for dementia patients. I visited her every week, often with Mylène, and one day I asked the resident psychologist for advice about my own situation. "You can't start a new life in a house where you've lived with a former wife or lover," she said. "It won't work. The legends about homes being occupied by spirits of the past are not that ridiculous."

As a scientist, I didn't want to believe this talk of ghosts. Until I learned that my children didn't like the idea of Mylène using my deceased wife's desk, a stylish wooden piece of office furniture which in fact Mylène stayed away from, and that she didn't like the lack of space for her belongings compared with my mountain of my books and papers. Neither the Eiffel Tower area nor the Place de Clichy seemed acceptable.

Our finances allowed us to take long trips abroad, to Britain, the

Caribbean, and South Africa. This was stimulating, but we always had to return home. But to which home? The problem became acute in the summer of 2011, when we had to cancel a trip to China because Mylène didn't want any more travel. We had no centre of stability, and the rest was escapism. Our life project was falling apart, and that's when we began talking about trees and forests.

Mylène had always lived in an apartment in Paris, never in a house, and never with a garden. She'd dreamed of a new, more open environment for years and had visited the Fontainebleau area several times. So, in the summer of 2011 we rented a furnished one-bedroom apartment in Avon (sister town of Fontainebleau) for a few weeks to explore the greenery. The forest was only a few hundred metres away and we dived into its mysterious trails. There was no pollution, no human debris, just magnificent trees and rocks. Follow the trail-blazed trees and we were in a new world of colour and silence, kilometres and kilometres of forest surrounding the centuries-old Fontainebleau chateau of past French kings. A town where things moved gracefully.

Years before, I had been a runner. When Colette died, I lost eight kilograms in a few months and felt debilitated. The attraction of the forest for me was breathable air and more exercise. I had passing regrets for Paris cinemas, restaurants, and stores, but these dissipated rapidly in the quiet of Avon. The traffic was gentle, and cars stopped for pedestrians. You could find everything you needed on foot. While renting an apartment there, we attended an open house reception at the local community centre and met the representatives of an outdoors club called RSAG (short for Retraite Sportive Avon Gatinais, or Sporting Retirement for Avon and the Gatinais region).

Mylène had been fed up with Paris for some time and was attracted by forest areas. Several years earlier, she had visited Fontainebleau. She was already wondering how to escape from the capital and the past. She had encountered a group of hikers from this sporting club in the forest, and greeted the group leader, John.

"What are you doing here, Parisian?" he queried. "It's not your forest!"

Mylène made a face and approached a fit-looking woman on the edge of the group.

"Is your chief always so edgy?"

"Just a façade," said Jacqueline, and gave Mylène the hiking club's visiting card.

While renting in 2011, we found Jacqueline on the open house day, and she explained that the sporting group was for seniors over sixty years of age, and forest hiking was only one of many activities, though one of the most popular. The club also offered swimming, gymnastics, Pilates, Nordic walking, cycling, table tennis, mini-golf, martial arts, and more.

"How many members do you have?" I asked.

My question was addressed to Martine, whom I later discovered was the club president. Her face was lined; her body rock hard; her movements supple despite surgery on both hips. With forty years as a gym instructor behind her she was used to welcoming the public.

"About three hundred, and it's increasing each year."

"We'd love to join but we don't have a permanent address here, just a rented place."

She said this was not a problem and she could update our details at any time, so we signed up. At last, almost seventy, I accepted becoming a senior. And looking at all the fit club members I could see that new projects and adventures were possible. At this point we were riding a wave of enthusiasm and didn't want to return to Paris. But then the practical details of lodging took over. We couldn't leave all our belongings in Paris and had to find a larger place to live in. We debated rental or purchase.

"If we purchase, I can't contribute much—my money is tied up in my Paris apartment," I said.

"I'm willing to buy a place," Mylène said. "I've been planning this for years but didn't have the courage without a man I loved. I've got enough savings; if necessary, I can sell my place in Paris."

Up to this point we were in harmony.

"I dream of a large garden near the forest with lots of trees and flowers!" Mylène said.

"You mean a house? Isn't a large apartment more practical?"

I distrusted houses. I had been brought up in a pleasant, sprawling Caribbean house as a child, but now I preferred apartments, knowing how much more work it is to maintain your home building, manage heating, waste water, garbage, roofs, gates and windows, and the garden—oh, the garden!—unlimited hours of work for a few undeserving flowers. But Mylène saw things differently: she had never had her own house, and that's what she wanted.

I had read that changing homes is one of life's greatest traumas, comparable with losing your job or a loved one. We had already suffered the other two and now we were in line for the third trauma.

So, we visited houses and apartments in Avon and debated our options for weeks. After some tense reflection, I said: "Look, as long as you don't expect me personally to do any gardening, what matters is the location. I like Avon, but my family and friends are in Paris. I'm okay for a house if we are within walking distance of the Fontainebleau/Avon train station."

This settled things, but now we needed to *find* a suitable house. We continued searching for several weeks with no result. The houses were either in Avon but not very attractive, or lovely but far away. Our small rented flat, however, was perfectly positioned, just five minutes from the station, three minutes from the shopping centre, banks and post office, and seven minutes from the forest.

One day, we saw a FOR SALE notice appear on a house just opposite our flat, on rue Antoine Cléricy. The door was closed, but we noted the agency in charge of the sale. Several phone calls and letters over the next week produced no result. We gave up and continued searching elsewhere. Then, one evening at close to 10 p.m., as we were walking back to our flat, we noticed a light in the house for sale.

"Let's knock," said Mylène, always enterprising.

"No, it's too late!" I replied. "Don't—we'll disturb someone."

But there was no stopping her; she had already opened the gate and shouted, "Anyone there?"

After a few minutes, a clean-shaven man in his forties opened the door.

"We saw your light and wondered if the house is still for sale."

"Yes, it is. Have you seen the agency?"

We explained the lack of response from the agency so he said he could show us the place himself the next day. The practical location excited us.

The next day the owner showed us a house which was about eight metres by eight metres, on three levels, with a sizeable back garden. The basement included a workshop, a laundry room, and a dusty wine cellar. On the street level, there was a cluttered living room and kitchen; and on the first floor were three bedrooms and a bathroom. The house was not new, nor especially elegant, but clean. A new owner would have very little initial refurbishing to do, though we might want improvements later.

I felt a personality in the house. There were airy windows in each room and the main bedroom looked out over the back garden with an impressive weeping willow which seemed to pull me into its branches.

The owner suggested returning the next day to see the garage.

"And could you give us an idea of the price?"

He named a much higher figure than we had expected.

"But we can discuss this tomorrow."

That evening, Mylène and I worried about the high price of the Cléricy house, and the next day we questioned the owner on the possibility of a direct owner-to-buyer sale, avoiding the agency.

He agreed and lowered the price by twenty thousand euros.

"It's still too expensive for us," I said.

"You are forgetting that in addition to the house my garage is worth another one hundred thousand euros!" the owner said. "But I forgot, you haven't seen it yet. Let's go outside."

We followed him into the garden, and with three clicks of his remote control he opened the three automatic doors to his treasure trove, fifty square metres of white-tiled floor and three expensive vehicles. The walls were covered with shelves and the "garage" also had electricity and running water.

"Not just for cars, almost liveable, you see? It only needs a bit of heating in the winter."

Mylène whispered to me: "His estimate of one hundred thousand euros for the garage probably includes those cars, which he certainly won't leave for us!"

Impressed nonetheless, we followed him back up to the living room. Boldly, Mylène continued her negotiation, but the owner would not budge.

We agreed to think about it and asked him about the technical inspections of the house, a legal requirement. He offered to produce all the papers at our next visit, a week later, at which time we could sign a preliminary contract to preclude other buyers.

During that week, we thought about the family repercussions if we bought a place like this. On my children's side, both living in Paris, there appeared to be no problem. My only real constraint was the presence of my mother in a nursing home near Paris, which would now be sixty kilometres away instead of six. But on Mylène's side it was different.

One son lived to the west of Paris with his wife and three young daughters.

"The forest is just as good near us, and you could help with your grandchildren!" he said.

Mylène's eldest daughter lived even further to the west with her husband and two children.

"Small villages are best, and we have a beautiful lake nearby. And you could see our sons more often!"

Another daughter in Paris and a son near Toulon were neutral.

The first two children disliked the geographical separation, putting us almost two hours away by car. In their eyes, the main role of a grandparent was to step in and take care of grandchildren at beck and call. A negation of our freedom, we thought. Still, we investigated homes nearer to them and confirmed to ourselves that the Avon area was our best opportunity. But to our chagrin it seemed to be slipping away because of the cost.

On our third visit, we examined the rooms more closely. The owner had too much furniture and too little open space, but what struck us was the number of wall pictures and paintings, in the living room, the bedrooms, the kitchen, and even the entry. Some were country scenes, and many featured horses and horse riders; there were also dried flowers and ornate little mirrors everywhere. There was a striking painting of a woman in her late thirties in the living room, dark haired and attractive though not beautiful, with light brown skin.

"Why are you selling your house anyway?" I asked him. "It seems a pleasant place to live and you say you work nearby."

He looked at the picture of the woman and bowed his head. There was a long silence and I began to wish I hadn't asked something so personal.

"That's my wife," he said. "Died five years ago, and I've only just now got the courage to leave. All the pictures and paintings are hers. She loved horses."

He looked at us sombrely. "I don't suppose you know how it is, but it feels impossible to leave all those family memories. Then suddenly you wake up one day and feel the opposite: you must break away and start all over. Now is the time."

We were silent for a while.

"I do know how it is," I said. "My wife died only three years ago and I've been trying to adjust ever since."

Mylène continued: "My husband died eighteen years ago and only now am I beginning to feel healed. It takes time!"

We looked at each other, all three of us, and began talking rapidly. It was a rare and profound occasion that with a complete stranger, the owner, we could open our hearts to the pain still there. We talked about loss, about loneliness, about the rupture of relationships, about paralysis, about memories.

Then, unexpectedly, the owner said, "Okay, I'll drop my price another twenty thousand euros, for you. It's my last and best offer. I'll also leave all the kitchen appliances and the paintings."

We knew that whatever else happened afterwards a bridge had been built and we could meet in the middle. And he knew his paintings with their associated memories were in safe hands.

We glanced at the inspections and the owner explained that the only negative point concerned some of the electrical fittings outside of the kitchen, which had no grounded plugs. But, he said, there was fuse box protection. The gas-fired boiler was top German quality and had been serviced when necessary. The Internet connection was perfect and the TV roof antenna worked well.

We signed the preliminary agreement.

In the weeks that followed, we hesitated. Had we made a mistake?

Wasn't this a dangerous life choice? At our age, would we be able to make the best of that house?

However, Mylène duly signed the next stage of the sale with the owner's notary and the final closing took place in Paris in the first days of 2012.

Then, we started to move in. A house in Avon at last! A home! The emotional weight I had been carrying since 2008, already diminished when I met Mylène early in 2009, now became feather-light. My lungs filled with the fresh forest air and I felt my spirit becoming part of this new world. What could go wrong now?

We immediately had some surprises. The technical inspection was inaccurate and by a strange coincidence the inspection company had gone out of business one day after giving the owner the reports; no legal procedure was possible. We discovered that the waste water connection to the town's sewers was not authorised—rain water was being mixed with other waste—a large potential expense to correct. The roof antenna did not work well. The electricity defects were worse than indicated and would require complete rewiring. Most critical, the gas-fired boiler for heating and hot water stopped working after a week; it had not been serviced for five years and would have to be quickly replaced.

After the sale, the owner tried to help us, but only up to a point. He left lots of furniture and a huge American fridge-freezer. He assured us that the local town hall wouldn't bother us about the waste water problem, and he hadn't known about the false inspection data. We were momentarily angry, but there was no real recourse. Houses are more complicated than apartments and misrepresentation is common even without the intention to cheat.

Above all, we now had the house, the garage, the weeping willow, and all the wall pictures except the painting of the previous owner's deceased wife. Once the boiler was fixed, we could move in for good, and our dream of a new life could begin, on condition we had really left the old one behind.

What was in store for us in Avon? It was mid-January of 2012 and we were eager to join this world of seniors and sport. After three years together, we were hoping for many more. But we had another, more sombre, companion on this journey of exploration, the Dark Angel, to reckon with. It was a last matter to be settled.

"Promise me one thing," Mylène said. "Promise that you won't get ill and die before I do. I couldn't stand it. Not again."

"Agreed," I said slowly, knowing that the shadow of her past hung over her, like mine over me. "The day I fell in love with you I accepted the pain to come. I promise I *will* live longer. But for the next decade or two, let's just be us, no Dark Angels allowed. Three is a crowd."

2

BY ANY OTHER NAME

It was late January in 2012, at the beginning of a ferocious winter, when Mylène and I tried to move in to our new house in Avon. After spending a night there without heating, at near zero temperatures, snuggling against each other to keep warm, we moved back to Paris until the heating could be restored. Then, a week later, I was alerted to a new and much more serious situation. My mother Elsie, now almost ninety-five, had developed a lung infection, was on antibiotics and a permanent drip, and had almost ceased eating—a radical change in behaviour. I visited Elsie with Mylène and my children the next weekend in her Champfleury nursing home.

When we arrived, the home's medical supervisor told us Elsie's fever had gone but she was still on medication and wouldn't swallow more than two teaspoonfuls of food per meal.

Under our collective encouragement she ate seven spoonfuls that night—a small miracle—and we breathed a short-lived moment of peace. I was able to put the family in America and Britain on alert. Then, a fortnight later, just when it all seemed like a false alarm, the nurse tore down our curtain of hope.

The last Saturday in January was biting cold and we had just returned to Avon. All afternoon, I had been working on the house. The misfunctioning boiler in the basement had given up and a service company was busy replacing it. Then, at 5 p.m., the phone rang.

"Your mother is on morphine and breathing with difficulty. Better come quickly."

I closed the door to the basement, leaving the technician to urge the new condenser-heater into life. When he had finished, I shooed him away and Mylène drove us the sixty kilometres to Paris. She judged me unable to confront the motorway in my state of tension. We arrived at the nursing home after my children, who had also been alerted, just after 6 p.m. Elsie was motionless in bed, neither seeing nor hearing, but taking a deep rasping breath every fifteen seconds. At first, it was difficult to stay in the same room, but gradually the scene took on a hypnotic fascination, quelling conversation. It was clearly a matter of hours. Her nurse Maria had more work to do comforting my children than checking Elsie's drips. My daughter Chloé was wracked with tears, seeing not only her childhood granny disappear, but also remembering her own mother's death some three years earlier. My son Cyril was supportive and silent, having seen far more of danger and death as a TV foreign correspondent reporting on the Arab Spring than the rest of us. Mylène, who had lost both of her parents six years earlier, was grave but in control. I was a stone, with deep internal fissures. We all stayed until 9 p.m.

Sitting there, staring at my mother's closed eyes, her pale face, listening to her laboured breathing, I tried to escape my grief by letting the vivacity of her past life float through my mind.

WHAT A DETERMINED FIGHTER she had been! Born on the island of Dominica in 1917, she lost her English mother at birth and was fed by a local wet nurse. Her lawyer father Cecil Rawle took special care of her in memory of his departed wife. She grew up vivacious, with a step-mother and many half-sisters, but haunted by the unseen presence of her real mother and determined to found her own family.

She couldn't go to university because she was a girl and her Caribbean father thought it was not appropriate. They moved to

Antigua and Elsie did the next best thing—she studied hard at school and fell in love with her teacher, five years older, my father-to-be, Ralph Vanier. Cecil scornfully rejected any such engagement. Couldn't she find someone better than a school teacher? Elsie refused and said she would prefer to be a nun rather than give up Ralph. I could imagine her stamping her foot and standing up to her father, the most prominent politician on the island. But how could she improve Ralph's pedigree? He was the son of an Anglican priest with no financial resources, so Elsie had to wait a year before they found a benefactor to fund Ralph's studies abroad. Then she waited another three long years while Ralph qualified as a barrister in London.

Ralph returned to Antigua in 1941, his ocean liner narrowly escaping German submarines. He and Elsie were married by Ralph's father, but sadly Cecil had died during Ralph's studies and never knew his daughter's joy. Against all odds, her dream was coming true. The couple migrated to St. Kitts, and the next year I was born, followed by my two brothers, Peter and Noel, and my sister, Hazel.

Elsie's house in St. Kitts looked out over the bay of Basseterre and had a large tropical garden. My father planted the fruit trees—guava, mango, avocado, cherry, and paw-paw—and Elsie cultivated her roses. Later, I was delegated to pick up fruit every morning and I even climbed the coconut tree.

While Ralph pursued his legal career and provided for his family, Elsie became an accountant and then treasurer of the St. Kitts historical society. She read insatiably and worked for charitable organisations. Her ready smile made her known and loved all over the island.

Challenges never stopped my resourceful mother. She dedicated her energy to her four children, reading stories to them every night, studying the latest manuals on child care, founding her own school for young children as there was no alternative on the island, taking my motor-handicapped sister to America for treatment so she could walk, then years later finding a special school for her in England that eventually led to a university education. As for the boys, myself included, her early teaching and our father's prompting inspired us to win scholarships abroad and thereafter be self-financing all the way to advanced scientific careers. Where would we have been, born on a small, little-known island, without our parents' keen minds and constant encouragement?

However—there was a catch. Elsie focussed on her children. Their education was everything that mattered. And they succeeded. But this involved leaving their home in the Caribbean and starting new families abroad, hardly ever coming back. A high price to pay. Peter became a research physicist in the USA, Noel a research chemist, while I gained my PhD in chemical engineering. After moving to France, I tried to visit Elsie and Ralph every summer, but it was not enough.

Integrating that pale face and the laboured breathing in front of me, I remembered the photo I had taken of Elsie and Ralph at their fiftieth wedding anniversary in St. Kitts in 1991 when—at least once—all their children and grandchildren were assembled. Her smile was beatific.

In our world of today, distance and family dislocations often make children remote. But in the twilight of parents' lives, an adult child must often become the parent of his parents. As the eldest child this was my responsibility. I found a care home for my father Ralph on the island of Nevis and later brought Elsie to Paris.

Jumping forward in time to Elsie's old age in France, I thought of the day when I had first taken Mylène to see her.

Elsie was then ninety-two, and in the same nursing home at Sèvres, near Paris, where we were currently sitting. It was three years earlier, 2009, a year after Colette's death.

"Are you happy?" I asked my mother.

"Happy? Of course, I was born happy!"

This was Elsie's second intelligible statement during the hour we had been in the home. Legs twisted in front of her cradling wheelchair, bony hands gripping mine, she answered my question without moving her head, just a smile. I looked around the well-lit room where residents were brought for meals. A TV set sat staring at them. Bay windows stretched across a wall, framing the wintry garden outside. Two supine figures occupied reclining chairs while a nurse hovered in the background.

It was hard to tell whether Elsie's sensors were functioning; certainly not very well. I examined her eyes, which were half-open, unfocussed, and not directed either at Mylène or me. I wondered, not for the first time, whether I should have had her glasses replaced when she broke them a year earlier. But it was the same story for all the little personal objects which help an elderly person adapt to failing faculties. Hearing aids, dentures, and spectacles—she had either stamped on them or flushed them down the toilet, as if clearing the decks for oblivion. I whispered into her right ear, the one I knew heard better, "That's good. Stay happy, Elsie."

I don't know why I asked Elsie if she was happy. It might seem a futile question for someone with profound dementia in the special ward of her retirement home, what the French call a *Cantou*. She had attained the lowest possible disability grade, GIR 1 (Group Iso-Resources), meaning totally dependent, confined to wheelchair and bed, no treatment possible. Was her reply meaningful or just a chance conjunction of a few stray words rattling around in her head? Could the word "happy" apply to her state? Even for the rest of us, it's hard to say what the word signifies. Well-fed? Calm? Trouble-free? Aware? Jubilant? Certainly not the last two in her case. Yet I couldn't deny the occasional sparks which intimated some inner life, intuitive and sensual rather than rational. At ninety-one, a year earlier, she had even had a sort of romance with another Alzheimer's resident aged eighty-five. I had surprised both sitting on Elsie's bed, and I left quickly, embarrassed.

On the same day in 2009, earlier in the afternoon, we had parked outside the nursing home in the wooded Parisian suburb of Sèvres and entered via a lobby packed with the wrinkled faces of more mobile residents waiting for their next meal. Then we penetrated the security doors of the Cantou (there to keep the residents in) and found Elsie in the common room with three other Alzheimer's sufferers, two immobile, the other walking in circles.

A nurse, Maria, approached us.

"How has Elsie been?" I said in French.

"Quite lively today."

"Is she eating well?"

"Oh yes, Mrs Vanier has an excellent appetite. She even eats some of her food by herself."

I looked at Elsie from the back, saw her cheekbones sharply outlined and her thin body that was decades away from the days when she worried about being plump. I had read that dementia consumes a great deal of internal energy and most sufferers lose weight.

"Mrs Vanier! Your son Christopher is here to see you!" Maria said.

Elsie made a small movement of her head but did not turn, as if locked in her chair. As we approached, she babbled in French, *"Masher, masher. Merger, merger. Manger, manger."* Often, she would switch to English after I'd been there for a few minutes, but this was no more comprehensible.

I pulled up a chair and took her hand gently, avoiding the places where her skin was paper thin. My companion brought up another chair and then peered solicitously at a red bruise on Elsie's forehead; she had fallen despite efforts to secure her in her chair.

"This is Mylène, Elsie, who has come to see you." I gave Elsie a kiss and then, in a surprising movement, she clasped our hands in hers and said, "Be happy together."

Maybe this first use of "happy" caused me to ask the question later. But how could she know of our love? Between the clasping of hands and my question thirty minutes later Elsie said nothing we could understand. Could we communicate with her? Looking for emotional keys, I gave her reminders of her four children, five grandchildren, her deceased husband, her homelands in the Caribbean islands of Dominica, Antigua, and St. Kitts, and her own long-dead father Cecil —each ingredient of memory spiced with a kiss on her cheek. She gave no further sign of understanding except for a barely discernible lessening of tension in her grip on my hand. The Alzheimer's fog had enveloped her. I had played out this scenario many times over the past three years and even then—by an act of faith—I believed that someone still inhabited her body.

We left the Cantou with the word "happy" tingling in the background. Mylène felt this one word was enough—Elsie's instincts and most of her perceptions were still there. Mylène was curious about something else. "Why do you call your mother by her first name?" she said. It was a question my sister Hazel had also asked a year earlier on a visit from London when my son Cyril was married.

"Distance," I replied, "interior distance. Ever since I brought her to France years ago, I've been struggling with the weight of care. It helps if I feel I'm talking to an unrelated person, like a doctor to a patient, and not the person who gave birth to me."

Mylène didn't ask why I had brought Elsie to France, but images of our medically-impoverished island home in the Caribbean flashed into my mind. When my father had died in his care home in 1997, there was nothing left for Elsie in St. Kitts so I and my three siblings had debated what to do about her. She needed our love and care. My brothers in America—Peter and Noel—couldn't take her in because of the enormous health costs to come. They were right. My sister Hazel in London was too handicapped to be her caregiver. This left me to take the responsibility, and luckily Elsie had a British passport (inherited from her English mother), the key to EU residence. So, I brought her to France in 2001, aged eighty-five, and found her a studio a stone's throw from my Paris apartment. Always up to a challenge, she did her own shopping, upgraded her school-girl French, and began painting. She lived in her studio for six years before going into a nursing home for dementia.

Mylène looked at me quizzically, but I said no more, not wishing to disturb the feelings caged inside me—pity, sorrow, guilt, and anger. Of these currents, the first three—the oldest—were linked to my role as a son. Some of the anger was old, too, coming from my difficulties as a caregiver without much help from my faraway siblings, but a lot of it was recent. When my wife had died a year earlier, I had stopped visiting Elsie for several months. I couldn't accept that a non-communicating ninety-one-year-old continued to live, while my precious sixty-five-year-old spouse had been snatched from me. I knew this was illogical but my anger did not subside. I had invested much time and energy looking after Elsie during her seven years in Paris before Colette's death. Without this responsibility, I might have been able to care for my wife better.

～

AT AGE NINETY-THREE, in 2010, Elsie was taken into a nearby hospital for emergency treatment. Her pulse rate was bouncing out of control and causing chest pains, according to the nursing home.

Called urgently to the hospital and having worked my way through the maze of corridors and wards to Elsie's room, I found her weak and silent. I looked at the monitors next to her bed but failed to detect anything excessive; no spikes or chasms in the wavy green lines.

"We'll record a four-hour scan tomorrow," the hospital doctor said.

When I returned the next afternoon, he called me into his office. From behind his desk littered with papers he said quietly: "It's arrhythmia. The real problem is not the high pulse rates—though it does shoot up well over one hundred from time to time. It's her base rate. It's in the low forties, too feeble to maintain most physical functions properly. Eating, moving, talking, become difficult. We need to boost her base rate."

"How?"

"She should have a pacemaker to increase her rhythm and keep it at seventy."

"But aren't the occasional spikes dangerous too?"

"They can be controlled by appropriate drugs, if they recur."

"Seriously, doctor? You're recommending pacemaker surgery for a ninety-three-year-old?"

"It's simpler than you think—an implant just under the skin, on the chest near the shoulder. More and more elderly patients have it done. But we can't do it here. She'll have to be taken to the specialists at Percy Hospital."

The local hospital arranged for Elsie's transfer to the more specialised Percy establishment. I thought it was all settled, but the medical team at Percy had their doubts. The next day, I was called in for an interview with the top surgeon, ostensibly to sign family information papers, acknowledging that we knew the risks of the operation.

"Why do you want us to do this?" the surgeon said, staring hard at me.

"So she can live longer."

"You've been misled. Statistically, a pacemaker implant at her age won't increase her lifespan significantly. And she won't be able to communicate any better afterward—she'll still be in dementia."

Surprised, I asked, "So, she won't live longer? But she'll still be more comfortable, won't she? Pain-free, more relaxed, a better quality of life? Happier?"

He raised his eyebrows. "Okay, a better quality of life, as you say. We'll do it."

I shivered as I left the hospital, realising that as Elsie's surgical expenses were all paid by the French welfare state (though not her nursing home costs), the Percy medical team had to verify that a family in my situation really needed the benefits of a pacemaker. Otherwise, they were proposing 'benign neglect', even indirect euthanasia of the demented.

What had I done by insisting on a 'better quality of life' for Elsie? Perhaps it was a synonym for happiness. Whatever the word for it, two weeks after the operation Elsie's energy had returned. She ate better, slept better, and babbled better. They even tried to get her to walk again. Her nurse was pleased. Another year went by. Elsie turned ninety-four. It was in that summer of 2011 when we first thought of leaving Paris to rent off-and-on in Avon.

ELSIE MUST HAVE MADE A SOUND, for at last I returned to the present. As we prepared to leave, I asked Maria to call me during the night if the situation worsened. Before going to sleep near midnight in Paris, I changed my mind. I was overwhelmed and had to shut the world out. I sensed the coming shock wave and switched off the sound on my cell phone. It recorded a message at 5:20 a.m. which I didn't receive until 8 a.m. Elsie had died at 5 a.m., Sunday January 29, 2012. Now, like many seniors, I had no living parents left. The ending of a life story can over-shadow its high points. Who was Elsie, she who had given birth to me and my siblings? I saluted, not the frail person in dementia, but a strong woman, a literate woman, an optimist, a courageous mother—the origin of my existence. But there was no time for tears or any of those repressed emotions. To begin with, I needed all my energy to contact my brothers and sister with the news of her death. My voice would not break that day, not until I spoke of her several weeks later.

Elsie was a foreigner in France and her death entailed many formalities, most impossible on a Sunday. The immediate problem was to cool the deceased body, for which the nursing home had no facilities beyond opening the windows to the winter air. Fortunately, it was cold. I obtained a contact number for the local funeral home and set up an appointment for 2 p.m. the next day. Before her body left the Champfleury nursing home the four of us—my children, Mylène and I —reassembled in the same room as the night before, looked a last time at Elsie's quiet dignity. Her face was composed and beautiful. I took pictures. The nurses had dressed her in simple white and the agitation of the past few weeks had disappeared.

I banished fatigue. Angry that I had carried the burden of Elsie almost alone for the last twelve years, guilty that I had not done better, immensely sad that a loved one could be mentally so far away in their last years, still hurting from my father's death fifteen years earlier, I was now the eldest of my family, next in line for the grim reaper, and I still had a job to do.

It all went quickly but stressfully from that point on. I groggily signed papers with the ambulance team, the funeral home, and the nursing home the next day. We pushed the planning for the cremation to its legal limit of six days, the next Saturday, to allow any children or grandchildren from America to attend.

But first I had to obtain an official death certificate from the Sèvres Town Hall. Mylène and I found ourselves sitting in front of a large wooden desk surrounded by filing cabinets and computer printers.

Then some Kafkaesque administrative problems began. Elsie was British and had no family papers in France. To obtain a proper death certificate we needed the equivalent of a French *Livret de Famille* (Family Record), with birth certificate, marriage certificate, and the death certificate of my father. Then it should all be translated into French and witnessed. Otherwise the Town Hall couldn't write "widow, deceased". I had to get several of these papers by mail over the next few days—very difficult!

There were only three days to go before the cremation was scheduled. But the cremation couldn't legally take place without the official death certificate. I couldn't imagine what would happen if there was no death certificate.

My luck, however, was in. A day later, an ingenious niece in the USA was able to piece together the old documents into files which I promptly printed. The only remaining problem was whether the clerk would accept copies, and would she require certified translations into French. She accepted the lot, this time without a translation.

FOR THE CREMATION, I chose the simplest of coffins but requested the maximum beauty care for the deceased's face and body because that's what Elsie would have liked. The sealing of the coffin took place on a Friday, the cremation the next day, attended by Mylène, three of Elsie's grandchildren, two friends, and me.

The crematorium conveniently adjoined the funeral home, and this time I insisted on driving there, despite my companion's offer to let me relax.

Grey and cold was fitting, I thought. We entered the guest area where I filled out obscure forms and contracts. The official spoke very slowly and seemed to repeat everything.

"You have three months to recover the urn without charge. We can keep it for up to a year before dispersal of the ashes, but it costs more. You have three months to recover the urn."

"Is there a ceremony today?"

"Whatever you like. I can officiate or the family can participate. Whatever you like."

"We have short eulogies to read."

We moved into the ceremonial room containing Elsie's coffin and a speaker's rostrum with a microphone. I organised the order of reading by my son Cyril, my niece Sophie, Mylène, and me. A poem from my sister Hazel and letters from my two brothers were waiting. The busier I could be the less I felt the tension. Addressing those present, I read— without pausing—the eulogy I had written the day before and my younger brother's letter.

Afterwards, I thought of my late father; I had helped manage his bees, and he had taught me to absorb pain. Every two days he would place a bee on my forearm and encourage it to sting, and then quickly remove the stinger, killing the bee. Small, regular doses of bee venom gradually immunised me until the sting was quite tolerable. Eleven years of painful reminders of my Elsie's drifting away had similarly strengthened my resistance to her final departure. I was too close to her last years of dementia to cry. My cage was still safely locked.

In the chilly crematorium, the tears of my daughter Chloé were far more expressive than my numbness.

Then one bar of my cage, one constraint, came loose. Before the coffin was conveyed to the flames, I saw my mother as she had been.

I was a child and she was reading a fairy story to me in bed, one of many. The hero was afraid the sky might fall on his head, and I asked if this could happen. "No," she laughed, "not very often."

This was not just a box—it was Elsie Cecil Veronica Vanier, née Rawle, called Vera as a child, then Elsie after marriage, and Granny late in life. She had dedicated her life to her children, knowing that her own mother had died giving birth to her. She had done all she could for my handicapped sister Hazel. She had been without my father Ralph for the last fifteen years of her life yet had tried to make the best of things. A precursor of our new, long-lived senior generation, she had started an entirely new life in France at age eighty-five, and stayed alive, enjoying most of it, until almost ninety-five.

I could only do so much. My heart went out to her, happy in her way. A name was missing, one which I hadn't uttered for a long time.

"Goodbye, Mum."

3

BEWITCHED BY HEARTLESS SPIRITS

Coming to terms with the community of seniors in Avon was one thing, getting used to our elderly house in constant need of maintenance was another. I used to be a well-qualified engineer, but could I repair new and varied problems at my age? I had some trepidation, but then again, what was the worst that could happen?

The heating having been fixed, my next trial concerned doors. At first, these seem straightforward—a means of protecting our homes and privacy. However, as I became increasingly aware, the power of the door, or gate, is reputedly under the control of an ancient and duplicitous spirit, the two-faced Roman god Janus.

When we'd acquired the house in Avon, the mischievousness of the house's doors and gates wasn't at first apparent. With the arrogance of city dwellers from cosy apartments, we assumed that things should work, especially if they had worked before. Heating, electricity, windows, and most especially doors were the responsibility of others. We had already paid to renovate the gas heating, and we knew the electricity would have to be reviewed, but doors? Janus was far from my mind.

First, the automatic electric gate system installed by the previous owner abruptly ceased being automatic. We had been proud of this part of the property: one jab at the clicker and the heavy swing gates would gracefully open to let our car in or out of the driveway. Until . . . until the day we clicked and nothing happened. We were imprisoned (or at least our car was).

I had never looked closely at these gates. Now, I saw that each half of the gate was powered by a motor with a long, jointed arm, and the motors were connected to a black receptor box with a radio antenna. Probing frantically at the motors—we were late for an appointment—I found a way to open the top compartment. Under a thick layer of dirt and dead insects, I found a lever marked ON-OFF. I was thus able to open the gates by hand and let our impatient car with my impatient companion careen onto the street. I closed the gates, hoping they would stay that way.

We had to fix our automation. I was too lazy to keep opening and closing the heavy gates manually. However, I could find neither documentation nor maintenance contract. In addition, we were no longer in communication with the previous owner to ask him about it. Had I listened carefully, I might have heard Janus laughing. At last I found the guilty manufacturer's name, under the pile of dead insects. Internet research then led me to a service phone number. What could ail a faulty gate? I phoned and complained.

Two days later, a youngish repairman in blue jeans appeared.

"You broke your gate?" he said casually, in French.

"What, me? We've just moved in. Your motors don't work!"

Not replying, the repairman proceeded to ignore the motors I was so proud to have discovered and looked at the black box with the antenna. "Not well wired," he said. "Power cables must be protected by plastic sheaths for all-weather conditions." So, it was going to be our fault.

Then, with difficulty, he proceeded to dismount the front panel of the black box. When it opened, he jumped back as a horde of ants tried to defend their territory. One could almost smell the formic acid on their stingers.

"Holy cow! Don't you use insect repellent?"

Not wanting to admit I had had no idea of the black box's importance, I said nothing. Then, after a pause and while he was brushing the ant army away, I said, "Strange to find ants attracted by electronics, isn't it? Nothing to eat there. But surely they can't do any harm?"

He looked at me and sniffed, then patiently eliminated the last of the ant insurgents and removed a green electronic card covered with fancy-looking components which might have come straight out of my computer. It was the hidden brains of the automation system. He sniffed again.

"Don't know," he said, and pointed to a few soldered connections on the card that appeared discoloured. "May have to replace this, but let's try it and hope for the best."

A few minutes later, the gates were happily opening and closing again, apparently quite satisfied with their previously brain-damaged controller. I said, "How much will this cost?"

"Not much," he replied. "You were lucky with the card. But I don't do the figures. You'll get our bill in the mail."

I breathed a sigh of financial relief. "But will it continue working?"

"Buy some spray repellent," he said. "Warm weather's not over yet."

This I did, but the bill was nevertheless for 250 euros to cover an hour of the repairman's time. Doubtless Janus would have chuckled, because a month later the automatic gates broke down again, just after some summer rain. Maybe it was water leakage into the black box? Or some other type of insect? Previously, the doors had stuck closed, imprisoning us temporarily. Now they had stuck open.

Our property was entirely enclosed. Behind the house was our main garden, still waiting for me to cut its lawn, with fences to keep the neighbours in place; between the house and the street was a much smaller garden. This front patch was protected from passers-by in the street by a stone wall. There were only two means of access: a stout wooden gate for visitors on foot and the large swing gates for cars. Having this latter entrance gaping wide left us queasy. We might be burgled. I could disconnect and reconnect the motors the way I had done before, but who could tell when the automation would throw them open again?

I phoned the same company for more help. A few tense days later another repairman arrived, this time bearded and dressed in brown corduroys, and after he had heard my story he didn't hesitate. He made no remarks about the power leads because we had fixed this in the interval. No remarks about insects either because none were left. He opened the black box straightaway and plucked out the master card.

With a dismissive gesture he said, "No way to fix this." Then he produced a new card, replaced the old one, and recalibrated the system with new opening/closing speeds and clicker codes. He handed me the old, soiled card as a souvenir and said, "Don't know why you even tried to use this."

I wondered how much the job would cost this time but knew better than to ask. Doors cost what they cost. The answer came a week later—a hefty 450 euros for another "hour" of work plus the new card. Mylène haggled to gain time, but finally we paid. Later, I added a sliding bolt to the bottom of the car gate to ensure it wouldn't open without being asked to. Naively, I assumed my gate problems were over. But Janus would think otherwise.

We were expecting visitors for Christmas. One rainy morning in late December, Mylène called to me from the street outside our front garden in Avon. She was standing in front of the small wooden visitors' gate and complained that she couldn't get in and was getting wet.

"It's not locked," I said from a window. "I left it open."

Nonetheless, I had to go down and manhandle the rebellious gate. After much pushing and pulling it opened at last with a grunting sound.

"We'll have to call someone to fix it," Mylène said.

"I'm supposed to be an engineer!" I replied.

She gave me a quizzical look. "You so-called engineers know maths and computer, but not much do-it-yourself."

I tried to reply, but she continued: "From a top engineering school, my husband when he was alive couldn't fix much in the house. You're neither carpenters, nor handymen!"

In a way, she was right: "Engineer" in France is a management qualification, not necessarily a practical one, and even with my post-grad training in chemical engineering in the USA I'd never had any DIY at university. But . . . my thoughts went back to childhood, to my father's large workshop where, though a lawyer, he enjoyed repairing everything. Did he guess the heritage he was leaving us? He schooled me and my brothers in this treasure house of lathes, drills, saws, hammers, and all manner of tools. We made beehive frames for him, and built play houses, rockets, and race carts for ourselves. I had loved that workshop and when grown up I created a tool shelf in each of my lodgings.

"I'm sure I can do it!" I said.

"Surprise me!" she teased.

Hinged, made of solid brown wood, and fixed between two thick stone walls, the street door had no motors or anything fancy, not even a doorbell. A look at the uneven wall on which the gate fastened showed sticking points. The rain had caused the wood of the door to swell and it could no longer close. I collected a heavy-duty wood file from my tool kit in the basement and got to work. The wood was easy to file and in fifteen minutes I'd shaved off a millimetre or so where it touched the stone wall. I left it rough, because I couldn't be bothered to mollycoddle the thing. Doubtless, Janus was not satisfied. There was still mist on my glasses as I entered the house. I had succeeded, but I felt glum at the idea of slaving over an expanding gate every time it rained. I distrusted houses in the winter, which is why we'd debated apartment or house so vigorously. As for the summer, it might bring more insects.

Trying to think positive, I decided not to wait for more door problems to startle me, but to anticipate them, to make a complete survey of the house. Maybe this was a kindly nudge from Janus. But did I remember enough of my youth to fix tougher problems? I hesitated, but there was a high priority. We had planned to have seventeen overnight guests for Christmas, making it a very bad time for doors to stick.

I examined the house from the bottom up. No two doors were alike. On one side of the door there would be a brass handle and on the other, more brass (with luck), or porcelain, plastic, or—nothing. First, I inspected the old wine cellar in the basement, now converted into a compact bathroom. The workers had forgotten to repair the door lock. There were two white handles, one of which had gone AWOL, leaving the other free to drop off at the slightest aggravation. If someone were to shut the door from the inside of the bathroom with the bad handle on the other side it would be impossible to get out. Laughable, I thought. I didn't try to find a companion for the lonely handle; instead I bought two new ones. The hardware store said I was lucky to find the right size. It fit perfectly, pleasing both me and—possibly—my Roman overseer. What next? Xmas was now only two days away, and the tension mounted.

The kitchen had no doors to worry about and the living room doors on the ground floor worked, giving me fresh confidence. Next came the first-floor bedrooms, and that's where the final battles took place.

We had three bedrooms and a bathroom on the first floor. The largest bedroom, looking out over the back garden, was where we slept and I didn't need to check to know that door and lock worked. Most nights, somewhere between midnight and dawn, we opened and closed the door several times on our way to the bathroom. That's what two litres of water per day does to you. The bathroom door itself needed a little oil on its hinges to avoid announcing our visits with excited squeaks.

The second bedroom, with a street-side view, wasn't really a bedroom any longer. We called it the study, filled with books and papers, so I passed over it for the moment.

The third bedroom, adjoining, was where we would have guests in about twenty-four hours. It was Sunday, December 23, so this room got priority. I couldn't see Janus looking over my shoulder, but he may well have been there, putting me through the final hoops.

This third bedroom door wouldn't close. The front gate had dimensional problems on its vertical edge, but this one stuck on the top with a scrunch. It was made of wood in a solid frame, dating back sixty years to when the house was built. It seemed to have been mistreated. Up on a ladder, I saw that the top wouldn't fit under the lintel. Perhaps the whole house had shifted; or maybe it was Janus's next ploy. In response, I started filing. The misfit affected at least half of the top on the door, and this wood was dry and hard, so it was heavy work. After thirty minutes without success I tried sawing off the excess wood, a few millimetres, but the only saw I possessed could not cope with decades-toughened wood bewitched by heartless spirits. So, I was forced back to my wood file and a further sweaty hour of work. I told myself, 'Damn it, you're too old for this sort of thing. Forget your dreams of boyhood.' The wood dust irritated my nose and my shoulder ached before the door slimmed down enough to close. At last! I felt relieved and cheered myself down the ladder.

This was when I noticed that although the door had closed, the latch hadn't clicked shut. Anyone could push it open without using the handle. Why was this? Well, the catch was situated too high for the metallic opening it should slide into. Sighing, I exchanged my wood file for a metal file and went to work for a further twenty minutes enlarging the opening for the catch, pondering on the significance of open and closed doors.

I was repairing them because it looked slipshod to have sloppy doors which couldn't shut properly. And, above all, to prove I could do it. Moreover, guests like to have some control over their privacy. There had already been a minor scandal in the house when an adult guest wandered into the bathroom when a sensitive teenaged niece was in the shower. It's not unreasonable to shut a door with a latch and expect any potential visitor to knock first. For more privacy, our doors could be locked—but first, they had to close properly.

The most famous door of Janus in the Roman world was a gate to the ancient Roman Forum. When the city was at war, which was almost always, the gate was left open. During the rare periods of peace, it was closed. I wanted peace in the bedrooms.

A last task remained: check the closure of the study door. Though I didn't think this was as important as the bedrooms, the study contained all our computers, books, and files (paper, this time). And we would have to put an extra bed there for a guest on Christmas Eve. I spend a lot of time writing in the study without bothering to close the door, but on occasion I had pulled the door shut from the inside to help my concentration. Mylène likes to play music at a "meaningful level". There was never any problem closing that study door from the inside, and so I wasn't expecting any further work when I tested the handle from the outside.

Surprise, surprise—when I closed the door the handle went dead on me. By this, I mean that after the latch clicked shut, the handle I was holding offered no more resistance, clockwise or anticlockwise. It was no longer conspiring with its beloved spindle and just hung there, laughing at me, attached only to the brass faceplate of the lock. I could not open the door.

At first, I was just annoyed at my predicament: no immediate access to my books and papers. Then Mylène reminded me about the extra bed needed in that room the next night, and I began to gently panic. Having unstuck the other doors and made them close properly, here was a door that had closed obediently but intended to stay that way. What was the solution? I unscrewed the faceplate of the lock on my side of the study door and the lifeless handle promptly fell to the floor, leaving a round, gaping hole where once the all-important spindle had lived. It was hiding, probably protruding on the other side of the door. Not able to see into the aperture, I needed a torch. But my favourite torch was in my backpack, in the locked study. I hurried to fetch another torch from the basement. With its help, I was able to make out the end of the spindle, about two centimetres inside the hole. I can get that traitor, I thought. I need a thin, long-nosed pair of pliers. My basement tool kit, however, had only thick, short-nosed pliers. My only pair of needle-nose pliers was unfortunately inside the locked study.

I tried to avert that gentle panic, and plans buzzed through my head. I would go out and buy a new pair of pliers—but it was Sunday, December 23, and our guests would arrive the next day for the Christmas celebrations. If I couldn't find a tool to open the door, then maybe I could climb in by the window. No way, I objected to myself: we had recently replaced the old glass panes with solid double-glazed ones, too expensive to break. And to get to the window would require a perilous climb up the outside wall. If all else failed I would have to break down the door, or at least the area around the lock. But even for that, I would need tools which I didn't have.

I wanted action to counteract this growing tension. I explained to Mylène that I might have to break down the door if I couldn't find the right sort of pliers. She gasped, interrupted her vacuum cleaning, and came to stare at the lifeless lock. I dashed out to the Carrefour Market, five minutes away by foot, to check out its limited tool section. It provides bulbs, batteries, multi-socket plugs, cables . . . but no appropriate pliers.

Increasingly frustrated, I put on my reading glasses to better evaluate the hole where the spindle lurked.

"Why don't you go to BricoMarket?" Mylène asked, "It's only ten minutes away by car."

This was the nearest hardware store, and they would surely have this tool, but would they be open on a Sunday afternoon? I should ring and check. Janus would have been by now quite pleased with himself, because the phone directory and the computers were all behind the locked door, so there was no way to find out the store's number. I put on my jacket, grabbed my wallet and keys (at least these were available) and rushed out to my car with a hurried goodbye to Mylène. She herself was occupied, helped by an eighteen-year-old female Tunisian student, tidying and cleaning up the entire house, including the mess I left behind after battling with the doors.

"Back in thirty minutes."

"If you're lucky."

However, when I turned into the BricoMarket parking lot, I realised my luck was out. The lights were off, the store was closed, and there was just a band of punkish youths shouting at each other, or maybe at me. I parked the car and phoned my companion with the bad news.

"I'll have to go a lot further, to Melun, to the big Castorama store there."

"Will it be open?"

We agreed to look for the phone number any way we could and call back in a few minutes. This time I made progress. Maybe Janus wanted to keep me in the game. In my wallet, I found a receipt from Castorama and on it the store's phone number. Normally, I would have filed this stuff in the ever-locked study, but for once my untidiness paid off. When contacted, the store admitted they were indeed open on that Sunday, until 8pm. It was by then close to 5pm so I warned my companion I would not be back until much later.

No sooner was I at the wheel again than I realised I was still wearing my reading glasses. It was uncomfortable driving, but there was still just enough grey light to navigate. I would have given anything for a good pair of needle-nose pliers, even taking a motoring risk. When I arrived at Castorama half an hour later without mishap, my confidence began to rise again. I walked jubilantly into the store and searched for help.

"Needle-nose pliers, you say?" inquired an assistant. "Not sure we have any but you can have a look."

Well, what could I expect from an assistant working late on a Sunday afternoon on December 23? After about ten minutes hunting on my own I located what I had been dreaming of, a pair of slim pliers with at least four centimetres of nose. I ran my index finger appreciatively along the smooth polished surface. In case the demolition option came up again, I also bought other heavy-duty tools.

My pleasure in finding the tools was short-lived. Outside, it was *very* dark and wet, not good conditions for driving half-sighted. I phoned my companion before starting, sent her a kiss, but didn't tell her about the reading glasses. What could she do about it? I remembered having said a few weeks earlier that I liked driving at night because all the distracting scenery beside the road disappears and I could concentrate on the other cars and staying in my lane. True, provided I could still see my lane, and all the weaves and bends in the road.

I lowered my speed to sixty kilometres per hour on roads where the normal limit was ninety. This was tolerable for me, but traffic piled up behind. It doesn't matter, let them honk and push, at least I've got my long-nosed saviour, I thought. But it did seem a long way back to the house. On arriving, and explaining about my lack of proper glasses, Mylène said, "Silly! I could have brought them for you in my car!"

In fact, I was retroactively quite proud of my risky behaviour, and I rushed excitedly to the stubborn study door, brandishing the new pliers. I looked again into the hole for the elusive spindle. The trouble was, I couldn't hold the torch to see what I was doing and manipulate my magnificent pliers at the same time. Momentarily, I had the spindle, and then it slipped. I tried again, pushing the pliers further in until I realised I had knocked the spindle right through the lock, or at least too far ever to reach it with my beautiful but now ineffectual pliers.

No! No! I shouted internally. We needed that room for our guests. Now I would have to massacre the door and its lock! I was defeated and desperate. Mylène was right. Engineers are not good handymen.

Perhaps this ultimate confrontation didn't appeal to Janus. He just wanted to demonstrate how futile my pliers were. There are limits to human logic and brute force. The spirits still have a role in finding solutions. And perhaps Janus is ultimately forgiving. At any rate, what saved me from further combat was a remark from my companion.

"The cleaning girl says that there may be a *second* door into the study, hidden by some furniture."

Astonished, I suddenly remembered this other door. The previous owner had shown it to us before our purchase, saying that he had abandoned it, but it could be re-used, if ever needed. It was in a corner of the second bedroom, half hidden by a heavy wardrobe, and never opened by us. I had always seen it as part of the wall. A door only exists if we recognise its function.

I shifted the wardrobe enough to reveal the second door's lock. Though it had no handle, its mechanism was clearly visible without having to delve into the woodwork. I opened the lock in less than a minute with a screwdriver and pushed the door. Breathing heavily, I squeezed into our beloved study, and released the catch on the main door. The inner handle was indeed protruding awkwardly. It was missing the tiny bolt which secured the link with the spindle. I substituted a stiff piece of wire, reuniting the two handles into a harmonious couple once again. Our guests would never know how stressed I had been.

Janus seemed to have finally made peace with me. We could survive in this house on Antoine Cléricy and, despite my age, I had not forgotten all my fix-it skills. Mylène smiled at me, and I breathed thanks to my father and his workshop of so many years ago.

4

COMMUNITY

The spring after my mother's passing in January 2012 was the beginning of our life in Avon. We finally exchanged the familiar comfort of Paris for something very different. The next step was to discover the Fontainebleau region's strengths and weaknesses, to make it our nest. Birds of a feather do want to flock together, and our purpose in coming to this forested area was to begin a vital relationship with other seniors, to enter their sporting world. How and where would we meet new people, make friends, and become part of the community?

There is no separation between our newish town of Avon and the historic town of Fontainebleau. Both have a population of about fifteen thousand, and both have boundaries constrained by the forest. Fontainebleau has its chateau, a magnificent wooded park, two cinemas, and a glittering town centre. Avon has a huge Carrefour supermarket, a Corning Glass factory, the railway station linking the two towns to Paris, gymnasiums, and lots of higgledy-piggledy houses. French kings built Fontainebleau, and migrant workers built Avon next door. Twenty-five percent of Avon's population is over sixty.

Three hundred metres north of our house, the dark green forest begins. In fact, Fontainebleau/Avon is surrounded by one of the most majestic forests in France, about 280 square kilometres of trees reaching for the sky. The trails through the forest, the rock formations, the view-points, are so numerous that one could spend a lifetime exploring. Some forest lovers have done exactly that: a certain Denecourt has given his name to many of the trails. Today, I often climb up an old stone memorial tower in honour of him. I stare out at the nearby towns, half-hidden by the forest, and wonder how Denecourt would feel about his well-walked trails today. Too many hikers? Not enough? Too old? Were his paths well preserved? Are the trees in good health? And where are all the animals hiding?

When we arrived, I didn't know Denecourt's name, nor the meaning of the blue and red trail markers. Above all, I didn't know any of the other seniors walking the forest. We had joined the local sporting club of three hundred seniors (today four hundred), part of a national federation about which I had everything to discover. For a modest sum we subscribed for a year of sessions in swimming, gymnastics, table tennis and forest hiking (called "rando").

I've always preferred individual sports—no cricket, football, or other team stuff for me. I mistrust group activities and prefer to win or lose entirely on my own. But it dawned on me that, apart from my preferred game of table tennis, most of the senior sports proposed by the club were in groups, especially the forest walking.

"That's fine!" Mylène said. "My dream of old age is to live in a community, all in one big house, with everyone participating in what he or she can do."

"No way! I want my own dwelling, with no interference or depen-dence," I said.

Well, we did get our own house, with no close neighbours, but I remembered the previous summer, before my mother's death, when we had first visited Avon and rented a flat as an experiment, how we tried to explore the forest paths by ourselves. We lost the trail several times, even with a map, so maybe organised hikes with the club would be better to begin with.

One Tuesday soon after our house purchase, we tried to join the club walkers for the first time. Each hike has a rendezvous and finding the starting point on a forest map was confusing—we had to locate the forest "parcels" or area numbers and the nearest road or parking zone.

We arrived by car at the last minute when not one, but several, groups were starting. We recognised no one.

"Group level two? Anyone else?" said a large, cheerful man named Claude.

We gaped in confusion. Was level two tougher than level one, or the contrary?

"We're new here . . ."

Claude waved an impatient hand at us, and we followed him. He was balding, in his sixties, and preferred brief sentences. We were to discover that his passion was the forest and the life inside it.

Off we went, walking at what we thought was high speed with about twenty strangers. The trail was initially wide. At first, I stayed close to Mylène, and as we moved through the forest we were overtaken right and left. Soon we were at the tail end of the group, but fortunately Claude stayed with us. We found out this was no accident: a forest walk should always have two leaders, one in front of the group to choose the direction, and the other at the tail end to make sure no one gets lost (a *serre-file*, or file closer).

Getting used to the pace, I noticed strange trees around me with names I later learned, like tall oak, Scots pine, beech—and the silence, always that silence. No noise except a little gossip from our group. No apparent animal life, just silence. How different from the Caribbean jungle of my youth with its butterflies and monkeys. I had never considered myself a nature lover in bustling, elegant Paris but buried inside me lay memories and feelings from my tropical childhood, with volcanic slopes to explore and succulent fruit trees. My father had owned an estate in Nevis and taught me as a boy to hunt for doves with an air gun. In my childhood garden, or even our garden in Avon, I was used to the chattering of birds, the buzzing of insects, the wind rustling the trees. Now the sounds, smells, and movement were gone. They were all surely there, the birds, insects, and even animals, but well hidden. It would be months later, on warm days and in other parts of the forest before I heard birds chirping. I had to look at where I put my feet, so I couldn't stare much at those tall silent giants, but they fascinated me.

The path was sometimes easy and level, covered with sand, but often there were tree roots to cross, easy to trip over. The tricky places were those where the roots rose well above the soil, and you could catch your shoe, a trap for the unwary. And then there were rocks, of all sizes, to step up or down on. Some were gigantic, shaped like animals, or forming caves with corridors to navigate, often signposted by Denecourt. Going up or down over the rocks was difficult, especially on damp and slippery places. Even when there were no rocks, the piles of dead leaves on a slope could be treacherous.

I lost count of my slips and falls, Mylène doing not much better. After a while the rear guide, Claude, looked critically at us and remarked that we didn't have proper shoes for the forest.

I looked anxiously at my hitherto trustworthy tennis shoes. "Huh?"

"You need boots with proper grips." He leaned on his pole: "And you could do with one of these to keep you steady on the rough bits. At our age, it's all about balance."

A week later, we were equipped and our falls became less frequent.

Luckily so, because these forest walks were the club's main activity: Monday, Tuesday, Wednesday, and Friday. We chose five hours of walking, four hours of table tennis, two hours of swimming, and one hour of Pilates, giving us a twelve-hour physical activity week, and later we added thirty minutes of home gymnastics every day to keep our bodies supple.

But the forest walks were special. As we gained the ability to keep up with the others, we began to explore the social life of our walking community. Just as the surrounding trees were naturally green-leaved our fellow walkers and club members were unashamedly white-haired. And slim—regular exercise seemed to have its rewards. Right from the start, Mylène conversed more with the others than I did. Most of the time I was left happily to my thoughts, like that first day in the forest. Why should I talk to these strangers about trivia when this fascinating Fontainebleau forest was trying to tell me new things? Intriguing, confusing, even antagonistic things. It disturbed my childhood culture of tropical Caribbean trees. Growing up on an island with jungle on its volcanic slopes, I recognised none of these northern trees. Pine, beech, and oak were just names to me. It's hard to change an ingrained sensorial framework. Where were the mango trees, the coconut trees, eucalyptus, white cedar, calabash? If I didn't know the names and nature of these Fontainebleau forest denizens, perhaps I couldn't love them. Deeper down, the smell was not the smell of my tropical childhood. On one level these Fontainebleau trees impressed me with their novelty, on another I felt they were not real, just wallpaper. Much of the time, I kept my distance, and the wallpaper gave me time to ponder about family, writing, and how some trees would live longer than we would. Fine, but something was missing behind that wallpaper.

Mylène found walkers who had been teachers, had worked for telephone companies, or the army, or construction companies, or secretarial work, or had sales jobs, or hadn't had much of a career but were enthusiastic grandparents. The unwritten rule of the game was to keep up with a fellow hiker for ten or fifteen minutes, exchanging news, complaints, or jokes, then change company at the next break. Pauses were necessary at lookout points, and quite often for fluid input and output. The leaders of our forest hikes seemed to be experts in the Denecourt paths, but many trails were not marked. They carried detailed maps and smartphone trail-finders. We would stop at a complex path junction and the leader—Lucien (quite often)—would put his hands on his hips and shout with a grin, "Men on the right, women on the left!" and those in need would scatter behind the trees. The rest of us waited patiently for their return, sharing nuts, biscuits, water, and gulps of coffee. Lucien was slim and muscular with sun-browned skin, short hair, and a ready, somewhat sarcastic smile. He had travelled extensively in French colonial Africa before coming to Fontainebleau and, as we discovered later, his wife Christine spoke fluent English.

Often, Mylène preferred her own timing. She would drop behind the walkers and call me.

"I need a pause behind these trees. Stand guard, please!"

"Okay, but it's my turn next."

Then we had to run to catch up with the others.

I took to carrying two water bottles for each hike, one for me and one for Mylène.

Occasionally, I too, found someone to talk to. There was an ex-banker, Emilio, an Italian and one of the few single males, with whom I could exchange views on the stock market. I met a retired doctor, whom I consulted about my sister Hazel's handicap, and the differences between our health care system in France and the NHS in Britain. Tech-minded walkers like Jean-Marie and Christian showed me their smartphone apps to find the forest trails and our position on them. What amazed me in those first hikes was how the group leader not only never got lost, but always managed to get us back to our starting point after exactly two-and-a-half hours, whatever the weather, the terrain, and the group.

After forest walking regularly for a few weeks, the other hikers became acquaintances and then friends—a special sort of friendship. I asked one of them whether they ever met at each other's homes. To my surprise, the answer was no. The friendship was there—not just companionship on walks and other sports, but help when needed, shared cars for long trips, sympathy when ill, and other manifestations of care, but homes were out of bounds. Few club members invited others to their places, or if they did it was once a year, for a special occasion.

About three quarters of our club seniors were married or had a companion, like myself and Mylène. Quite often couples would do different sports—one would walk and the other partner would swim or play table tennis. Some singletons were discreetly looking for partners of their age, but the new wrinkled-to-wrinkled relationships didn't necessarily last long, though we would soon attend a seniors' wedding. Fortunately, the sporting community provided some comfort for those without a companion. Married or not, most had children and grandchildren who took up time and resources.

Family constraints have changed over the last few generations. My parents took my grandparents into their home for the last decade of their lives. For the next generation, the finances go the other way—we seniors often must help children and grandchildren to survive and prosper.

∿

APART FROM FOREST HIKING, I had signed up to play table tennis, but almost none of the walkers played this game, except Emilio and Gérard. The latter was an athlete who seemed to do everything—walking, cycling, swimming, you name it. I also did four hours of swimming per week, an hour of Pilates gymnastics, an occasional Nordic walk, but no more. Gérard was an administrator of the club. In addition, he was one of the very few who spoke English, having served several years in a joint UK/French military unit in Fontainebleau. He was three years older than I was and very active.

"How long have you been a club member?" I asked him, catching him up in the middle of a hike.

"Since the beginning, about twelve years ago."

I learned that there were hundreds of sporting clubs for seniors all over the country—something the previous generation had little access to. Nothing like this had existed in the Caribbean that I remembered. The French Federation for a Sporting Retirement (FFRS) hoped to soon have one hundred thousand members.

Bemused, because I had imagined I was just joining a friendly local group, I asked about the federal ambitions. Was there an overall policy?

"Well," said Gérard, "we are linked to the government's sporting objectives, but in a non-competitive way."

I avoided a large tree in my path and shook my head in disbelief: "Come on, how can sports be non-competitive?"

Gérard looked back at me: "We're elderly, remember? When you signed up with us, you were probably told that seniors should practice at least three different sporting activities, but in moderation."

I couldn't see the point of this lack of competition, though forest hiking was a possible example. Even here, there were energetic walkers who always pushed to be in front of the pack. "How can you eliminate competition in sports? In table tennis, for example, there's a winner and a loser in each match."

Gérard grinned and patted my shoulder: "Some club members don't want matches, just exchanges, as you'll find out, and anyway a friendly match is not really hard competition."

I remained doubtful and resolved to keep some competition in my veins.

"What about injuries?" I asked. "Aren't all these sports more dangerous for the elderly? And wouldn't the club be responsible?" I was wondering about sprained ankles, asthma fits, or even broken legs in the forest. I still slipped too frequently for comfort.

Gérard explained that our annual member's card required a medical certificate saying our health was sufficiently good for certain sports, and that—based on this—club members had good accident insurance.

"So, it's okay if I slip and fall?"

He laughed, "I'll push you if you want!" Looking around, he insisted that there were very few forest accidents. The club's riskiest sport was cycling, but even there a bad fall was quite rare.

"And all our guides and instructors have first aid training."

We had just climbed to the top of a rocky hill with a view over several kilometres of forest, and I searched for the philosophy of it all.

"Fine, but do you really believe that this picturesque walking, and two other non-competitive sports are going to make us seniors live longer?"

"Not necessarily live longer, but live *better*."

I liked that, but how could I know that my new-found friend Gérard, superbly fit, had just two years of good heath left to him before beginning his fight against cancer?

"Another question: how come our annual fee is so low? Who is subsidising our club?"

Gérard thumped his muscular chest. "I am," he laughed. "Unlike most big clubs, all our administrative work and—above all—supervision and instruction are carried out by volunteers."

"Volunteers?"

"Trained, qualified volunteers, themselves club members. Like me, and like the guides leading the hiking group today. They know the forest by heart!"

I digested this in silence.

∾

I WAS FAR from knowing the forest by heart, but when I stopped thinking of it as wallpaper, those trees could be forbidding, especially when it got dark. So, why did Mylène and I accept an invitation from the instructor Claude to hike in the forest at midnight?

It was because of the animals. We had been told from the start that the forest was full of wild boars (*sangliers*) and stags, but only the initiated could see them. I looked and looked during our walks, but they were completely hidden. If it were not for the tufts of overturned soil on some paths, I would have treated the animals as an illusion, a sad memory of Denecourt's days before all the hunters had exterminated them.

However, Claude told us this hidden population really existed, and the best introduction was to hear them rather than see them. He said that at mating season the magnificent stags would cry out to all the female deer, singing them songs of love and desire. All we had to do was to position ourselves at a good listening point, remain in total darkness, and wait for the stag mating cry (*brâme*). This usually happens around midnight in the two last weeks of September.

At 11 p.m., a group of us parked our cars just off the road at a rendezvous point chosen by Claude and listened to his instructions.

"Turn off all lights. Don't use a torch. No flash photographs either. Put on your walking shoes. I've chosen an easy path. But since you can't see the ground, walk slowly, heel first. Raise your feet to avoid tree roots. Don't talk or make any noise above a whisper. Those forest animals can hear much better than we can. We'll reach our listening point in an hour. Stay close! No wandering, please!"

It was fortunate the path was broad and almost obstacle-free, because without a moon there was very little light. Mylène and I held hands on some stretches. We finally reached our listening destination having only minor encounters with branches. We were at an elevation with an outlook, had there been any light, above the rest of the forest. Then we sat down and waited. And waited. Except for a light breeze, all was silent.

After about fifteen minutes, Mylène asked Claude, "How late will the stags continue their calls?"

To which Claude replied that the orchestra could continue until at least 2 a.m. Someone else then asked if there might not be another listening point lower down.

The answer was yes, but before we could move, one of our group gave a cry and came running towards of us. Against Claude's advice, he had wandered far away from the group and heard a frightening grunt in the bushes behind him.

Claude hushed him, "You disturbed a wild boar! Best for us to stay close together."

After another twenty minutes of careful walking, we heard faint sounds, barely audible, like "Ho! Ho! Ho! Ooh, ah."

"That's them!" said Claude. "Listen carefully." To me, it first sounded like aggressive moans, but the cries echoed inside me, thrilling, and finally gave depth to that elusive wallpaper of forest trees.

In a low voice, Claude explained that the stag's cry was competitive. The female deer could detect from the tonality what the size of the stag might be. Since these females had only one twenty-four-hour period of fertility per year, each wanted the largest, mightiest stag available. Sounds familiar?

We listened for thirty minutes, happily imagining the coupling soon to take place, then returned to our cars in the small hours of the morning.

The last words from Claude were, "Now you know the forest animals do exist, you should have respect. Our human community must live in harmony with the animal community. But be careful! Deer are impossible to approach and don't pose a threat. But the wild boars can attack and together with deer think they have priority on the roads. If you drive at night across the forest, never go faster than seventy kilometres per hour. That's your survival speed limit if a wild boar blocks you."

We drove home slowly.

∾

NOT SO SLOW and not so lucky was the nephew of our next-door neighbour a few months later. He was leaving home in Avon at 5 a.m. in a small car to go to work and probably never saw the stag which challenged his right of passage. The stag did not survive and neither did the young man.

OUR CLUB PRESIDENT Martine did survive her recent encounter with a wild boar. The animal, wounded by a hunter, penetrated her garden bordering the forest and attacked her dogs. When Martine intervened, the boar rushed her with its tusks and ripped her legs. The boar escaped, but Martine had to have several stitches in hospital that night.

5

THE ONE-LEG SQUAT

At my age, I had a hidden problem. It affected my forest walking but was only fully revealed in my favourite sport, table tennis.

Safety analysts are good at forecasting and explaining other people's disasters, not their own. It's an amusing thought if you are not in the process of plunging toward a hard floor. I was a retired engineer, trying to remain a competitive sports player. I had previously been a reliability analyst, now coming to grips with a new and personal safety situation. This was a moment of reckoning. First, I had lunged at a white ball on two feet, then pursued my trajectory on just one foot, right arm and racket outstretched, then finally flown solo, realising that not only had I missed my target—those forty-six millimetres of plastic sphere—but also that a shock of unknown severity awaited me, every bit as dangerous as slipping on leaves in the forest.

I knew only that I was falling, but I am now going to leave myself suspended in mid-air and search for the causes of my plight before shouldering (or kneeing) the consequences. If I could have frozen time in this manner, allowing me the comfort of speculation, I would first have blamed my opponent. We were, you see, in a large gymnasium in Avon playing a tense game of table tennis. In response to a relaxed top-spin drive on my part, my opponent had smacked the ball down the diagonal far to my left. I'm good at retrieving on the right, but less prepared on the other side—that's my style of play. So, there's my first explanation: I was falling because of a venomous shot.

On second thought, however, my worthy opponent had simply done what I was trying to do—put the other player in difficulty. So, it wasn't venom but skill. And anyway, this wouldn't have been the first point I had lost by not being in the right place at the right time. So, why was I falling *now?* Have pity on me, still flying through the air, and conducting a virtual search for the origin of my predicament. My next explanation relates to equipment. Perhaps my progressive lenses had misled me about the ball's trajectory. That could be it. Then, when I realised my error I would desperately have tried to compensate, forcing my centre of gravity into an impossible orbit. And yet—I remembered telling myself I could always recover and stop in time when I made that fatal lunge. So why didn't I stop? Impossible orbit be damned.

Finally, I focus on my tennis shoes. Why hadn't they prevented me from sliding? That evening I had rashly worn an old pair, more suited to jogging than to a slippery gymnasium floor. I had just resumed playing table tennis after an absence of ten years, and now in this frozen moment of introspection I remembered that special anti-slip shoes were necessary for match play. I had no idea where my last pair had gone. So, there it was—the perfect culprit—poor shoes which let me down, or rather up in the air, still waiting for impact.

But think again, I said to myself. It's never so simple. This was not my first unexpected fall. Where were the precedents, table tennis or not? Think about the stairs. Didn't I remember the day I left my apartment lugging a heavy backpack?

Yes, three years earlier there had been a very nasty precursor to the current fall. I'll leave myself suspended in the gymnasium and examine what may be the event which explains it all. Tennis shoes indeed! More like overconfidence. What happened that other time should have made me more careful, but pride goes before all sorts of bad stuff. I was in a great hurry for an appointment on the other side of Paris. A publisher friend, Laurel, wanted us to talk about publication of my work. Everything I had to show her was on my laptop. My writing needed tidying up and I didn't feel happy mailing it, so I packed the three-kilogram Toshiba into my new backpack, something I'd never done before. Together with papers and odd stuff, the pack must have weighed at least six kilograms. It doesn't sound like much but carrying it around on my back was one load too many. No prudent camel would have accepted a similar straw on its back.

I opened the door to my apartment in a state of excitement (would Laurel help me get to publication?), ignored the lift, and charged down the stairs. The backpack plummeted faster than the rest of me. Three steps from the bottom I tried to slow my descent but the momentum of the pack was too much. There I was, again flying, just as in the gymnasium, this previous time with an ultra-hard tiled floor ready for combat a metre below. Why couldn't our building have had a carpeted landing? Forget about the aesthetics of marble.

I'm going to freeze the action again, because once more some speculation on the causes of falling could be useful. Let's leave me doubly suspended and waiting for judgement, because I must now explain about the metro. I have fallen several times in the metro. It's a dangerous place, not because of the whizzing trains on their screeching metal tracks and the bustling, shoving passengers, but because of all those long corridors and the infernal up-and-down stairs. Like many voyagers, I'm always in a hurry to get down to my train or get out of the grimy, dimly-lit underground. Who wants to spend more seconds of his life there than he must? Going fast in the metro is also a macho, competitive thing. Why come second? I knew my legs were strong because of my jogging and I wanted to prove it. So, unless I was carrying a lot of shopping, my habit was to charge up the steps two at a time (three if I could). This worked up to the age of fifty-five. And then, something changed for me. One day, either I slipped, or the step was not where it was supposed to be. I started falling, and I'm not going to freeze myself this time.

I was fortunately going *upstairs* and my hands went flying out the short distance needed to break the fall. There were no notable consequences apart from a slight elbow bruise and my embarrassment at passers-by wondering if I could get up on my own. I didn't want help. It's a random incident, I thought. But a few months later it randomised again, and though I tried hard to dismiss it, my ability to take the stairs at a run was impaired. It kept on happening every few months. At first, I ignored it, and then I put it down to lack of flexibility or bad luck. Strangely, I never considered the consequences of a fall in the other and more dangerous direction, going downstairs. It is even stranger when I remember those reliability and safety studies in my past. Rockets and spacecraft fall apart in a catastrophic manner when there are several simultaneous defects. The problem is to avoid the combinations of minor mishaps which may cause large-scale failures. I now had to become a better sleuth for my own balance problems.

This brings us back to the day in my apartment building when I was suspended above the marble floor on my way to meet Laurel. I hit the floor with a horrible bang on my right knee and rolled over a few times. The pain was intense but with an effort I was able to stand up. It couldn't be so bad then, could it? My computer had survived, so why not me? I dismissed the idea of going back upstairs to my wife and cancelling my appointment. There's nothing like a good dose of courage to sink the ship. I left the building and struggled to the metro nearby. At least, I used to think it was nearby—only three hundred metres—but right then it seemed much further. During the thirty-minute train ride I massaged my painful knee and told myself it would soon calm down. Then I spent an hour talking with Laurel, not moving an inch. I can't remember anything we said. When we had finished, I couldn't get up. Laurel helped me to a taxi and I returned home to much deserved reproaches from Mylène for being an idiot. We phoned a French clinic specialised in knee injuries and other orthopaedic care.

Mylène drove me to the clinic for emergency treatment. Before I saw the surgeon, my knee was X-rayed and I had masochistic fantasies about the possibility of an operation. When I limped into the surgeon's office assisted by Mylène I found a distinguished-looking man in his forties—an age at which I hadn't known the meaning of falling. Would we get along?

He examined the X-ray carefully and said, "Ah! Interesting—you have a clean, vertical fracture of your kneecap. How did you say this happened?"

Somewhat disconcerted by the notion of a fracture, I gave him my story, backpack and all. How stupid of me—did I really need the heavy computer? The more I talked, the more I could see him shaking his head, as if he didn't agree with something.

"I know I shouldn't have carried such a top-heavy load," I said.

"No, you've got it wrong. I don't think the fracture occurred today. It's much too clean and neat. I operate frequently on kneecaps which have fractured horizontally, much nastier. In my experience, a vertical break like this is a birth defect. You were born incomplete, happens all the time. There's no splintering or even fluid fill of the gap. You've simply aggravated a natural defect."

"Are you sure, doctor? I've had other X-rays and no one has ever noticed this before."

"Think of yourself as lucky—you won't need surgery. Take the pain killers and anti-inflammatory pills I'm going to prescribe and come back in a week. Use your knee as little as possible—no walking except with a crutch. We'll see how the fissure develops. Oh, and if you find any old X-rays for comparison, do bring them next time."

The next week, still in much discomfort, I returned with X-rays of the same right knee taken four years earlier after a cartilage-swelling incident. It didn't take much medical expertise on my part to see there was no evidence of a previous fracture. So much for the birth defect—my mother's honour was safe.

"Ah!" the surgeon said. "So, you did fracture it last week. How clever of you to fall just right, in perfect alignment, so that the injury will heal by itself. I can now see the beginning of the fluid fill. Lucky you!"

"How soon can I run again?" I said.

"No more running," he said. "Not on the stairs, nor in the parks, nor anywhere for six months. Then you can begin again, slowly. Come back in two months for a fresh X-ray."

This was bothersome because I knew if I got out of the habit of jogging, I would put on weight and lose form. But every time I cheated and moved a little faster, my knee told me the surgeon was right. I had two further X-rays done and returned to jogging near the end of that year. After twelve months, there was no more pain and no trace of the fracture. No physical trace that is, but it left a memory which should have saved me from future falls. No more heavy backpacks, I decided at the time. But was it just the pack? What does it take to convince a sinner that it's his own fault?

Let us now return to the Avon gymnasium where I am still suspended in mid-air over a hard, slippery, wooden floor, barely more accommodating than the marble landing in my apartment building.

Ready? Crunch! This time I managed to fall on my left knee and slide. I slid a long way. I paused before trying to pick myself up, fearing the worst, and hating the idea of seeing the orthopaedic surgeon's smile again. But to my pleasant surprise the pain was far less than in the previous accident with the backpack. I returned to the table and was able to finish the game, taking no more risks and losing comfortably. Once back home, I rubbed an anti-bruise ointment over the knee area and hoped for the best. After two days of rest, I had just a huge black-and-blue to show for my adventure.

However, more than my pride was at stake. Something fundamental was wrong. The first precaution I took was to buy adequate shoes. The sporting goods salesman suggested a light, cheap pair for table tennis, but I made him find more efficient lawn tennis shoes. Why should a champion like Federer be served better than us Ping-Pongers? I found a heavy model that wouldn't slip on the shop floor. Indeed, when I forced it to slip it screeched in resentment. I suspected that even this was not going to be enough. Out there in the cold, hard world of the over-sixties, stairs, slippery floors, and other obstacles had declared war against me. I had to find a comprehensive battle strategy or risk another disaster. I was lacking more than proper shoes.

The breakthrough came a week or two later during an outdoors gymnastic session in the forest of Fontainebleau. I had hoped this sort of activity—light jogging, jumping over obstacles, horizontal bar hanging, stretching exercises, and walking on logs—might do me some good. I found this easy, except for the last. I was faced with a set of innocent-looking forest logs, about fifteen centimetres in diameter and supported forty centimetres above the ground. Several sports addicts were traipsing atop these logs, waving their arms, more or less at ease. Some, like me, held back in trepidation. When my turn came, I put one foot on the nearest log (good shoes this time), tried to stand with the other, and immediately fell off. No harm done, but equilibrium was impossible. I tried repeatedly, in vain. I thought wistfully of the tightrope walkers in movies and circuses who have no difficulty balancing on ropes far thinner than my frustrating log.

At this point, our gymnastics instructor, Martine, looked at me critically and uttered the word *proprioception*. It sounded like a curse. That's what I needed, she said. She explained that after an illness or simply as we grow older, we can lose our ability to balance properly, especially those who live sedentary city lives. Anyway, balance is always temporary—we move from instability to instability with every breath. I remembered that in addition to falling on city stairs I had slipped many times in the forest.

Forget about spectacles, tennis shoes, flexibility, endurance, or even hubris as excuses. Past sporting prowess is no help—it may even make things worse if we ignore the risks and exceed our capacity to control our balance, resulting in serious accidents. Proprioception is said to be deep, conscious knowledge and awareness of our bodies—where you are in relation to other objects, especially the ground, perception of our internal stimuli, how to balance, how to avoid falling. Let's follow this thinking some distance, remembering that we humans are complex chemical-mechanical systems, but systems nonetheless. Analysing the reliability of the system formed by my body might be like studies of mechanical systems (cars, planes, the Eurotunnel) from my previous professional activity, despite my crying ignorance of the neurological and other processes involved.

What makes us fall, anyway? Or rather, what mechanisms are available to keep us upright? That night, I did research on the Internet and in my Pilates textbook. The vocabulary is arcane: Golgi tendons, muscle spindles, the vestibular system, the gamma feedback loop, and proprioceptive neuromuscular facilitation (PNF). Sadly, ignorance of all this may result in falling flat on one's face. It is as if man was not meant to be upright (as babies probably suspect), and a complex chemical messenger system is all that keeps him standing.

The muscles which control posture from our ankles to our thighs are not just passive soldiers. They are surrounded by a supporting army of spindles and special tendons which communicate with headquarters in the brain. When a muscle is tensed, a signal is sent in a millisecond. Instructions then return, telling the muscle what to do next. Underlying this circuit is vital information generated by the vestibular system—parts of the inner ear that detect acceleration and rotation. Miss the right cue and a fall is likely. I once believed all I needed for good balance was my eyes and the necessary muscles. Think again!

My research showed me that the eyes are quite secondary. In fact, they themselves depend on the movement detection, or vestibular system, to function. You can focus even when your head is gyrating. Fortunately, the balancing system can learn. The blind and the deaf can rediscover how to stay upright, showing that the magic is all inside us. The overall system can also *unlearn* as we age. For a start, some important muscles may no longer be doing their job. What you don't use, you may lose. Even if the necessary muscular force is there, we may forget how to react to a stability threat, like a lost platoon behind enemy lines. Neck straining and back contortions from slouching in front of a screen can do this—writers, watch out.

Fortunately, I found specific training to recover a semblance of my youthful balancing ability. I started with toe control. Toes are our primary ground contact, and it seems weird that we might not be using them properly. After all, we walk with them every day! The problem is the shoes we wear. At first sight, shoes improve our balance by their rigid soles. They have a flattening, stabilising effect on the foot, aside from keeping all the city crap at bay. However, compressing the toes together can make them lazy, and they no longer report their positions individually to the spinal column. Since we rarely go barefoot, the result is that many adults, let alone preoccupied seniors like me, can't control their toe movements.

Yet, each toe has its own muscle, just waiting to be revived. I learned what is called the Mexican Wave, though why the Mexicans should be better at this I don't know. First, I had to practice moving the little toe by itself, keeping the others still, then the big toe. Finally, it became possible to immobilise both big toe and little toe and make the others dance and wriggle. It took a few weeks, with daily exercises. Curiously, I now *feel* my toes when walking. They keep tensing and un-tensing as if determined to assert control over my shoe, and not the other way around. The rest of my training was done barefoot.

After this initial success, the key exercise I latched onto was the simple squat and reach. There are many types of squat exercises, but this one seemed the best for re-educating my proprioception. I hoped it would work well for running, table tennis and stair challenges, but I had doubts. During my runner's career, I had exercised sporadically—pull-ups, push-ups, sit-ups—so I felt I knew something about exercises, but always with the goal of strength and speed. Recently I had taken up Pilates exercises with quite a different focus, on breathing and stretching. I still couldn't see how an "exercise" could improve something as intangible as balance, but whether the squat was a curse or a cure, I didn't have any alternative.

What follows is an important survival strategy for seniors, especially those over seventy like me. When younger, we can do many things easily and automatically, like balancing (and memory). I tried some of my exercises on Mylène's ten-year-old grandson and he had no problems. The challenge for us elderly is to understand what we need physically (and mentally) and find ways to retrain the body (and mind) by exercises (and methods). An active senior can compete with the next generation if he or she adapts to their age with appropriate training.

To begin with, I would place a box or a low stool about fifty centimetres in front and to the left of my left foot. This was the squat target. Fire away! In my bare feet, I would balance in a standing position on my left foot, while raising my right foot behind me. Then, slowly I would bend my left knee as I lowered my torso towards the squat target. Sounds simple? Well, initially I could not do a squat at all, not even this first movement. I lost balance at once and had to put the free foot down. Even just standing on one leg and bending its knee was a problem—that knee insisted on trembling from left to right like a crazy pendulum.

Next, go for the target: I would reach forward with my *right* hand and touch it, twisting my torso as needed. I would try to maintain my balance by extending my right leg behind me. I had to keep my left knee central over my left foot. Having touched my target, I would pause, and return to an upright position. Often, if I managed to place my hand on the target I *couldn't* return upright. I would lose control and find the other leg crashing down like a plane on a forced landing. Most days, I felt I was wasting my time.

Furthermore, one squat is just the beginning. I would try to maintain slow and controlled movements, keeping my right leg off the ground throughout the exercise, and repeat the sequence five to ten times. Then, I would switch feet and repeat on the other side. Surviving a first shaky squat did *not* give me any consistency. Any changes in noise or lighting—or even *thinking* of falling—would throw my concentration off; it was impossible to train with the TV on. It took me three weeks to painfully succeed three successive squats on each leg. It was hard to remember I had once been a 3.5-hour marathon runner, but with perseverance I began to see where the elusive squat was leading.

How little did I know my body in space! I needed three months to carry out the full ten squats on each leg without error, on good days, that is. I discovered my legs were not equal in their ability. My right leg is a centimetre shorter than the left and takes a disproportionate fraction of my weight when standing. It adapted more quickly than its lazy partner on the left. I had to educate neglected stabilising muscles on the outer left thigh.

I do these squats almost every day now and sometimes add weights. I must give credit to the exercise: no more falls to record; no more visions of a hard surface snarling up at me. My companion says I now walk in an almost straight line. I wonder how my zigzags went uncommented on before! My sports reactivity has improved. Today I can carry not one, but two, heavy backpacks up and down several stairways. But a word of caution: even with better proprioception, I have abandoned my ambition of taking the steps two at a time. No point pushing my luck. At least, not going down stairs!

Here's a final test if you're curious about this one-legged stuff. I finish my exercises by balancing on one leg with both arms extended outwards, sideways. Then I close my eyes and count the seconds during which I can remain upright. It's humbling! Most seniors don't survive a count of six. But even this can be improved by more work on proprioception. I've done it. On the one occasion (so far) when, eyes closed and one leg reaching for the stars, I was able to count to a hundred, it felt ecstatic. Most days, I'm happy to reach a count of thirty.

There is a price to be paid for this well-being, the time spent on daily training—toes, squats, abdominals, neck and shoulder stretches. This amounts to 3 percent of my waking time. Is it worth it—becoming an exercise freak—I ask myself? Not every senior will agree. Maybe addiction to the squat is a curse, as I first suspected. But I don't want to lose its benefits, whatever the cost.

Balance is not everything and cannot take into account the disruptive events around us, whether external or internal. When descending treacherous stairs, over-sixties would do well not only to light up their proprioceptive lanterns but to grab the handrail. Don't be the fall guy.

6

FIRST AID

At my age, I am careful with my health, none of that daredevil stuff for me. Younger, things were different. When I was a teenager, over sixty years ago, I cycled down a hill without brakes, smashed my bicycle into a car, and had to be carried home. These senior days, if I'm hurt, I get up, lick my wounds, and go on my way. When I come across an accident in the street, I check that other people are taking care of the injured but I try to walk away as soon as possible. Minimum service, if you like. Blood is bothersome, especially other people's. And yet, here I was, embarked in first aid training, and all the red stuff. Blame it on table tennis.

Having painfully resolved my balance problems during early sessions of table tennis in our new club for seniors, I began to take the game seriously again. A decade before, I had been a ranked player and regional umpire but had stopped competing because of injuries. Now in retirement I turned the clock back. I even changed my grip from penholder to shake-hands. The table tennis group was quite a different community from the forest walkers. To begin with, sessions were in the evenings, in a gymnasium. The activity catered to players—like me— who had known the game years earlier and preferred it to walking, a few still-working club members who were happy to smash a ball in the evening, and finally those elders who wanted a reactive sport to wake them up. Our youngest players were in their sixties and the oldest near ninety, though I couldn't tell this at first—they looked very active.

I made many friends. André, short and stocky, lived close to us and had built one of the few all-wooden houses in Avon—he played well despite recovering from a cancer treatment in his right arm. Sishir was our star player, a dark-skinned Malaysian who played penholder close to the table and had enjoyed the game from age six to nearly eighty— very reactive but don't ask him to jog. Jean-François was our artist, a tall smiling player always in-between photo exhibitions and foreign travel. The names of other table tennis friends indicate their international origins: Emilio, Carlos, and Friedhelm.

I found myself adapting my play to have simple fun with my opponents, bringing out their best. Only occasionally during an evening session could I let myself go against a good player like Gérard and work up a real sweat.

After a few months Gérard said to me, "I need more club instructors for table tennis. Would you be interested?"

Caught off guard, I responded, "Not especially, my friend, I'm too busy with other things." I was thinking of my writing and family obligations.

"Well, consider it," he insisted. "The club would pay for your training."

Training? What training, I wondered. What's there to learn in a non-competitive environment?

Two weeks later, at a swimming-pool session, our club president, Martine, personally invited me to become an *animateur* (instructor) for table tennis, certainly at Gérard's request. Taken aback, with a mixture of reluctance and excitement, I felt I couldn't refuse the president's offer. I accepted, and thus moved a step deeper into the seniors' sporting community.

How could I know that a year or so later I would oversee the whole table tennis operation, and the recruiting of other instructors? How could I know I would become part of the club management, with so many friends I would forget half their names?

Mylène warned me that it was a big step—I would have to give up other activities like La Vie Devant Nous in Paris—but she warmed to the adventurous side to it.

~

AFTER A FEW ADMINISTRATIVE PRELIMINARIES, things changed radically in my sporting life. Suddenly, I was in a high-stress zone, enrolled in a first aid course as part of my training. The national sporting federation (FFRS) decreed that, like all trainee instructors, I first had to learn how to take care of the players in my charge in case of accident. Hopefully, my first aid training would never be needed, and none of my sporting colleagues would do anything foolish. Still, I was nervous. I wondered what my first aid lessons were going to entail.

The training facility was in a fire station just outside of the town of Melun. I was greeted by a man in his mid-thirties, clean-cut, slightly balding, with a serious, military look. "I am Gaétan," he said, "your guide for today. We have seven hours to study life and death."

It sounded grim, so I stared curiously at his uniform but couldn't figure out his rank.

Gaétan escorted me into an antechamber where a few other grim-faced volunteers from our sporting club and others were waiting. "You have all come here to learn how to save lives. Welcome. We shall see what you can do for the injured; I'll call them victims. None of you are medically trained, I presume?"

We shook our heads, me emphatically.

"We are going to talk about the bad stuff you may have to deal with: choking, wounds, burns, loss of consciousness, heart attacks, broken limbs and so on. We will learn by example and you can't be squeamish."

I tried to tell myself this was a challenge, nothing disturbing, and surely nothing to do with table tennis, but I began to conjure up unpleasant images of mangled bodies. There were five men and three women in the group of trainees. If they could stomach it, so could I. And there might be intriguing aspects. I was a scientist, after all.

Gaétan fixed us, one by one, with his green eyes. "No insult meant, but right now you are all incompetent in an emergency. When we're finished, you'll know a few vital things but the 'first' in first aid is especially important. It doesn't mean you can save an injured person on your own—it means you need a 'second'. So, the thing to remember is: you must have medical reinforcement quickly. How will you get that?"

"Telephone 18," a fit-looking man said.

"No, 112," came from a sturdy woman.

I had never bothered to learn these phone numbers which most French people were familiar with, though I had vague memories of my wife Colette calling 18 when our apartment was flooded some thirty years ago. We lived near the Bichat hospital in Paris and once when I had an asthma fit at night, we walked to the emergency ward together rather than bothering the emergency medical services (SAMU).

Gaétan seemed amused rather than concerned at our lack of precise information. He cleared up the mystery on a paperboard. "For medical help anywhere in France, you'll need to call 15, the SAMU; the number 17 is for the police; 18 is for the fire brigade; 112 is a European-wide help number; 115 is for homeless persons. Obviously, you must carry a phone whenever on service."

I took it that "on service" was occupation related, which meant whenever I was responsible for sporting activities at my club, and only then. This was initially a relief: I could continue to ignore street accidents and other nasty stuff, as before. But what if there was a public injury and no one else volunteered?

Gaétan then told us that first-aiders should be prepared to help the injured in the event of a public emergency—fire, earthquake, radiation —signalled by a siren of three one-minute blasts. So much for my hopes of limited service.

"Here is your first challenge," he said. "Imagine entering a damage zone, or even hearing a cry from someone nearby. The victim appears to be choking. This could result from an explosion, toxic gases, a fall, allergy, or an object stuck in the throat. What's to be done?"

We looked at each other, imagining signs of suffocation, but remained silent. One friend from our club, Jean-Claude, a good walker but overweight, seemed even more concerned than I was. He kept on examining his body during the exercises as if to prevent this or that happening.

"Well, as with most first aid, to begin with you need to *assess* the victim's situation and confirm the degree of choking. If he or she can speak, it's only partial choking, so encourage him to cough and then leave the victim to it. If you shake up a partially blocked throat it may make it worse. But if you ignore a totally blocked throat, death will quickly follow.

"So, if the victim gasps, clutches his throat, is not able to talk or breathe, or looks blue in the face, you *need* to intervene. First, get behind them and bend their head and shoulders slightly downwards. Check the mouth for obstruction. Then administer five firm blows between the shoulder blades with the heel of your hand."

Thumping is aggressive, I thought. But then I pictured *myself* as a choking victim having wolfed a spicy hamburger too quickly, and the use of force made more sense.

"The five impacts are sometimes sufficient, but if not, you should pump air up through the victim's throat from his lungs, which is called the Heimlich treatment by abdominal thrusts. Grab the victim from behind around the waist, between his navel and his sternum, your stronger hand made into a fist, the other hand reinforcing it, and squeeze hard, very hard, moving upwards, five times in succession."

I had not heard of Dr Heimlich, and his abdominal thrust sounded violent. Despite the German-sounding name, I found out later that Heimlich was American and his technique was widely accepted.

Gaétan added, "If this works, the foreign object may be expelled and the victim may vomit." He paused. "If the victim is still choking, return to the five thumps on the back, and repeat."

It was time for practice. Gaétan gave five tepid blows to a volunteer's back and showed us where the abdominal thrusts should be applied. "I won't complete the Heimlich manoeuvre on you because it can itself cause an injury."

Fortunately, no back thumps or injurious thrusts came my way.

"What if the victim is fat, or pregnant?" a small woman with grey hair asked.

"Grab them a little higher, around the chest, and thrust for the best."

"What about children? Aren't they the ones who choke most often?"

Gaétan smiled, anticipating this question. "Children from one to eight years can be treated like adults, but please lighten the blows. A baby under one year is a special case. Its lungs and chest are not completely developed. The Heimlich squeeze is carried out with two fingers gently pushed into the middle of the chest slightly under the baby's nipples."

Next, we were asked to do this exercise with a baby-sized doll. Its chest moved in and out in a realistic way. When it was my turn, the exercise suddenly felt personal; my son had a three-year old boy Adam and his wife was expecting another baby. I tried to imagine doing this for my grandchild but shied away from the responsibility. Yet the idea of not being able to help a small vulnerable being was difficult to accept. Then again, surely this would never happen—would any imprudent baby choose my presence to have a choking fit? But how could I know what future disasters fate might throw in my path?

I was still digesting all this when Gaétan led us through a door into a larger victim room. "Now, about blood," he said.

Before describing Gaétan's next shock treatment I need to step back and question my state of mind. What was the origin of my negative attitude to giving first aid? Was it fear, or was it something else? I had not always been averse to medical acts. For thirty years I had bound up my family's cuts and bruises as a father should. Nor was I always indifferent to the call of medicine itself, as the technical guides on my bookshelf suggest. But my recent interventions had seemed futile.

Some years ago, there was a six-month period during which my late wife had needed complex injections to stabilize the levels of her red blood cells and platelets. At first, a nurse came to our apartment to administer the treatment. Afterwards, I had to do it myself. I can see my old living room, Colette reclining on the sofa, and I manipulating a syringe filled with red stuff. I injected my pallid wife awkwardly, rereading the instructions each time. It seemed to help her at first but her haemoglobin level stayed below normal. A few weeks later, she was hospitalised.

I still had faith in her doctors. Previous hospital spells had been successful. Then it all went wrong. Instead of haemoglobin levels, the word leukaemia was used, acute myeloid leukaemia. It was mid-August, French holiday time, and her doctor was absent. The palliative services were also absent. On the nurses' advice, I telephoned an outside doctor in authority for higher morphine doses. With my children, I stayed in her hospital room day and night, and we were there when she died. The nurses cried with us. When her doctor returned a day later, we'd asked why a bone marrow transplant had not been tried. It rarely works, they claimed. In my anger and despair, I lost confidence in those doctors.

But all of this was seven years earlier—surely, I could now make my peace with illness and injury situations. Sporting accidents, like my recent bruised knee, had nothing to do with leukaemia.

Ahead of us, on the lawn, were a few prone bodies and two upright victims. One of them staggered up to me shedding fake blood in a stream of strawberry red. Gaétan took the victim's right hand. The palm from which the blood jetted was split diagonally by an eight-centimetre gash with a shiny object in the middle. Glass, a razor, or a nail? Although I knew it was a simulation, my stomach tightened.

As if sensing my agitation, Gaétan said, "First aiders must be able to look at a spurting arterial bleed and not faint. The main arteries are on the right side, where the heart pumps oxygenated blood to the rest of the body. But some veins on the left can result in profuse bleeding when severed."

It's only an "incident exercise" as they call it. Just a simulation, I kept on thinking, a table tennis player can't hurt himself like that with his racket.

"You must lay the haemorrhaging victim on the ground." He helped the injured man down and lifted his wounded hand. "Loss of blood will lead to fainting and possibly death. You only have six litres to spare! Elevate the source of bleeding and then compress the area. Also raise the legs above the heart level, if feasible."

"Shouldn't the wound be cleaned first?" I asked.

"No! That might open the cut and accelerate the flow of blood. The same is true for a knife stuck into the body—leave it in place until medical help comes. If there is an embedded object, press on either side of it to close the edges of the wound. In the present case, I will cover the wound before compressing it: a handkerchief, a plastic bag, or a strip of shirt will do."

Not my shirt, I thought, taking a step back.

"Avoid direct contact with the wound." He squeezed the injured hand with a cloth which rapidly turned pink, and he continued, "Now call for help."

"What if I have no phone handy?"

"Then bind up the wound with a knot and search for someone who can call."

I had hardly recovered from the sight of so much false blood, and was reeling from images of knives, saws, hatchets, and all sorts of sharp instruments severing veins and threatening death, when Gaétan said, "And now for burns."

A fresh victim approached; his face contorted. This time it was the back of his hand—he appeared to have a large red-and-black oozing area of blisters and pustules. Not much blood, but no skin left, either. It disgusted me more than a deep, bloody gash.

"What should we do?" Gaétan said.

"Clean it up! Disinfect with mercurochrome. Spread soothing creams on it . . ."

"Wrong! No oils or creams or bandages or supposed disinfectants. Only use cold running water for ten to twenty minutes. And call for help at once."

This was an accident about which I had some knowledge. When I was a boy, my baby brother Peter had overturned a kettle of boiling water and scalded his lower body, loins and testicles included. The maid in charge did not know where to find any medication and plunged him into cold water. I shivered when I remembered him crying, so long ago. All his burned skin came off and my mother was furious, but this was the right treatment. The skin grew back, and his future sexual ability was not impaired, as proven by his healthy family of today.

I asked a female club member how she had found the cuts-and-burns exercises. "Nothing much," she replied, "it's all body cream and tomato ketchup!"

Then, we went back inside the classroom for trauma and cardiac situations.

"Each of you has to do the next exercise," Gaétan said. "It's central. Onlookers tend to panic when someone falls unconscious, but *you* must act. The cause may be trauma, illness, or drugs. Remember to protect yourself from unnecessary contact."

It had not occurred to me that an injured person could contaminate me. And how could I not panic, just a little?

"First, and always, analyse the victim's situation. Remove any dangerous objects nearby. Distance the crowd. Reassure everyone. Check for wounds and bleeding. Bear in mind the victim's limbs and perhaps his neck may be broken. Your objective is to know whether resuscitation is necessary. Is the victim breathing?"

But how can one verify this?

"Ask him! Gently hold his shoulders or his hand and question him. 'What happened? 'Can you breathe? Can you open your eyes?' If the victim responds, he has passed the first test and *is* breathing. Call for help. He can be left where he is until medical services arrive. Don't try to move him.

"If, on the other hand, the victim doesn't respond, you can't conclude he's not breathing. You must tilt the head back, then put your own head close to his face and look, listen, and feel for breathing. This should be quick—no more than ten seconds."

Suppose the man was dead? I found this increasingly disturbing. I had only touched one corpse in my life. I remembered the dimly-lit hospital room in the small hours of the morning. I was holding my wife's hand when she died. I didn't want to let go. When her heart stopped beating, I felt her fingers grow cold—not in ten seconds, but less than ten minutes.

Don't be an idiot, I said to myself, forget your personal traumas. This is not going to happen during table tennis.

"If you have established he's unconscious but breathing, you may have to put him in the *recovery position,* on his side or his stomach. This is the best way to keep the airway open."

I had more qualms. There was a very fat man in my group whom I was sure I couldn't turn over. Why was he doing first aid instead of slimming, anyway?

"Kneel beside the victim making sure his legs are straight and place the arm nearest to you at right angles to his body. Then bring his other arm across the chest. Grasp his far leg above the knee and pull it up."

There were too many legs and arms involved! I was a bit confused.

"Now hold one hand to his cheek and pull the far leg towards you so the body rolls over on its side. Adjust his upper leg so both the hip and the knee are bent at right angles. Tilt his head back and move the chin to ensure the airway stays open. Wait for help."

Though I didn't grasp all of this explanation, it was easy in practice. The raised knee gave a lot of leverage. I rolled one heavy man over, and in turn was rolled by a tiny lady. But the sequence wasn't finished.

"Now," said Gaétan, "we have to know what to do if the unconscious victim is *not* breathing. We can't give up."

This was the tensest moment of the day—who dies and who survives. "There are ninety thousand deaths by cardiac arrest in France each year," Gaétan told us.

I imagined that perhaps a few of them might be saved by the apprentices in our group. Then I tried turning the tables and wondered who would intervene on the day my own heart stopped beating. I first dreamed up a slender, romantic female first aider leaning over me and then I realised a lot of strength would be needed; better a well-muscled plumber.

"Emergency services take ten minutes or more to arrive. Each minute of heart failure without help decreases the victim's chance of survival by ten percent. Figure it out!"

I took this literally and couldn't stop myself calculating—engineers are like that. Gaétan implied a 100 percent chance of death. My own probabilistic calculation started with a 90 percent remaining chance of survival for each minute lost; thus, 0.9 raised to the tenth power yields a 35 percent residual chance of life after ten minutes of neglect. It's better than nothing.

When the heart fails, I learned it's usually because of something called ventricular fibrillation, an abnormal rhythm caused by injury or lack of oxygen. Gaétan explained what the usual first aid tools were: cardiopulmonary resuscitation (CPR), which consists of pumping the chest area, and rescue breathing, which is inflating the victim's lungs with our own oxygen-depleted-but-still-useful breath. Fortunately, we would not practice on each other but on a life-sized dummy. Each of us was issued a face mask to place over the dummy's head for the rescue breathing. This was not romantic or amusing. I imagined a real victim with a vomit-streaked face and a failing heart. Could I do this?

In addition to Gaétan's techniques it would mean taking charge of the crowd situation; reassuring the onlookers, though I might well be in a barely-controlled fluster myself; recruiting someone to phone emergency services; and pumping the victim's chest like the devil.

Gaétan then produced a yellow box he called a defibrillator (more precisely, an AED, or automated external defibrillator). It contained a measuring device for the heart rhythm, an electrical shocker to bump up the slow rhythm, a speaker, and a computer to control the procedures. This magical device costs only about fifteen hundred euros, making it worthwhile in many public places. From being distrustful of the whole first aid setup I became indignant that there were not more defibrillators available to get some of those ninety thousand arrested hearts beating again. The heart which stops beating triggered a family association: I remembered my late wife had been an enthusiastic first aider in her company, as was my daughter, Chloé, for the Red Cross. They could be relied on to intervene if needed in their daily life. I had been an outsider. Now, could I render the same service?

I was one of the last trainees to carry out the exercise, which should have given me confidence, but didn't. The body was lying on its back. I had to kneel beside it and position the head, slightly backwards with the airway opened. Then I placed both hands on the chest, the right one in the centre and my left hand on top of it. I leaned over the body with my arms straight, pushed down hard, and then released the pressure.

Unfortunately, I had recently injured my left wrist by falling on a patch of ice, and it hurt to press on it. I forced myself to pump up and down thirty times, quite fast—wishing I were elsewhere. In real life, I hoped the victim would have responded by coughing, and opening his eyes. With a dummy, there was no respite.

Next came the rescue breathing. I covered the mock-victim's mouth with mine, pinched its nose, and breathed out deeply. The cold plastic lips were quite unwelcoming, but I had to make the dummy's chest move. Several times! On my first try I didn't pinch the nose properly and my breath came right back out in my face. After this, I began the next round of thirty CPR compressions. A slog.

Gaétan opened the defibrillator box. It immediately shouted instructions, beginning with: "Connect the electrodes." I placed them one on each side of the chest and the defibrillator announced its first jolt of current—its voice ordered me to step back. Since the electric shock didn't produce results, the machine began a two-minute waiting period before its next measure of the victim's heart condition. During those two minutes, the first aider (me) had to continue CPR and rescue breathing. This would be exhausting, equivalent to about a hundred partial push-ups. Then, the defibrillator should give another jolt or (optimistically) announce a renewed heartbeat.

My training stopped arbitrarily after one two-minute session. The true first aider should continue indefinitely until medical help arrives. Torture! But only a doctor can pronounce the victim dead, though in our training session we could be more brutal with a dummy. I now understood why no one with a heart condition could get a licence to play table tennis in our sporting club.

Despite trying hard, I felt I was not very effective at heart pumping. And I couldn't translate the plastic model into a real victim. It was time to decide what all this effort was worth. "What are the chances this will save anyone?" I asked Gaétan discreetly.

"Hard to say. When a first aider like you does basic CPR, it's like suspending a death sentence, not cancelling it. Defibrillation can change the verdict. Sometimes, that is."

I liked Gaétan's "sometimes" for its realism. Perhaps it was this and the intense physical stress which made me look more closely at my fellow first aid club trainees. I hardly knew most of them, but I felt they were good people, not there just out of obligation. If faced with an emergency, sometimes their actions would be vital, although they might not be enough. But they were prepared to try. I, too, had made the training investment, even if table tennis had been my main goal. My fear and distaste had been largely shaken out of me.

We learned about other injuries, but none as serious as heart failure: bee stings should be scraped off with a plastic credit card; ticks should be uprooted with tweezers; asthma treated by a "reliever inhaler" (typically, a bronchodilator).

Chief Sergeant Gaétan closed the day. "Unfortunately," he said, "you will forget most of today's details, and you may have to repeat this training. But please retain Heimlich, CPR, and the SAMU phone number. Much of the population in Norway has had exposure to first aid training at school or the Red Cross. In Germany, this knowledge is necessary to obtain a driver's licence and eighty percent of the population knows the basic techniques. In Britain, schools don't teach first aid and companies are only required to have one first aider present for every fifty employees, so less than ten percent of the population has had the equivalent of our one-day training. Here in France about forty percent have some first aid competence. You volunteer seniors represent a significant part of this."

I became eager to memorise the techniques and read books about first aid. I am not a doctor, and my technique is limited, but I am now a part of the 40 percent.

When leaving the classroom, I asked a smallish woman what she had made of the training. "I can thump someone on the back," she replied, "but I'm not strong enough to do the squeeze or the chest compression. And if you ever call the SAMU, I'd advise not giving the age of the victim. They take longer coming to help the elderly because they think it's too late anyway!"

Fortunately, table tennis sessions almost never produce an accident, and we haven't had any air raids or public emergencies, so in the following year I had no chance to test my skills. When our star players were injured, it always happened outside of our sessions, like our ex-policeman Bernard doing fancy mountain climbing. At most, I saw a train passenger in difficulty, fainting, and alerted the railway security services. Despite my good intentions, Gaétan was right, my senior brain soon forgot most of it, except "call 15 for the SAMU".

7

NO PLACE TO HIDE

At three o'clock in the morning I was ripped from sleep by a cater-wauling.

"Yaroo! Miaow! Take that! Eeargh! Yowee! You too! Sss! Arou! Yagagh! Meeahow!"

The racket slammed through the double-glazed windows two floors above our back garden in Avon as if the carnage was taking place in our bedroom. Mylène simply groaned in her sleep, but my hairs sprang to alert. I sat up, pulse accelerating. Who was being slaughtered, the cat or some feline stranger? Could I practice first aid on a cat?

I slipped out of our blankets, stumbled to the window, pushed it open and peered at the moonlit scene below, expecting to see the combatants. I took in our weeping willow, grass lawn, gravel drive-way, and shadows. A cold gust blew in through the window. Nothing else.

"Hey! You, down there! Shoo!"

Still nothing.

It seemed as if the fight had never occurred—no sign of human or animal life. I stared out of the open window for several minutes, panic ceding to curiosity, and considered going downstairs to get a better look at the aftermath. Finally, sloth and sleep got the better of me and I returned to bed. "Tomorrow, I'll bury any corpses," I thought. Mylène had not stirred.

Before breakfast the next morning I went down to the ground floor. The door between the laundry and the guest bedroom was closed. Inside the bedroom area I checked the folding bed and the small bathroom. No sign of a fight, but the sliding door to the garden was open. This room was where we had lodged the cat.

This was not *our* cat. It belonged to Mylène's daughter, Dorothée. A week before the cat fight, just before leaving for a holiday in far-away Bali, Dorothée had phoned Mylène and asked us to take care of her pet while she was away. "My neighbours are all absent and I can't leave The Cat confined for two weeks," she said. Beyond the parental link with her mother Mylène, there was the underlying idea that two senior citizens have no better demands on their time than to foster a feline for a fortnight.

What does it mean to be a senior, anyway? We are mostly over seventy and have grey hair (or no hair), and often still in good health. We've retired and have thus lost the daily group of communicative co-workers and finicky bosses who used to frame our lives. Maybe, like Mylène and me, we've replaced this group with some other community. But we've also lost our family bulwarks. Our parents are no more. Our children are remote, themselves grown up and mostly married, with their own careers and interests. We feel this void of contact, if not of affection—but what can take its place? It's not simple to help adult children while avoiding parent-child postures. Mostly, our opportunities for new family relationships lie with grandchildren. Or maybe even their pets! All this before we ourselves get so old that we need help ourselves.

So, taking care of Dorothée's cat was natural for Mylène. And seeing the depth of affection her daughter had for her fourteen-year-old pet, we were hopeful that someday she would find an even more inspiring human partner. Love, in short. Three years later, this would come true.

If Mylène had asked for my agreement on this project, I might have said no, but she didn't. It's not that I don't like cats, quite the contrary, but I am averse to taking care of one. I find them fascinating creatures, but with a strangeness linked to violence. When I was fourteen, the same age as Mylène's daughter's animal, my last cat Simba was shot dead by a neighbour in the Caribbean and I vowed at the time never to own a cat again. But there was no escaping this pet.

Dorothée lives in Paris and has no car, so soon after her call we bought a cat litter, feeding bowl, and some food "for choosy cats".

She arrived the following day by train with a heavy animal basket, which she placed on the floor of the downstairs bedroom.

"What's its name?" I asked, trying to get a peek at the funny voyager.

She hesitated, "The Cat is what I call her."

"But her real name?"

"Pollen, I guess. From long ago."

Pollen is a neutered, fourteen-year-old female, and weird. Dorothée's refusal to use her name is also weird.

When Dorothée opened the cat basket, Pollen immediately scurried under the nearby bed. Only when I went down on my knees could I see that her fur was white, caramel, and black. Two large, scared eyes stared back at me.

"She's like that," Dorothée said. "Not very sociable—always hiding somewhere." She glanced dismissively at our food for choosy cats and said: "I've brought *special* food for her, and if you want to spoil her, she appreciates small bits of ham mixed in with her croquettes."

I exchanged glances with Mylène.

"She can be hard to find," Dorothée said. "Last time I left her with someone she stayed under a bed, in a dark corner, or stashed away in a cupboard the whole time."

"We'll take care of her, don't worry," Mylène said. "Why don't you spend the night here?"

"Alright, but I have to get back to Paris by midday tomorrow. And then leave the madmen and hyper stress in my office. I'm going far away to forget it all."

We accompanied Dorothée back to the station, wondering what we had got ourselves into.

A neurotic cat—just what we needed!

Before taking the train, Dorothée's last words to us were: "If something happens to her while I'm gone, I won't be mad at you. But please don't tell me until I come back from my holiday!"

Of course, this only made us more concerned about Pollen, whom we refused to depersonalise by any other name. During our first twenty-four hours of guardianship, we never saw her.

Many cats like to be petted, strut around, and chase things, even their own tails. True, they sleep for more than half the day, but this is to compensate for their intense activity when awake. Not Pollen. We could detect no activity, no sounds, and no movements.

We closed the doors to her room and left some food and water in bowls. The food disappeared during the night, and the next morning we found Pollen under the bedspread. When her hiding place was discovered she scrunched herself up inside it and looked at us with cautious round eyes. We tried to pet her but she recoiled each time.

We speculated that Pollen had been scared at birth and had therefore concluded that her goal in life should be to hide. But I had my doubts. Cats are strange, which is why they fascinate us. Attributing a human-like childhood trauma to Pollen was perhaps too simple. Unlike dogs, who obey orders, cats have a sense of freedom which makes a mockery of our everyday concerns. What was it with Pollen?

In any case, by small encounters, our relationship with Pollen developed. We would leave the room, close the doors, and a few hours later the food would be gone. The only thing which changed was Pollen's hiding place. Sometimes we'd find her under the bed, sometimes under the bedspread, and sometimes beneath the sheet which was under the spread. Never a sound, not the slightest meow did she make. On the second day, she started using the cat litter. I sniffed, but the odour was just about tolerable. We took to going down three or four times a day, "to check", but in reality, to see if we could catch her moving. Maybe she couldn't even walk properly.

The third day, two things happened. First Mylène sprinkled some bits of ham on the hard, brown croquettes. Next, I opened the sliding door onto the garden and left it ajar. The weather was fine and we wondered whether Pollen could be tempted outside.

The bits of ham disappeared, and so did Pollen.

I scanned the room, scouted our garden, and found nothing. Disturbed, we phoned the last person in Mylène's family who had hosted Pollen and inquired about the cat's movements. Had she ever left the house?

"Pollen? Oh, you mean The Cat! No, she never went outside. But she did disappear. We lost her for a whole two days, just before Dorothée's return. Then she reappeared an hour before her owner arrived. Very bizarre cat."

This was not reassuring, but that evening we spied a cat-like hump on the bed. It was Pollen, under the sheets again. It may have been my imagination but, looking under the covers, I thought I saw a glint of excitement in her round eyes. Where had she been?

The next night, Pollen disappeared again, and we were pretty sure she was having adventures outside. A boyfriend? A walk on the wild side? There were at least three other cats who sometimes crossed our garden. Her appetite seemed to improve the next day and Mylène had to empty her litter box.

Then came the night of the hideous caterwauling. I blamed the neighbours' cats. One of them in particular frequently slept on a patch of uncut grass under the weeping willow. He was probably the warrior who had confronted Pollen. Who had won the fight? And had there been any injuries? Since we couldn't approach Pollen, we couldn't check whether she had any bite marks. Clearly, the neighbourhood could be dangerous for a new cat on the street. So, that night I took the decision to close the door to the garden with Pollen inside the room.

Next morning, day six, came as a shock. No Pollen.

I checked the doors to the bedroom—all had been closed. The attached bathroom was empty. She was not under the bed. Nothing was under the bedspread, or under the sheet. The only other furniture in the bedroom was a large table against a wall with heavy cardboard boxes stored underneath. These contained books and papers recently moved from my apartment in Paris. There were two large cushions on top of the table which had served once or twice as hiding places for Pollen. But she was not there. The six boxes underneath the table were stacked on top of one another and covered the space from floor to table top. There was no gap between the boxes and the wall behind the table.

In short, *there was no place to hide!* Where was Pollen?

For an engineer like me, an unsolved mystery is a terrible thing. It mattered more that I couldn't figure out what had happened than to know whether Pollen was alive or dead.

"I suspect an intruder, who opened and then closed the sliding door to the garden," I said to Mylène. "Remember the Korean film about a weird man who stalked houses at night? He would climb over walls, open doors, or windows, and walk silently around people's homes, not waking anyone and not stealing anything. For him, it was the thrill of not being discovered. On our street there are a dozen houses like this one, all with gardens and low fences. A night-time prowler might be invading all of us. And he (or she) would have thought it funny to let Pollen out—the one witness who couldn't testify against him."

"Hmm," said Mylène. "Are you sure you closed the door to the rest of the house?"

"Yes."

I reopened the door to the garden to let Pollen back in, if and when she deigned to show herself, and we tried not to be worried as we went about our affairs—fiddling with computers, pretending to write, shopping for more ham, and so on. Near the end of the afternoon I heard a cry from Mylène, "She's back, Pollen's here!"

We found her under the deepest sheet cover. And perhaps—my imagination again—she looked tired from her adventures. Mylène dared her hand under the sheet. "Sweet Pollen, how are you?" Pollen retreated, and then surprised us by allowing herself to be petted on the head for the first time. I tried ruffling her fur myself, with partial success. Perhaps wild love was changing her nature. Or perhaps her real nature was not what we thought.

That night, I modified my security strategy. All the doors to Pollen's room were shut, then locked and double-checked. We slept soundly; no intruder could enter. At breakfast time, around 9 a.m., I strolled downstairs with some bits of salmon Mylène had prepared. I opened the door to Pollen's room and approached the hump in the bed.

If this were a murder mystery, I'm sure you could guess what comes next. The hump was empty, and there was no Pollen, neither the live cat nor her corpse. I called for Mylène and on hands and knees we looked everywhere. Once again, Pollen had disappeared into thin air. And no exotic intruder could be responsible. I remembered Houdini's vanishing tricks but it didn't bring me nearer to a solution.

Mylène frowned: "Dorothée did say The Cat is quite ingenious in choosing hiding places."

My inner engineer was profoundly frustrated. We searched all the places we had already searched. We found only a lot of cat fur which would take days to clean up. My rationality began to waver, and I wondered if some animals might not have special invisibility powers.

She *had* to be outside, even if we didn't know how she had got there, so I opened the door to the garden again. And we waited, going about our business. Patience is a virtue, virtue is a grace, and Grace is really a cat named Pollen who vanishes in the morning and then reappears each evening for her food.

As it happened, we had no more time to be concerned because we became host to one of Mylène's grandchildren, Eliot, for the next few days of his summer holidays. When he had been duly welcomed and fed (not on croquettes!), we took him down to see Pollen and told him about the mysterious disappearances. We encouraged him to be Sherlock Holmes and help solve Pollen's vanishing act. He watched while Pollen quivered under the sheet and I locked all the doors to her room.

The next morning, armed with a magnifying glass and a notebook, our young Sherlock tried to solve the mystery which had defeated us. He accompanied me down to Pollen's abode. I opened the door and, as before, the cat had disappeared. Now we were three to witness the puzzle. After fifteen minutes of searching, Eliot wanted to know what was in the boxes under the table.

"Just books," I said and lifted the top rightmost box down from under the table top. Its contents seemed unstable and I put my hand inside the cover to open it.

"Miaow! Psssst! Grrrrr!"

This was the first time I had heard Pollen emit any sounds if you don't count the night fight. She had been hiding inside the cardboard box all along. I won't attempt to describe the gymnastics she had to carry out to enter the half-closed box with less than ten centimetres of leeway between the box cover and the underside of the table top, but somehow, she had done it. A collective sentiment of relief went through us and I congratulated the young Sherlock.

Since I didn't have to bother about supernatural disappearances any more, I began remembering other strange cats I had encountered in the past, and the relationship between a cat and its owner. I had once known someone whose behaviour was the inverted mirror image of her cat's. The person in question, my deceased wife's elder sister, was shy and polite to excess. Her cat was ultra-aggressive, climbing up her curtains and ripping holes in them, snarling at visitors. Maybe a cat can pick up the inner vibrations of its owner's character, hidden personas, and act them out. One day, astonished, I witnessed this friend lose control and throw a glass of water in a visitor's face. Soon after, she was committed to intensive psychiatric care for bi-polarity, and I had to find another home for her cat.

Could it be that when I looked into Pollen's hypnotic eyes and thought of her as "scared" or "cautious" or "excited" that Pollen was evaluating *me* and wondering what my alter ego was?

This alter-ego response might also be the case of Pollen and her owner, Dorothée, who is normally a confident and talkative person. Pollen might have been reflecting Dorothée's concealed timidity, a search for a hiding place in life. And when Pollen let us pet her, she may have been wondering (if that's what a cat does) if we were her new owners. Should she adopt new behaviour?

If a cat can sometimes play the role of an alter ego, I had to rethink the significance of *my* long-ago cat Simba. I was considered calm and self-controlled as a boy, but Simba was a night-time marauder and chicken thief. The day he was shot down I became so angry I wanted to kill the next-door neighbour who had blown him to bits. So, was my own alter-ego a secret pirate, given to fits of anger when things go wrong? Maybe I, too, was stealing chickens from someone! Maybe we all have dark alter egos which feed into the warriors of the night.

Foolish speculations perhaps, but the oddness of cats would never be the same for Mylène and me. Moreover "alter ego" is not a sufficient insight into a cat's behaviour. What if there is no hidden persona? The cat remains an emotional sponge for whatever vibes are in the air and performs a feline version of its master's mood.

When Dorothée returned from Bali she came to recover Pollen from us. We joked about her cat's creativity. Before leaving on vacation, Dorothée had been very tense about her job and had been in deep conflict with her dastardly manager for months on end. Now, the wonders of Bali had made her mood much more positive. The world was again a good place to be in, provided one could scoot off to the far and beautiful corners several times a year.

That afternoon in Fontainebleau, I looked out of a window and saw Dorothée in the garden, under our weeping willow, typing enthusiastically on her phone. It was a warm return of summer weather. Pollen was there, out in the open, for perhaps the first time. She strutted about her mistress, vociferously meowing, and rubbing against her legs, "normal" cat behaviour we had never seen before. Dorothée stroked The Cat with a smile, as if to say, "How can I work with you sticking to me like glue?"

Pollen seemed to have no worries or fears about anything. Sticking? Hiding? Who, me?

8

KEY TO THE GAME

There were no more cats to look after. Instead, I was on the long road to Bugeat, five hours of driving, and I had time to wonder why I was going there. To boot, my companion Mylène was not with me, a separation we disliked strongly. Still, there was table tennis ahead, my favourite game.

I concentrated on the road and figured I would have to stop twice, once every two hours, to stay alert. My GPS, I realised afterwards, had decided to keep me off the motorways, and routed me through narrower and more tiring secondary roads, via Bourges and Montluçon, to the East of Limoges.

The French have this curious word *animateur* which in their sporting world means *instructor*, and not just organiser and coach but also entertainments officer. Since volunteering to become a federal instructor for seniors' table tennis I'd had one surprise after another. First had come the gory one-day first aid course where I learned how to detect injuries (is he dead or alive?), and above all, to call emergency services. Then, my second training session was a three-day administrative brain-bashing in Paris where I was made aware of the chain of responsibility from the instructor via his club president, to the regional management, and then to the French Federation for Retirement and

Sport (FFRS). It was drummed into our heads that the elements of being a good instructor are conviviality, training skills, and safety. He or she has an obligation to try not to lose any senior citizens along the forest trails, nor at the bottom of a swimming pool, nor even under a table tennis table. To try, with due care, or else the insurance won't pay.

After I had driven two hundred kilometres, I pulled into a parking lot for a fifteen-minute rest. I stretched my legs and recalled my third training session, which had dealt with the health of cantankerous seniors, plus a lot more about accidents and insurance policies and how to privilege good humour over competition. It was a week of management information. Our federation is multi-activity and the third training centre purposely had no specific equipment for each sport, so each trainee had to contrive a virtual glimpse of his discipline to the others: an archer showed how to shoot with invisible arrows, a Nordic skier how to march without poles, and in my case, I pretended to bounce Ping Pong balls on a tiny stone table. I kept on thinking back to our federation's slogan—senior sports are not so much about adding years to your life (though this happens) but about adding life to your years.

Now, I was off for five final days of theory and practice dedicated uniquely to the table tennis instructor. A pity it had to be held 450 kilometres away from Avon. I hoped it would make me a better player.

That Sunday afternoon in October 2013, lonely in my car as I weaved along the road, negotiating roundabout after roundabout, slowing to fifty kilometres per hour in villages, trying to justify all this effort, I needed to stop again and eat the ham-cheese-and-pickles sandwich prepared by Mylène. There was no official parking at hand, so I pulled into an area off the road in front of a decrepit house. As I sat in my car and started eating, a rough-looking man emerged from a van near the house and approached me.

"Hello," I said to him in French.

"You can't stop here," he said grimly. "It's private property."

"Sorry, I couldn't find an official parking place and I'm tired."

"Well, you'll have to leave, old fellow," he said. He turned away and halted in the doorway of the house to glare at me.

Old fellow? Who did he think he was? Surprised and annoyed, I didn't start the motor at once, but slowly finished eating my sandwich —pickles and all. I felt I certainly wouldn't enrol *him* in my table tennis team. No conviviality.

Accelerating away, I felt destabilised. Should I have reacted differently? Shown more anger or more politeness? How would I have dealt with the man years before? Not for the first time, I felt several personalities inside me corresponding to significant periods of my life. Who was I today, and how should I live? What would it mean tomorrow to become a table tennis instructor? I didn't feel old at seventy-one. I felt the same *me*, as if nothing had changed since youth. Yet this was untrue—any mirror could show the difference. My body was slower, less resilient; my muscles were weaker, though I tried hard to maintain them; my balance needed daily maintenance; my sight needed more correction; greying and wrinkling had to be concealed. To my astonishment, people sometimes gave me a seat in a bus or the metro, though I often refused.

On the other hand, I knew more about my body and what it could do. Experience counts, even if I was no smarter. You might call it a small dose of wisdom. A younger person can't measure the consequences of apparently innocent choices (inactivity, smoking, poor diet). Vivid images tickled my memory as I drove onwards. When did I first play table tennis?

IT WAS many years ago in my school in St. Kitts. I'm holding a book in my hands and staring at a play area where there is a scratched green table with a low, sagging net surrounded by my boisterous classmates lunging at small plastic balls. I am not a participant—I don't know the game. Then, I saw myself the day I arrived in England in 1961, a raw-but-proud Caribbean student admitted to a prestigious university. There I am, disembarking from an Atlantic passenger boat at grey-and-rainy Southampton, looking for my baggage, and not knowing where to turn. I'm feeling cold in this strange country and have almost decided to abandon my stuff and seek shelter when I am accosted by two smiling faces.

"Are you Christopher from St. Kitts?"

"That's me! Who are you?"

"British Council, come to see you don't get lost."

"I just don't know where my bags are."

"They've already been put on the train to London. Can we help you find a seat?"

"Well, thanks, but don't bother. I'll find it."

After all, I knew about planes, boats, trucks, and cars, though on reflection I had never taken a train in my life.

"It's no bother. We're supposed to see you to Kings Cross in London, where you can catch a second train to Cambridge."

I was both flattered to be met and insulted that they didn't think I could find my own way. Finally, menaced by the complications of not one but two of those strange trains, I accepted temporary help. But I would have to find ways of showing the Brits—not just these two—that I was self-reliant. This feeling hasn't changed much with age—I prefer to solve my own problems unless the mathematics becomes impossible.

My first opportunity came two days later, freshly installed in Pembroke College, when a fellow student, Robin, took me on a tour and showed me a sports room. On the ground floor of the college library, a chapel-like cavern with a high ceiling and walls of polished oak, I could feel the age of the place, smell the years.

"This is the table tennis room," Robin said. "Do you play?"

I didn't, but when I saw the easy-to-use bats and the little celluloid balls, the urge came over me to make this game *my* sport and show those staid Brits what a Caribbean student could do. It couldn't be that difficult compared with cricket, which had always daunted me. Who wants to face up to a hard leather ball thrown at you at high speed? Some islanders were inspired by Calypso, limbo, and Rasta music— why not Ping Pong for me?

"A little," I said, so Robin handed me a bat. I fingered it curiously.

"Outside of Asia," he said, "most players shake hands with their bats; they grasp the blade between thumb and forefinger and wrap their remaining fingers around the handle. Like this."

I tried it.

"On the other hand, the Japanese and Chinese grasp the handle like a pen, with thumb and forefinger on the same side of the blade; they use only one face of the bat. No one around here uses this grip, so I don't know if it works well."

I chose the Asian penholder grip on my bat, just to annoy my orthodox opponents.

This was a key contrarian decision—because with my enthusiasm and my unusual penholder style, I would play against Oxford three years later (captain of the second team, lost 0-10, but let's forget that bit). Robin shared in this inglorious defeat. We played together in the college team for several years and in later life he represented a New Zealand provincial team.

I would continue vigorous competitive play in England, the USA and France for almost four decades in local tournaments. One tiny thing changed when I left England—most other countries talk about a table tennis racket and not a bat. Whatever you call it, the excitement was the same for me.

Now, en route to Bugeat in the Corrèze region, all I had to do was to find new strategic ways to approach the game, and my life as a coach, organiser, and player would rise to new heights.

As if to sober me up, my mind jumped to 1999, and sat me down in a doctor's office in Paris with my neck giving me hell.

My burly doctor shrugged his shoulders and said, "No, you can't continue. It would be damned foolish. You have arthritis in both shoulders and your table tennis aggravates the cervical area."

"But, Dr. Krott, table tennis is a gentle sport. All the health guides recommend it."

"Not the way you play it! You told me you were constantly smashing with your crazy penholder grip. Do you want another paralysis of your right shoulder and arm, with six months of a restraining collar around your neck?"

I didn't and took his advice.

Temporarily—a twelve-year break.

STILL ON THE ROAD, the key moments of my table tennis past kept coming back in emotional rather than chronological order. The next invasive image surged from earlier on, as if provoked by the face of my pessimistic, overweight doctor.

It's several years before my shoulder problems, and I'm now a young fifty-year-old in the 1990s, ranked at 65 points by the French Table Tennis Federation scale of the time (lowest was 80), and quite cocky. On a Saturday morning, I'm getting special training in table tennis from an ex-French-champion, Marcel Barou. We are in a small gymnasium in Paris, near Place Monge, and have the place to ourselves. Marcel no longer plays in competitions but runs a garage. He loves national holiday weekends because there are so many smashed-up cars to repair afterwards. But he can't repair my faulty table tennis smashes, and after a vigorous exchange I hit the ball clumsily into the net and shout in frustration.

"Don't worry," my coach says, "you may not be able to improve your game right now, but when you are my age, over seventy, I predict you'll play better than ever in your life. You may be a bit slower, but you'll have time to think about the game and your body movements."

I laughed in disbelief.

HOW COULD I have forgotten that? I came back to the present and smiled to myself while slowing down the car for some serious bends in the road.

I thought about key events and causality, about how my table tennis career had progressed in one direction rather than another. Having abandoned the game for twelve years, I might never have taken it up again seriously, despite the optimistic prediction of my coach Marcel. Yet, I had accepted the role of instructor after a chance encounter with the President of our Fontainebleau sports club at the swimming pool a year ago. I shook my head, mocking myself—I wouldn't have had to take the emotionally disturbing first aid training, nor to be on this lonely trip going to strange places if I hadn't felt ambitious. Did my past duties as an official table tennis umpire and regional tournament organiser justify all this? And there were other consequences—to be on the safe side I changed my grip on the racket from penholder to the orthodox shake-hands style. My game had suffered at first, and I had had some new balancing difficulties, but at least now there were no shoulder pains.

THE IMAGE of my recruitment faded, and I was back in my car *en route* to Bugeat, for my final training session. In the dying daylight, the last roads through the forests of Corrèze were full of turns and bordered by massive trees. I couldn't see much ahead, even with headlights on. It got darker and foggier and I was glad to arrive at Bugeat.

The receptionist gave me a magnetic key-card to my room. I thought the residential sports centre looked comfortable, though the lights over the stairs up to the living quarters didn't work. The first thing I discovered was I had a room with two beds all to myself. The next (and I kicked myself for not knowing) was that for a small extra sum I could have brought my companion along. It would be the first time in five years Mylène and I had been apart for as much as a week. Very annoying, since at least one couple had registered, but separation can make feelings grow stronger.

We were sixteen trainee table tennis instructors from all over France. A lot was crammed into that week. I was up at 6 a.m. for my own personal exercises, then outdoor gymnastics after breakfast, lectures throughout the morning, gym sessions with table tennis after lunch until 6 p.m., and evenings looking at video playbacks of the day's matches and national tournaments.

Mylène was visiting her children and grandchildren in Avignon while waiting for me to finish my training, punishing those little celluloid balls. We telephoned each other every evening and then I looked at the late-night news to keep the past in balance with the present.

Sadly, you can't teach people a great deal of technique in a week, though you can motivate them to share ideas and make table tennis a fun activity in seniors' clubs. You can also alert them to safety issues. It's true the risk of getting injured while playing non-competitive table tennis is small, but what about the players who have been injured or ill *before* entering the gym? Our elderly population is full of knee problems, shoulder problems, neck problems, eye problems, prostate problems, or recent strokes, and some surveillance is necessary. Any accident must be reported to the club, the federation, and the insurance company.

But had we come all the way to Bugeat just to learn warming-up and cooling-down exercises (which, in any case, we would have difficulty enforcing in our clubs)? Many of the trainee instructors were there more for the club organisation than the skills of the game. For me, it was like being presented with the icing on a cake but no cake underneath.

When thinking about my future role of table tennis instructor, I had hoped to acquire more *technical* skills in the game, but there was little said which I did not already know: topspin, backspin, sidespin, the pendulum service, the hammer service, were all cited but it would take months to perfect these fine points. Most of the trainees had been selected by their clubs to manage the activity rather than be skilled players themselves. Only a few (four or five—including me) had previous competition experience, and I felt the others were less interested in fine-tuning their games.

One trainee instructor with not much playing experience asked the course director how to choose a table tennis racket, and how to advise other players.

"The choice of a racket is intimate," the director said, "it's easier to suggest a new lover! Fortunately, for beginners any standard racket at about forty euros will do. For the more ambitious, it might cost one hundred euros."

"But suppose the player wants to know about racket surfaces and things like that, are there guidelines I can suggest?"

"The key is to know the player's psychology. Confident, assertive types will want to develop an attacking game and need a fast surface. The more hesitant types will favour defence and thus they need a slower surface with more control and perhaps more tackiness. You can tell by the way they behave."

The questioner, my fellow trainee, acquiesced, but I objected.

I looked at the affable director and said, "Isn't that a bit naive? What if the goal of a player is to develop a new personality, a quest for freedom? Think of a diffident, polite, British type (don't look at me!) who wants to liberate himself on the table and be ultra-aggressive! Or consider teachers, doctors, social workers who spend their days helping others and now want the luxury of hitting out. Better allow the undecided to test different types of racket."

"Hmm" was all the director would comment on this, but he continued, "and who knows an easy way to detect an old or ineffectual racket?"

No one responded, so he said, "If your racket can't be used like a hairbrush, it's no good! Place it on your head and drag it across your hair."

This test was no problem for most of us and certainly not for the two women trainees, but I saw a few balding seniors uncomfortably scratching their scalps.

"Does your racket adhere to your hairs and pull them the way you want? That's called tackiness. If your racket surface is smooth and slides over your hair without resistance then it will have no effect on a table tennis ball either. Time to buy a new surface! This is the key!"

However, keys are not always so accommodating. The next day, after a morning lecture, lunch was a stodgy potatoes-and-ground-beef mash-up which took time to digest. I finished late and ran up to my room to change into my gym kit.

My door would not open. My electronic key-card had stopped working. Angry, but trying to keep calm, I set off for the front desk.

"Ah, your card gave up, did it? Too close to your mobile phone, perhaps. Happens sometimes. You should take more care! We'll need ten minutes to fix it."

It took them thirty, and I was late for the afternoon session. I remained suspicious of the key-card until the end of my stay.

However, this misadventure didn't stop me from getting my licence as a federal instructor for table tennis. During the week, we were tested for our ability to organise innovative practice sessions for the other trainees. In one of them I had the group play with their left hand (except the left-handers who had to switch to the right). This produced an intriguing disorder, because now the weaker players often did better than the stronger ones. To extend the chaos, in my next exercise I converted them all to penholders for a rowdy fifteen minutes. Deprived of the movements we take for granted, we must rethink our place on two feet and find a new relationship with a moving ball. Maybe we seniors should change other habits to keep us adapting.

At week's end, certificate in my pocket, all that remained was the long drive home and some reflection on my future in table tennis. The autumn weather was perfect for the first half of the trip and I began feeling pleased that my game skills were adequate, at least as good as those of my new instructor friends. But as I drove through the forests, golden leaves carpeting the roadside, I wondered whether "adequate" was good enough. Didn't I once have higher goals?

ABRUPTLY, I saw myself at age twenty-two, seven kilos lighter and a lot faster, during summer vacation at a Butlins Holiday Camp in England. I had been playing table tennis there for a week, at the end of which I took part in the English national tournament. I'm in a huge gymnasium/stadium with dozens of tables. Though struggling valiantly, I'm unranked, and easily eliminated in the preliminary rounds. However, the organisers recruit me to umpire some of the later matches, one of them featuring a certain Chester Barnes. I gulp. Now perhaps forgotten in the archives of table tennis, Chester Barnes was a brilliant player, already considered among the best in England at age sixteen.

As the ball whizzes by from one side of the table to another, my umpiring confidence, normally strong, is shaken. Suppose I make a mistake scoring such an important match? These players are so rapid I could easily miscount.

My memory is blurred on this point. I may have made a scoring error with a ball which nicked the edge of the table, but the players corrected it themselves and waited for my acquiescence.

"Barnes to serve, twenty–fifteen," I remember announcing. Barnes then flicked his way to victory, and he went on to win the tournament, the youngest English champion ever, and he won it again every year for the next four years. At the end of the match both players shook my hand and some of their electricity must have entered me. I couldn't *be* Chester Barnes, but at least I had gotten close to him, and surely my game would improve in the future.

In the next four decades, I would never meet a wizard of the game as talented as the young Barnes, I thought, looking at the darkening road ahead. It began to rain and would rain increasingly heavily all the way back to Fontainebleau. It felt strange, this brief immersion in my young man's layer of identity almost fifty years ago.

NEXT, I remembered a day in Seattle, America. That score of twenty–fifteen is still in my mind. I look around me, and there is no gymnasium, there are no table tennis tables, just a large auditorium filled with people dressed in suits rather than tennis shoes and shorts. I'm dressed alike, and I'm on a stage in front of the auditorium with a big white screen behind me. The intricacies of table tennis are far from my mind. A projector assistant is displaying slides for me on this screen, and I'm delivering a scientific paper, all about heat transfer by natural convection around ice surfaces. It's about the way water behaves near its maximum density of four degrees Celsius. It's why lakes and rivers don't freeze to the bottom during the coldest winter and all the fish don't die. The research project is the background for my master's thesis. The talk goes well, and at the end I begin to pack up my slides and notes. The projectionist, a young Indian in his late twenties, comes to shake my hand.

"Your paper was good, but do you remember being fifteen–twenty down and winning?" he asks.

"No," I say, but then it comes back in a flash: Pembroke College table tennis team against Caius College, five years earlier and a year after the Chester Barnes match. We are in the basement of our college library, the table tennis room I know so well. I am the club secretary and we need to beat Caius to get our team promoted, but the match is deadlocked and I seem certain to lose my game with the Caius captain, a young Indian of my age.

I am five points down, fifteen–twenty, and my opponent only needs one point to win. Never in my fifty years of playing have I turned the tables in such a losing situation, except that day. I serve five aces, making it twenty–twenty. My opponent is then so rattled he loses the next two points and the match, twenty–twenty-two. And there he is in front of me, shaking my hand in Seattle.

"I was so shaken up by our match," he said, "especially by the fearsome look on your face, ready to take me down to hell. But I got over the defeat, and in the following weeks I said to myself if you could do it then so could I, and my game has continued to improve. You inspired me to my present success in the game!"

While driving back to Fontainebleau, I don't know if it's the warmth of remembering an old acquaintance or reliving the thrill of competition which moves me most.

WHEN I RETURNED home from this epic trip to Bugeat, I put all this soul-searching aside because Mylène was waiting, equally tired from her journey back from the South of France, and we had much to discuss. She was happy my daydreaming had not resulted in any accident on the motorway.

The next day, I decided to remedy the lack of competition in my Fontainebleau senior's club. I was nagged by the low level of playing technique in our instructor's training. The dictum seemed to be: "This is the equipment, these are the rules, this is your organisation; the ball can spin but we don't know why, now just manage it for us."

Our national organisation, the FFRS, thinks that serious competition is not the best objective for seniors, and thus does not sponsor this aspect of our sporting activity. But I *had* to compete again, not simply train and organise. The philosophy of training techniques between coach and learner is in three phases: cooperation—uncertainty—duel. Without a duel, the cycle is not complete. So, I registered with another club at Fontainebleau which catered to all ages and sponsored competitive table tennis. I paid my fees and asked to play in the monthly tournaments. Maybe I could bring back useful ideas to the seniors I would train, or maybe I was too old and would look ridiculous. But if old age was not to be a wilderness after retirement, I needed new goals.

My first tournament was open; meaning any licensed player over eighteen could compete. I started in Division 3 and lost every match I played. I was the oldest player in the gym. Most of my opponents were aged twenty to forty and showed no compunction at walking over a seventy-one-year-old like me. I didn't see myself as slow—they were just quicker! One of my first adversaries was named Monsieur, Serge Monsieur, and he laughed every time he made me run after the ball. But I returned home strangely satisfied with the taste of blood. I could see why these competition players were so much better, and maybe I could learn to anticipate faster and counter their aces.

My second tournament was organised by age group. In France, the word "senior" is ambiguous. In the sense of "senior citizen", it implies oldies of over sixty, and retired. The FFRS will only accept senior members over fifty-five. In French companies, workers over forty-five are often considered seniors, on their way out. The table tennis sporting classification is more detailed. Seniors are aged from eighteen to thirty-nine. Players over forty are *veterans*: my age group, seventy to seventy-nine, is V4, and a new category, V5, has been added this year for players over eighty. There is at least one known competitor in Australia who is 102 years old (V7?); it's clearly a rejuvenating sport.

I was to compete in the town of Chelles, about an hour's drive from Fontainebleau. I looked enthusiastically at the list of my opponents and discovered that for the first time I would be meeting other V4 players, and even a few V5s. This, at last, could be my moment of fulfilment, with no age differential to handicap me. To comply with the check-in time of 1 p.m., I planned to leave at 11:30 from home.

First, I stopped at a service station on the outskirts of Fontainebleau. It took more time than planned to fill up on gas and check the tyre pressure, and I used the service station restroom.

The shock came as I was hurrying back to my Ford Mondeo and felt in my coat pocket for the car keys. Nothing there. Puzzlement, then increasing stress. I was wearing three layers of clothes—shorts and T-shirt to play in, gym trousers and pullover for warmth, and a jacket on top—all with pockets to search. No keys.

Keeping my panic under control, I figured I must have dropped the keys in the service area. My jacket pocket was a little shallow, so I retraced my steps to the payments counter. Still nothing.

"Have you found a set of keys?"

"What keys? Where?"

The only place I hadn't searched was inside the restroom, fortunately unoccupied. My eyes darted fruitlessly around the floor, the corners, the bin, the washbasin, and at this point I almost gave up. My keys were lost and I would have to call Mylène and borrow her car, leaving mine to an uncertain fate. Damn, damn! Consequently, I might miss the tournament.

Glaring frantically everywhere, something inspired me to check the toilet bowl. And there they were, black plastic and metal floating calmly in a forbidden sea. Relief and distaste. What to do?

The water appeared clean. This meant the keys must have fallen in during or after flushing, maybe when I zipped up my trousers. Slightly reassured, I fished the keys out and washed them thoroughly in the basin. Then I dried them in paper towels and examined the result. My key ring had two attachments, a black plastic electronic clicker to open the car doors and a green clicker for my garage. Satisfied it was all there, I breathed deeply and ran out to my car for the second time. How lucky I had been.

Near to my car, I pressed the clicker, but to no avail. I pressed repeatedly, and still nothing. The doors remained locked. Nearby drivers seemed to detect my disarray as I fiddled desperately with my keys.

I was back in the panic scenario where I would have to leave my car and miss the tournament. I, who was always looking for keys to everything, I was to blame. This was the writer in me, stuck in his symbols. Keys are worthless if you don't know how to use them.

Then my inner engineer took over. The clicker was not the only means of unlocking the car doors. It had a metallic key attached to start the engine. This key might also unlock the doors, although I never used it that way. Blessed key, eureka, it worked!

I was so relieved I went back to the restroom to pee again.

An hour later, I was seated in the mammoth Chelles gymnasium, munching my sandwich, and admiring the zealous competitors smashing away at each other on twenty-odd tables. Most were seniors and young veterans. My own age group V4/V5 had seven players allocated into two pools, due to start at 3 p.m. Now, at last, I could be at home with my own.

Well, not exactly. Two players in my pool were ranked way above me and I was duly hammered; I won just one game out of seven. My third adversary was, for the first time, distinctly older than me; a V5 with a slight limp. It should have been easy, but I was hard put to win. Taking stock, it looked as if the only competition players I could beat were more impaired than me!

Ah, where had the Chester Barnes electricity gone? What was I missing? And what good was a third-rate instructor? Could I be satisfied with coaching in my club if I failed to improve my own game? Weary and seriously down in spirit, I barely heard my name called from the side-lines. It couldn't be for me, I knew no one in Chelles.

"Christopher, it's me, Roger!"

It was a friend from my Fontainebleau club among the spectators. Surprised and revitalised, I jumped over the ball barrier and shook hands with him.

"Great playing!" Roger said, "I've recently joined the club here, but don't forget to invite me to Fontainebleau for your next annual tournament."

I was in a hurry to leave, but I looked with tenderness at my grinning ninety-year-old friend, a survivor of several medical crises, and I talked with him for a while.

I told him how brilliantly I had just lost, and he laughed.

Roger had, like me, taken up writing after his retirement, so I asked him how his work was going.

"Funny you should ask me that in Chelles, a place where we've never met before. I'm working on a novel about beginnings and endings. Every story starts in one town and finishes in another, revealing a new protagonist who will continue the story."

"I'm writing essays about Fontainebleau," I said, "where we seniors try to get our lives in perspective."

Or at least I thought I was, and about table tennis in particular. I admired Roger and wondered if I would have as much enthusiasm for the game in twenty years' time when I was his age. Helping other seniors like him to play was worthwhile, largely compensating for my static competition skills. I felt my elderly ambitions changing. When playing, I could exercise my body, help my adversary to improve, and have a whale of a time.

What kept Roger going? I remembered how Mylène and I had skirted panic when she had had a bad result from a tumour marker test. She had had a melanoma on her back removed many years earlier, and then in Avon her dermatologist discovered a suspicious mole on her abdomen. Confusion and fear! Fortunately, fresh surgery was successful. On the other hand, how easily Roger shrugged off his three cancer operations and even the possibility of yet another! It wasn't bravado. I felt he had accepted mortality, and thus in Socratic terms, accepting his death allowed him to learn to live.

This was my real quest, I realised, not just finding a key to better table tennis. In my declining years, striving and losing could be worth as much as winning. Well, almost.

9

MY ENEMY, THE SNOW

Table tennis wasn't my only challenging activity. I grew up thinking snow was a myth. I could not imagine our vigorous Caribbean sunshine replaced by fairy-like feathers floating down from the sky. When I first encountered the white stuff, far away from my birthplace, I shivered in the cold and hated snow. Unable to banish winter, I have since tried to keep snow at a comfortable distance. Yet today, I am much older, and it has trapped me once again.

First, let me explain the bias of my student days, how I froze when I first arrived in England. Coming from the tropics, I expected nature to be generous and accommodating. I was well prepared scholastically, but no one had explained the principle of warm underclothing to me. Or else I hadn't listened. My first real winter, in 1961, brought burst pipes and snow. Even the Brits slipped and fell in the slush. University heating was minimal. When I complained, a Scottish friend, Sandy, pointed to his open windows and nonchalantly displayed a glass of frozen water by his bedside. How could I accept living in a refrigerator?

And yet, I had once been a little climate rebel. I hadn't respected the static world of my tropical youth—sun, sun, and more sun. I liked hurricanes, perhaps because I had never experienced a major storm.

My island seemed too quiet, lacking in magic. I hungered after change. So, why hate the snow? When the river Cam froze, the power of that icy transformation overwhelmed me. In that frozen moment in Cambridge, I could walk on water! I could skate on it. This new, white world was suddenly beautiful, and it fascinated me, until my fingers objected to the nipping cold. The ambiguity of my feelings about snow has its roots in that first winter.

Four years later, in 1965, I left the half-hearted frosts of Britain for the real thing in North America. I adapted. The campus at Syracuse, in upstate New York, where I began graduate studies was far colder, sometimes minus-twenty degrees Celsius, but the houses were warmer and I understood the importance of proper winter clothing. Each winter was thick with snow, but I walked everywhere in warm boots and even breathed in the cold air without freezing my innards. My first engineering research project was about the properties of ice.

It was natural for me to try skiing. If it was going to be cold and snowy, why not have fun like the natives? Skiing in New York State is easy. You don't have to take a train or rent a room in a resort. I could hop into my car after work and in less than an hour, I'd be on a lighted ski slope. I learned the snowplough technique, and then discovered how to parallel ski; extravagant behaviour for someone brought up on sunny beaches. This was a period of truce with snow.

However, when I immigrated to Paris in 1970, I found that easy access to snow had disappeared. The city received just enough to occasionally disturb the trains and put dirty ice and slush on city-dwellers' shoes. Still, one or two walks in the Bois de Boulogne, with the trees draped in white, softened snow's worsening reputation.

Until, that is, my two-year-old son stepped on the thin snow-covered ice on the park's lake next to those elegant trees and fell into the deadly cold water up to his neck. Luckily, I scooped him out in time. It was a black mark for ice and snow, and for the careless parent.

For a few years after this, winters came and went almost unnoticed. Then my wife Colette and I faced up to the February school vacation dilemma: what to do, where to take the children? That's when ski resorts raised their conniving heads. We tried out Club Med resorts, where organisers tend children and parents are free to ski. Thinking my skiing expertise learned in the USA was still intact, I tried one such season in Switzerland and realised how steep the mountains can be. Green-and-blue-rated ski slopes for beginners had my favour, while the near-vertical red and black ones gave me the willies. Never again would I risk a broken limb in this sort of activity.

In my mid-forties I had become a jogger and a marathon runner, something many lazy downhill skiers wouldn't dare. For me, exercise was essential after hours behind a computer screen. This involved gymnastics, high pulse rates, and hours of training on flat terrain—preferably at sea level. I tried cross-country skiing but it didn't measure up—too few trails, too far to go. Therefore, farewell to ski resorts; vacations were meant to be in the sun, not getting your toes cold.

ALL OF THIS was the past. Now that I am more than seventy years old, where do I stand with respect to snow and winter sports? Mylène had romantic skiing memories from her youth, a yearning for the grace of sliding downhill and the thrill of acrobatic turns on the slopes. So, when our Fontainebleau sports club arranged a trip to the Alps for a week in February, Mylène persuaded me to visit snow again with her.

Snow, snow, damned snow! I wouldn't have agreed to a week in the cold if it forced me to ski again. Some other club seniors were speed demons, risking life and limb on the slopes. It seemed crazy to me. I only accepted this trip because our club offered non-skiing members another option: snowshoeing. I had never tried this sport, but it seemed akin to hiking and jogging, more compatible with seniors, its purpose being to travel over deep snow without drowning in it, exercise more than risk. I wouldn't need to buy any equipment, just wear outdoor, snow-proof clothing; the Alpine resort would provide everything else.

At seventy years of age, broken limbs are not appealing. Furthermore, Mylène discovered that the fanatic skiers from our club were only looking for the most difficult slopes. There was no room for beginners within their ranks. To find out if *she* was good enough,

Mylène proposed we take a week of lessons at the same resort before our comrades arrived, her on skis, me on snowshoes. I hesitated—not one, but two weeks in the cold—but then, maybe I could do with some snowshoe preparation myself. And I could always pack another book to read.

~

WE WENT by train to the Alps. Would the snowshoes, plus Mylène's pleasure, be enough for reconciliation with the nasty white flakes? At my age, could I learn a new and demanding sport?

Our troubles began at the start of our trip. We were late catching our TGV train to Aime La Plagne, and then we had to eject the passengers who had taken our reserved seats. We forced our bags onto an already-full baggage rack and, wiping away the perspiration, collapsed into our retained seats, thinking, "Never again! We'll be earlier next time." Nevertheless, today we still seem to relish the challenge of last-minute arrivals. Stress, panic, combat, sweat, and beating the clock often feel like a rebirth of sorts. Now, reborn, I was ready to face those cold snowy peaks ahead.

The trip to the Alps took five hours. Outside, grey sky and nondescript countryside flashed by. No snow of any sort. The train climbed gradually. Then we stopped at the town of Chambéry, and I began to see medium-sized mountains (hills, really) with an occasional splash of white on top—not nearly enough for serious winter sports. I began dreaming of lazy mornings, Savoy cheeses, and time to read and write. I patted my laptop affectionately. Thank you, climate change, for keeping the snow away.

When our train passed through Albertville, I remembered it had been an Olympics centre for winter sports. White froth had contaminated a few more of the nearby mountaintops, but nothing much. I saw drab village houses, built in a hurry, concrete walls painted yellow or green and diminutive gardens. There were no stores, cafés, offices, or anything else in view, just a mass of dull looking bungalows. How did these people live, and what work did they do?

Finally, we reached our destination of Aime La Plagne. Abruptly, my hopes of a no-snow week were dashed. We had turned into a new valley with much higher mountains, and the snow was everywhere. That dratted white cotton wool covered the peaks; it clung to the roofs and the streets near the station. We were at eleven hundred metres altitude, and a bus took us up to our resort at Cap Vacances, Montalbert, at fourteen hundred metres. Everything was white, or dirty white, and we had to drag our suitcases two hundred metres in the snow to the resort's main entrance. There was no escape.

I had read about snowshoes before arriving, but I'd never actually seen a pair. The name "snowshoes" evokes images of North American Indians trekking great winter distances on wood and rawhide to hunt for food. The modern version, made of plastic and metal, is like a tennis racket under my boots. The French call the sport *la raquette*. I hoped the linguistic likeness to table tennis would give me courage.

We arrived late on a Sunday evening, and spent Monday getting to know the ropes. It was Tuesday before I saw a snowshoe.

While waiting for our Fontainebleau group, I signed up with the French Ski School, which proposed expeditions on snowshoes. Mylène opted for some preliminary lessons on the beginners' ski slopes. Having accepted my fate, I began to get interested in how the snowshoes worked.

I found my first snowshoes in a rental store called Snow 2000, a name I didn't appreciate. "Here you are," the store technician said, and handed me two blue plastic-and-metal frames.

"Why so many holes?" I asked.

"It's to let the snow through, so it doesn't accumulate. Haven't you ever done this before?"

I looked in a bemused way at the snowshoes. They were gently pointed in front and behind, about forty-five centimetres long by twenty centimetres wide. "They're big," I said, "much bigger than my boots."

"They're designed to spread your weight over at least four times the usual surface area of your boots. It's to stop you from sinking into the soft snow."

How deep could you get, I wondered.

"Let's find your size."

In the centre of the snowshoe was a hinged metal plate with a set of straps and buckles to attach my boots, one set at the toe end and another at the heel. My sporting club in Fontainebleau had advised me to wear rigid, waterproof boots with ankle support. The technician measured my boot and then adjusted the heel cup and straps.

Then I noticed that although the toe was fixed to the frame the heel end seemed loose and could flip-flop upwards.

"Shouldn't this be fixed?" I asked.

"No," the technician said, "the back or heel end can rotate upwards because the frame of the rear snowshoe should lie flat in the snow as you step forward and push off."

Then he turned over the snowshoe and showed me that underneath the plastic was a set of vicious-looking crampon cleats to keep the shoe from slipping.

I fingered the cleats and pointed at a small hinged metal bar at the end of the snowshoe.

He explained it was for going up steep slopes. It could be flipped over to fit under the boot.

"All clear?"

"I suppose so," I said. "How can anyone walk with these clumsy things?"

"Just follow the others," he said, laughing.

I didn't dare put the snowshoes on. Instead I carried them to the rendezvous point about three hundred metres from the store, at the bottom of the ski lifts. A group I didn't know from another ski resort was waiting there. Most of them were youngish women chatting with each other. They didn't seem afraid. Our instructor arrived, dressed in a red EFS instructor's uniform (Ecole Française de Ski).

"Okay, put on your snowshoes and let's go."

I fumbled with my things but couldn't seem to get my boot into the straps. Looking up, after a moment I found only another elderly man and I were still not ready. The instructor came around, helped my comrade, shoved my boots in place, then fastened the straps; it seemed easy when he did it.

"Now, start slowly, it's just like walking. One foot after another but slide the snowshoes rather than stride."

We set off without falling and I adopted a wide-legged gait so as not to hit one snowshoe with the other. It worked but was slow. The width of the shoes was more annoying than the length. The business of leaving the snowshoe flat on the snow while you raised your heel was no bother.

To start with, the EFS instructor took us across the bottom of the slope for about two hundred metres of level terrain. The snow was already compacted and we followed the tracks of the person ahead, one after another. Then we stopped near the ski lifts.

"Now we're going up," he said, "and not on the lift! We'll climb one hundred metres to the top of the first slopes on our snowshoes."

I looked up and saw how steep it was. Despite being in good shape I felt nervous about slipping. There was no trail. The instructor started tracing a path for us in zigzags, and we followed. I kept my place in the group and the crampon and cleats did their job. At the top, the group was puffing and panting but no one had fallen. The instructor paused to let us recover. I remembered hearing that in virgin snow the first three or four walkers who make the tracks have more work to do than the rest, so I didn't try to overtake, though I felt able to. From there on, we crossed field and forest until we reached a little restaurant where the owner demonstrated how to make a Savoy cheese, the Tome. He opened a large window in the back of his kitchens and curdled yellow cream in a copper vat while we stood outside looking on in fascination. I couldn't see much and all I can recall is how cold my hands got, standing around for thirty minutes. Then we retraced our path and I returned my snowshoes to the store. I realised with some pride that, although I was clumsy, snowshoeing wasn't too tiring and I hadn't fallen once.

Maybe the snow wasn't a bad thing after all. The locals called it white gold. After paying for the expedition and the snowshoe rental, I returned to our rented room. Mylène had had a short ski lesson and was complaining about the price. Counting the cooks, servers, cleaners, day-care centre, and evening performers, the ski resort employed a small army. Without the snow industry, this part of the country would be lost.

The next day, I tried to book another outing but it was not possible for lack of enough participants. I walked three kilometres down to the ski school's office in Montalbert and discovered the same was true for the rest of the week.

"Why don't you go on your own?" the woman at the desk said, as she produced a map of the permanent trails for walking or snow-shoeing.

I rented snowshoes from the resort in the evening. The next day was grey and snowing and I almost changed my mind. However, I dressed for the cold. Mylène was worried at the prospect of my solitary adventure but she too had an adventure in waiting—a ski lesson at an untested rendezvous point. Nervously, we put our faith in our mobile phones.

My first problem with being on my own was resizing the new snowshoes for my boots. There was no technician around but a bar acquaintance showed me how easy it was, a simple twist of the lock in the metal inset plate.

So, was I up to it? I studied the map and located the three nearest trails. I estimated seven to ten kilometres there and back for the first one. But then, I had to find the start of the trail. It was called Bief Bovet (the Bovet Canal). I snowshoed up around a beginners' ski slope area, avoiding the wobbling performers, and then to the top of the lowest ski lift. After much searching, I saw a sign in the distance. Sure enough, it read BIEF BOVET, but with a useless arrow which pointed into impenetrable (for me) snow and forest. Tempted to give up, I nonetheless climbed fifty painful metres further and at last found a useable trail. It wound along the edge of a frozen canal for about two kilometres, with further signs explaining who had built the canal and its past importance for the villages below. The trail was easy going for a beginner like me—flat, and a metre wide—with snow-covered pine trees on one side and water gurgling pleasantly under a sheet of ice on the other side. I was the only snowshoe learner in sight and I could test my movements, slow or fast. The canal flow was runoff from the slopes above, and no longer drinkable. I was told later that the ski slope operators used it to generate artificial snow.

A few trees had fallen across the Bovet trail but this didn't stop me. What did bring my solitary expedition to a halt was the need to traverse a busy downhill ski track, about thirty metres wide. The ski devils were whizzing down at high speed, no brakes, and I couldn't see how to force my way across without being massacred. Later, I learned that while the skiers always had priority, the safest way to cross their path was *en masse*, a whole group of earnest snowshoe users at the same time.

This expedition took three hours, as did the following two on Friday and Saturday. I had fun on my own in this strange white environment, provided I could find a clear path. Meanwhile, Mylène pursued her ski lessons and we treasured the lunch breaks and evening meals to recount our successes and failures. On my second solo foray, I explored the downhill paths to Montgésin and Montalbert. On the third, I did a long haul to a place in the woods called, unimaginatively, Le Bois. I found the three expeditions stimulating and I learned two things.

First, the positive: a more refined walking technique was possible to avoid one snowshoe stepping on the other. It's tiring to spread one's legs further apart than usual, and many trails aren't wide enough for this. The trick is to adjust the sliding movement of the snowshoe to lift it slightly above the edge of the companion shoe before placing it well in front. Then they can overlap comfortably with just an occasional click of contact.

Next, on some of the easier trails near Montalbert, I encountered whole families out for a walk in the snow—father, mother, children—and all in ordinary winter boots. This was embarrassing. Perhaps I could move a little faster with my cleated supports, and the uphill bits might be easier for me, but were the snowshoes necessary? With good boots, there was not much risk of slipping, so perhaps I could just do that and save on rental.

The answer to these questions came soon enough. The next day, Saturday, my club arrived and I found I still had a lot to learn, especially about deep snow.

That evening, I examined my snowshoes and had an unwelcome thought. Was there a right and a left one? They looked identical, but should they? On checking my comrades' snowshoes, just issued, I noticed one small difference—sometimes the straps were on the left and sometimes on the right. I had done all my previous snowshoeing with two left shoes! The straps and bindings should face outwards on each foot to minimise the occasions where you might step on them.

"Really?" said the front desk, "you think there's a right and a left? I'll ask."

A hurried phone call later, and she came back with a properly oriented pair; she was evidently not a snowshoe addict herself.

We had two groups of twelve snowshoe users, and two instructors, Matthieu from the ski school and Dominique from our sporting club. When I buckled on my shoes for the first time with the club, Dominique checked my fittings and complained I hadn't fastened my straps properly. There were two buttons, one black for release and one grey (which I had never understood) for winding the binding tighter, notch by notch. So, there it was: I'd been out for three days on my own wearing two left snowshoes, neither fastened correctly.

Concerning my query about the usefulness of the snowshoes: never did our instructors take us on such easy trails as I had practiced on. Much of the time, we were breaking new trails in deep virgin snow. There was rarely a predefined path. The instructor would cut his route through the forests and up and down the steep slopes, trajectories which would have been impossible with simple boots.

I began to enjoy myself. Matthieu, clean-cut and in his late thirties, knew the Alpine environment inside out. The first day he started by describing my enemy, the snow.

"How do you think it's made?" he asked the group.

"Falls from the sky . . . frozen water droplets from the clouds . . . scraped from refrigerators . . ."

"Not so simple. Frozen droplets are sleet, not snow."

He explained that first, there must be a tiny initial ice crystal. This happens in a cloud which is super cooled—say, minus-ten degrees Celsius—when water vapour condenses around a fine dust particle.

"You mean our dirty pollution causes all this pure snow?" said an ecologist throwing up his hands in horror.

"No, no, the particles concerned are much finer than that, it's clumps of non-water molecules blown upwards from the trees and sandy places."

"That's it? A seed particle hosts a blob of ice?"

My long-ago doctoral studies of melting ice got me interested.

"After seeding, the initial crystal draws in more water vapour and gets heavy enough to start falling. As it falls, slowly, slowly, more cold-water vapour solidifies around it in other crystal forms. The basic pattern is hexagonal, but no two snowflakes end up identical. The shapes can be thin plates or more like needles according to the temperature and the humidity during their flight downwards."

This was a new science to me.

I inquired about the hexagonal shape.

"It's to do with the molecular structure. The internal organisation of the water molecules is reproduced on a larger scale in the snowflake, approximately. Some 3-sided flakes have been observed, though most have six. How big do you think a snowflake can get by the time it lands on your head?"

I guessed one or two centimetres, maximum.

"Some have been observed up to ten centimetres in diameter! And what colour is a snowflake?"

White seemed too obvious an answer, but we said so nonetheless.

"Wrong! The crystals are transparent, not white, but the reflected light appears white. If you dig a narrow hole in the white snow with your ski pole, you may see different colours like blue at the bottom."

So much for my enemy / friend snow: it was multiform, complex in its evolution, not just a dumb frozen blob. I gave it a little more respect. Still, there was a negative side: the birth of a snowflake is due to contamination! Moreover, the fully developed flake doesn't even have an honest colour!

At our next stop, after an hour of snowshoeing, Matthieu addressed my concerns about the snow's cruel intention of freezing humans like me.

"What do you know about staying alive in the cold?" our instructor said. "Where are the danger points for heat loss?"

"The head?"

"Yes!"

I added, "And the hand, too, as every runner knows."

Matthieu clapped his gloves together and said: "No, the hands are not critical; it's a question of priority. The body's main concern is to keep the head—your brain and its autonomous control system—at a constant temperature close to thirty-seven-point-five degrees Celsius. If ever this temperature drops by one or two degrees, it's a case of hypothermia and collapse. Your control system will do anything to avoid this, including depriving places like your hands of blood circulation. This means that if you feel your hands freezing you should first cover your head warmly before worrying about your gloves. When the head feels less menaced it will restore circulation. Inversely, if your hands (or elsewhere) become too hot and sweaty, begin by taking the cap off your head so it can cool down. Then it will reduce the pumping of excessive blood to the hands. All of this is relevant if you are actively snowshoeing, skiing, or walking—if you sit still for some time *everything* will get cold."

I pulled my ski bonnet tighter and hoped my fingers would respond.

On the second day, Matthieu made us look critically at the flora, something I usually ignore. My native Caribbean background had already made most of the Fontainebleau forest a stranger to me.

The mountain trees looked all the same to my eyes: a fuddy-duddy green or brown with needles for want of leaves, just décor. Matthieu wanted us to look closer and distinguish species. With difficulty, I followed his criteria, mostly to do with the fruit they bore, or pinecones: if the cone is hanging down, it's a spruce; if the cone is pointing upwards, it's a fir. I tapped a snow-covered branch of the spruce nearby and, having dropped its load, it whipped upwards by a metre. Then there were the brown trees which looked good only for firewood. To my surprise, they weren't dead, but adjusting to the winter snow, and they are called larch. Their wood is much harder and more brittle than spruce and fir. Shedding their leaves diminishes the weight of snow which can stick to their branches and saves them from arthritic collapse. And about those pinecones—but this bit I can hardly believe —rumour has it you can predict the weather by the way the cone's scales behave; with dry weather coming they open, closing means rain.

Between afternoons of intense snowshoeing, I kept the first half of the day for answering email and writing. Often, however, the local WIFI system failed; maybe it was the snow's fault. In frustration, I wrote a story about the last two hours in the life of a man condemned to highly risky surgery.

In the café where I wrote, I observed a woman on crutches, waiting to be evacuated, one of several injured skiers that week who seemed to justify my fears of unbridled speed. She looked a lot younger than me, too.

On the fourth day of snowshoeing with my group of friends, it snowed heavily, more than on any of the preceding days. Early every morning I took pictures from our room. Sometimes, dawn over the white-capped mountains was a brilliant orange spectacle, sometimes mist and snow blocked out everything. This day was like that, nothing but sheets of white, curtains of drifting snow. Not a good day to venture out. Nevertheless, I did, and found myself with my group in the middle of the fairy-like feathers, flakes decorating my spectacles. We snowshoed up above Montgésin into an area of botanic experiments. There had been many plantings of exotic Alpine species, each with a notice along our trail, but neither the trees nor their names were distinguishable under the heavy snow. It didn't matter. Our snowshoe trail was fifty centimetres deep and sixty centimetres wide, with a dramatic view downhill on the right.

The slope was level or gently uphill. There was no sound except the occasional click of a snowshoe. The forest trees enveloped us, trunks dark and majestic, branches laden with white. The snow fell densely, soft packets over everything. Any tiredness or pain I had had disappeared. I felt a heightened awareness, telling me to remember that instant, the trees, the snow, my state of mind. It was the same out-of-body sensation I have felt before, like signposts in my life, looking out at spectacular sunsets, or moonlit seascapes, or gothic tree branches silhouetted on the horizon. Taste the moment.

I was ready to forgive the snow its vicissitudes, but the next day, Thursday, was an ordeal. We snowshoed for seven hours with just a thirty-minute break to picnic in a wooden refuge at two thousand metres altitude. It was sunny but freezing cold, almost too cold to handle my sandwich. However, the peaks on the other side of the valley were majestic.

"How close do you think the nearest one is?" asked the instructor.

"I guess, a few kilometres."

"It's about six," he said, pointing across, "and Mont Blanc on your right, how about that?"

"Maybe ten?"

"It's sixty kilometres away and would tower over us if we approached. Distances are deceiving from up here."

We descended six hundred metres on tensed knees. Did I forget to say that going down on snowshoes is more difficult than going up? I had not fallen up to this point, a matter of some pride, but that day I fell five times. Admittedly, three of the five close encounters with the snow were purposeful—I was glissading the trail, meaning sliding down on my buttocks. These were places too steep and slippery to proceed in small steps, though some others, notably Jean-Louis, were more courageous than I was. He was ten years younger, still working as a technical project manager, strong and supple, given to cheerfully jumping down small slopes shouting "Yahoo!" (with an occasional spectacular fall). Later, I discovered that in table tennis he would cry "Yippee" after a smash or (very occasionally) "Oops".

Once fallen, I had to get back up, and this takes practice. The snow-shoes encumber you and the snow around will not bear much weight. I tried to pull myself upright with my ski poles, but—frustratingly—this didn't work. Matthieu had to show me how to curl up, bend my knees, reach out over the snowshoes, and use my legs to stand.

The effort of this long day was exhausting and I cursed the snow again, and again, and everything to do with it. I forgot the good times and only my aching knees counted. At this point, the group was so tired we paused for ten minutes. Surprise—the instructor took out a metal flask with liqueur in it and passed it around. Rarely had a drink tasted so good, pumping warm encouragement into my tired muscles.

"What's it called?" I said.

"*Génépi*, an emblematic local plant steeped in alcohol. It does wonders for mountain sickness."

I gazed at my snowshoeing friends, Jean Louis, Alain, and others, feeling something more than the sweet liqueur binding us together. Several had taken off their caps, and for the first time I made the correlation between the colour of our hair and the snow under our feet. We were all older people but still doers, and how better to affirm this than in our present environment?

The last day, Friday, I started coughing and did not go out at all. I remembered a waiter in the restaurant, Valentin, who had boasted how ill he was and yet had the courage to come in every day to work, wiping the tables. I guess he wiped my area a bit too much.

On Saturday, it was all over. Mylène and I took a last walk on the icy roads near the resort.

"I liked it," she said. "I wasn't very good, but I learned a lot. I want to do it again."

I coughed, scuffled my feet in the snow, and struggled between my fascination and dislike of winter's magic in equal parts. I said: "Hmm . . . er, maybe . . . we'll give it another try." I picked up a pinecone.

Whether I would return to this inimical territory or not, I felt pleased that my senior's existence had allowed me yet another adventure unlike those in my youth.

The next day, we travelled back to Paris and Fontainebleau.

The cough inherited from Valentin proved difficult to shake off, as if to warn that winter magic has a cost. Despite two days of rest, both Mylène and I needed salutary doses of syrup for a week. My sore knees also protested against those hours of bending and twisting downhill. Our first sporting encounters in Fontainebleau took all our remaining energy and left us like rag dolls.

Eight days later, the exactions of the winter mountains dissipated, and I jogged comfortably for an hour. Climbing stairs felt effortless, almost as good as snowshoeing.

The next morning, I sat at my desk and emptied my holiday backpack. I found the carefully wrapped pinecone and placed it in front of me. A souvenir from the last days. It was fifteen centimetres long, exuding a forest smell, with brown *closed* scales. Not fir, nor larch, but spruce, and it would soon rain, or maybe snow.

10

THE WEEPING WILLOW

It was the summer after our expedition to the snow, and I could still see the tree from my upstairs bedroom window. Lying down, recovering from a recent cough and its asthmatic sequel, I stared out at the huge weeping willow in our garden. Or was it staring at me? Its leaves were a drab yellow-green, falling quickly in the autumn weather. The tree filled my horizon, shielding me from the neighbouring gardens and more distant apartment buildings. I took comfort from the willow and felt sympathy for it. But the whole tree, all thirty metres of it, was due to be cut down.

Some forestry experts had advised us that the willow was too old and dangerously weak. A bad storm might uproot it, damaging property or hurting someone. Also, we wanted to extend our house into the garden area and the tree was an obstacle. Still, at sixty years of age, the tree deserved respect, like all seniors.

The gardeners were already in the garden and would soon begin lopping off the smaller branches.

"Isn't it sad to see it go? We won't have anything near our window. No birds singing or nesting nearby, just sky, the lawn, and a few distant rooftops," said Mylène.

"It's only a tree," I muttered, not certain how I felt. "No tree, more sunshine."

"Sunshine! We're facing southeast and there'll be too much sun. And no more picnics in the tree's shade."

"Look, we've talked about this for weeks and *you* finally voted for the willow's execution. Forget the nostalgia and worry about possible accidents—those gardeners might fall off their ladders!"

I lay there in bed thinking about the tree, of the dozens of pictures I had taken of it over the past three years, dawn and dusk, rain and shine. There was a series of photos of a large nest which two magpies had built near the top, level with our window. As if anticipating the tree's future problems, the birds had never laid any eggs in their home. One day the wind blew too hard and the branch with the nest broke and fell, still empty. Later, a young cat visiting us, Igloo, succeeded in climbing the tree in search of adventure and pigeons. Clawing his way up was feasible but descending the vertical stretches of trunk without falling was another matter. To the awe of onlookers, Igloo slipped, scratched, and leaped his way to safety. I made a video of that, too.

Right now, the harmony of the tree with our bedroom window was about to disappear: the cutting had begun.

A crashing sound came from below and I leaped out of bed; the gardeners had just sawed through the first upper branches. I took more pictures. The gnarled and mossy trunk of the willow, decorated with mushroom-like parasites, was vertical for the first six metres and then forked into two massive stems. Whenever I looked closely at this lower part of the tree, I saw the willow partly as a distinguished elder and partly as an ailing patient. A further two or three metres up and it bifurcated again on each side. The upper branches were younger, still ten centimetres thick but curving over gracefully and sprouting thinner and thinner branches which could reach all the way to the ground. These were the objects of the first pruning, the bits that brushed against you as you walked under the tree.

I took photographs to preserve memories, as I often do. But was it necessary? Wouldn't I remember the weeping willow after it was gone, without the visual aid? This was a challenge and I deliberately settled down in bed again, closing my eyes. Yes, I felt things were being lost, like holes forming in a fabric. Images and episodes live on in our minds for months or years but slowly, or abruptly, some disappear.

Did I think as often today of my deceased wife as I had done five years ago? Should I? This was painful. Colette used to be in my mind all the time, a way of keeping a bit of her spirit alive. Then, after a year or two, I couldn't remember how she dressed, and she only returned to me in certain limited contexts. For example, she had never liked the smell of overheated coffee, so every morning I now throw away the used coffee filter as soon as possible and hope she is satisfied. Is it trivial to remember her dislikes? On the positive side, she liked doing the shopping, and prepared most of my meals for thirty-eight years. Now I do much of that for Mylène as another remembrance and take pleasure in it.

How would the weeping willow fare in my mental archives? I decided to test the permanence of my memories in a neutral framework—all the trees or other skyscapes which I could recall from previous bedroom windows, back through seventy-two years.

I plunged into the past. We had lived in this house, in Avon, sleeping in this bedroom for three years, since early 2012. From the beginning, the tree had created an atmosphere of intimacy: it was *our* willow, not shared with anyone else except the birds. It was the first thing we saw every morning. We dressed and undressed by the window, staring at its fluttering leaves. No eyes could see us but those of the willow. In the winter it looked sad, in the summer it looked thirsty, and in windy weather it thrashed and moaned. A senior citizen, like ourselves.

I probed behind those three years. It is now earlier, 2011, and Mylène and I are living in an apartment looking out over the rooftops of Paris. It is in the fifteenth arrondissement, and we have a breathtaking twelfth-floor view of the Eiffel Tower and Montmartre. Surely this was more spectacular? Why bother about an old tree? I delighted in the sun rising over the golden domes of the French capital and the crisp white trails of planes crossing the sky. It looked like a child playing with a crayon on a blue canvas above the bedroom. I have fond memories of this apartment because this is where Mylène and I started living together. I took pictures of those sunrises and sunsets.

But look down to the street level on Boulevard Garibaldi and you hear the rumbling above-ground metro and see the homeless sleeping under its supporting arches. There are few trees nearby, none visible from the bedroom. This had been a reason for leaving Paris after retirement.

Meanwhile, back in the present, I get up briefly and look out of the window. The long ladders of the two gardeners are now up in the first fork of the willow and their chainsaws are ripping through the smaller branches. One man works in the tree while the other clears up the debris. When a branch is too close to a neighbour's fence, the man on the ground pulls it away with a rope so it will fall on our land. Soon, the left fork is bared down to the thicker trunks.

Before the bedroom in the Fifteenth Arrondissement, I lived in another area of Paris, the Seventeenth Arrondissement, Villa Compoint, an impasse in a triangle of tranquillity, away from the busy avenues of Clichy and Saint Ouen, with a private garden just outside the second-floor window. When Colette and I moved in, you couldn't see the garden and its small trees from the bed, but I did take pictures from this window, too. I remember buying the four-bedroom apartment back in 1988 when a new building was erected on the site. An American who bought at the same time was upset because he didn't know Ho Chi Minh, the Vietnamese rebel leader who fought against America, had once lived there. Memories from those windows are vivid. Over the next twenty years we raised two children there and I watched the trees grow until they were higher than our windows. In the garden, we let our children bury their dead pets. I lived there with my first wife, Colette, until she passed away in 2008. Will her fond memory be reduced like that of the weeping willow, or can I keep all these slivers of life in mind?

Now I hear the gardeners readjusting their ladders to access the second half of the willow. The fallen branches have all been cut up and stored in neat piles. As I drift off to my memories again, I hope no one falls.

Earlier on, both our two children, the joys of our life, were born elsewhere in this Seventeenth Arrondissement. The youngest, a boy, Cyril, was born when we lived nearby in Rue de la Jonquiere, a cosy three-room place on the third floor with only a street view and absolutely no trees anywhere. From here back in my stack of European memories, the tree-views are rare, and perhaps that's why the weeping willow presence in Avon was so much appreciated. Rue de la Jonquiere, so narrow I felt I could almost spit across it, represents about eight years of life, from 1988 back to 1980. It had quaintly-shaped rooms and a large bay window in the bedroom looking out on a noisy school with chattering children. It was our first property purchase since arriving in Paris, a sign of confidence in the city. We had previously rented for eight years.

The memory trail is getting distinctly rough and winding. I almost jumped back to 1978 in another part of the Seventeenth, forgetting the memorable year of 1979 spent in Lima, Peru. I had been sent there by my engineering firm to do computer analysis for Electrolima. My wife and I and our lively four-year-old daughter lived in an enormous apartment of four hundred square metres looking out over a park in San Isidro. *Hay muchos arboles*, as viewed from our bedroom. I jogged merrily round this park most mornings. One day the earth shook with a 5.5 Richter quake and while we quivered by the window the trees in the park didn't budge and neither did our four-year-old our daughter. The mission to Lima only lasted a year but taught us all some Spanish and how trees can survive in a very dry climate.

This brings me to the period 1978 to 1970, when Colette and I were in Rue de Levis, and looked out on an exciting market street; no trees but full of all kinds of fish, fruit, vegetables, and pastry, with hawkers shouting their wares. Smells of cooking and fresh produce. That's where I first ate horsemeat, and where we lived when our dear daughter Chloé was born (no cause and effect). We rented successively three different apartments in the same building, two rooms, three rooms and finally five rooms. Moving up the property ladder, I suppose, just as the gardeners are now battling on their aluminium ladder with the second half of the willow.

It gets harder to picture as I go back further in time. Nineteen-seventy is the year I arrived in France, twenty-eight years old, newly married, and wearing a fresh PhD on my shoulders. I'll skip the Latin Quarter hotels while looking for work, and the voyage from the USA on the ocean liner *France*. Not much in the way of bedroom windows or trees there.

Now it's back to 1969, the magic year I got married in Syracuse, New York State, to Colette. We lived in a town centre group of flats while I was finishing my studies. There must have been a few trees, but could I see them from our room, or not? All I can recall is a Hollywood-style shootout in the complex. A holdup in the reception area brought the police and their guns to the rescue. Why don't I have any more images in memory? It's getting difficult to keep the years straight. The campus was undoubtedly green but, 1965 to 1968, I lived in low-cost graduate student lodgings and I can't recall any visible trees. Maybe the windows were too small or facing the wrong way, or maybe I took nature for granted.

THE GARDENERS HAVE FINISHED CUTTING ALL the secondary branches on the willow and the thick forked trunk is all that is left. It looks bare and lonely but I still take its picture.

It's the same bedroom opacity for my undergraduate studies in Cambridge, 1965 back to 1961. On days when we could get up late, we tended to sleep with all windows closed. Trees were not our priority, but the college lawns were an impressive green after hundreds of years of care.

The weeping willow was not the only tree in my life. To go further, I now must make an ocean liner sail backwards, removing me from English shores and sliding across the Atlantic to the Caribbean island of St. Kitts where I was born. It's 1950, I'm now eight, and I live with my parents in a large house with a veranda, overlooking the bay of Basseterre. The sea view was for my parents; my room was in the back of the house and the windows looked out onto a tropical garden. My cat would jump though this window from outside during the night, after its feline encounters, and dig sharp claws into my back to show affection. I was surrounded by mango trees, banana plants, bay rum and pawpaw trees—a small paradise, of which the willow would doubtless be jealous. Those Caribbean trees seemed young and eternal; a pawpaw tree could grow five metres in a year. Today, in faraway France, I eat a mango each morning for breakfast, to remember and preserve that arboreal eternity.

This is my last (first) distinct bedroom window memory. Going further back, from age eight to age four in various other houses in Basseterre, I can't recall where I slept. And younger than four years is a dispiriting blank.

RETURNING TO THE PRESENT, I've moved back to the windowsill in Avon and below me I see the weeping willow is now completely dismembered. The gardeners have sawn through the huge trunk in fifty-centimetre sections, and now they are chopping these up for firewood. I go down into the garden to inspect more closely.

"Look at the base of the tree," one of the gardeners says. "Rotten inside and couldn't last."

The base was eighty centimetres in diameter and only the outer five centimetres looked clear and healthy. As my gaze progresses from the bark towards the centre, the wood appears softer and more coloured until it becomes dark and powdery and terminates in a fifteen-centimetre hole in the middle. Something worm-like is moving in the brown, rotten part.

"What's this?" I ask, picking up the wriggling, whitish object.

"Cockchafers," the gardener says. "They're eating your tree!" He explained that the tree would have died from old age anyway, but the destructive insects had sped up the process by several years.

Just then, as I looked at the decayed core, a shiver goes through me. There was a disturbing analogy between the death of the weeping willow and my memory exercises. Just as the willow had deteriorated more and more at its centre as time went by, my early memories have become less and less reliable as I grow older. Just as the willow only kept standing thanks to the last ten or twenty years of growth in its outer perimeter, my own mental stability is essentially based on what I can remember from the past two decades. The more I considered this, the more worrying it became. If the willow could fall in the next bad storm, what might happen to me in a severe emotional upset? Was this how dementia begins, with a gradual loss of significant memories? We had cut the sick willow down with few regrets. The insects had had their way. What sort of demonic mental insects might be eating away at *my* substance, and what sort of gardener might come one day soon to cut me down?

I am not a tree, I told myself. I am flesh and blood, not wood and sap. I walked quickly away from the piles of branches, logs, and the decapitated stump with the hole and the insects. I imagined the willow not weeping but laughing at me. "Now you know how it feels, little man, to grow old and powerless."

Strange, I thought: as my mother went deeper and deeper into dementia in the last years of her life, she forgot the present and recent past and became a young girl again, while I am worried about forgetting details of childhood. Are the old memories simply hidden? Or perhaps there's no correlation between the recall process and the time lapse—it may depend on the intensity of the experience.

Some memory loss may be inevitable. One useful idea I hadn't forgotten from my university days was the effect of chemistry on the brain. Acetylcholine manages both short and long-term memories, and we can help the brain's resources with a proper diet. I did a mental check of our kitchen: wheat germ, eggs, salmon, broccoli, avocadoes— it seems okay, just missing some beef liver and soy products. Or was this just dreaming, against the possibility of an Alzheimer's bulldozer?

All I have to do, I thought, is to build new and solid memories, love my new companion, live new sporting activities, keep moving, and stop the insects from getting into my head.

As I stand boldly naked by my unprotected window each morning, clutching at any winter sunshine available, I force myself to remember the weeping willow's leaves, but I let the new landscape take precedence over the past.

11

ACCEPTANCE

Where do we seniors find our inner drive? An incident on a train set me thinking. Mylène came home from a visit to Paris and said, "I'm lucky to be alive!"

"Did you intervene in a train scuffle again?" I asked. I know she can't resist getting involved in public-conflict situations, and has sometimes interposed herself between two combatants, at great risk.

"A man on the line-fourteen metro nearly had his head cut off!"

"Come on, I thought the guillotine had been abolished."

"Listen, you remember there are two closing doors on that line, one on the train and the other on the platform. Well, this elderly fellow got his head into the train door, which promptly closed on him, and then— bang—the platform door imprisoned his body. I saw it before the others and shouted, 'Watch out!'

"The train was about to leave the station. Three passengers jumped up and heaved on the doors until the old man's body followed his head into the train compartment. Luckily, he was short and thin. I was very upset, and at the next station, I approached him. Closer up, he was balding, tremulous, and looked about seventy-five. 'You can't push through a closing door like that,' I shouted, 'you were nearly killed!'

"He looked at me soberly and said, 'I know,' and left the train."

On hearing about this incident, I wondered whether the elderly man was not semi-suicidal. Maybe his reaction to old age and perceived death was to take excessive risks.

At what age are we ready to accept the end of our lives? "Never," said Freud. Each of us believes in his immortality. Other people die, not us. And knowing what is coming doesn't mean accepting. However, this may be less true for the current ever-growing generation of seniors. The retired, pensioned over-sixties will soon comprise close to 30 percent of the French population. At age seventy-two, I am fully part of this demography, old and getting older. I feel the presence of death around me. It is not so much the wars and spectacular accidents I read about in the newspapers; these tend to be abstract, like impersonal movies. It is more the nearby examples of family, friends, and acquaintances who disappear. Two decades ago it was my father, more recently my wife, then my mother. Now, my table tennis partner Gérard (seventy-five) has bone marrow cancer and long-term chemotherapy. My friend Georges Quélin (eighty) has just succumbed to heart failure; he was president of my association La Vie Devant Nous. We are transients: here today, gone tomorrow.

I asked myself how can we, the retired seniors, adapt to a future in which our remaining time is short, maybe one or two decades, maybe a lot less, but more time than our parents had, before the big stop sign? First, accept the stop sign. Had I accepted? If so, how? What does acceptance entail? For the young, life is a ladder to climb: childhood, education, career, love, marriage, children, family, more career, then retirement. However, for many of us seniors after retirement there seem at first to be no more rungs left, only our rendezvous with the dark horseman. How to face this? Outside of Europe retirement may not have the same significance; in the USA it comes later, often after the age of 70; in poorer countries people work until they drop. For us in France, it can be a frightening transition. Since coming to Avon, where there are many retired seniors, I have tried to understand the attitudes of the people around me—and my own—towards death.

I found that when thinking about their mortality, people often fall into two groups: the first is more afraid of loss of faculties, dependency, terminal illness, and suffering, than death itself; the second objects more to the notion of extinction, whatever the prior conditions.

The man on the train might have been in the first group, afraid of illness but not thanatophobic. If he were indeed seventy-five, then perhaps he had come to terms—bad terms—with his mortality by taking deliberate risks. Nevertheless, I feel there are many positive ways to live out our last years. I seemed to have little death anxiety, though this may be a temporary affair. I needed to find out more.

I looked back for examples in my family. When young, or even middle-aged, we do not really believe in our parents' death any more than we believe in our own. When my father died of pneumonia on a small Caribbean island at the age of eighty-five, it was a shock for me. I was living in France at the time, age fifty-five; I had thought I would see him again. At the funeral, I remembered his preparations. He must have understood several years earlier that his time was running out rapidly. He was bedridden, had suffered from several small strokes, had high blood pressure, and was developing an untreatable hydrocephalus. On a visit home, he called me to his bedside.

"Chris, please promise me something."

"Yes, Dad, what is it?"

"Promise me!"

"Yes, okay."

"Promise me that when I'm gone, you'll take care of your mother. She won't know what to do."

"Of course, Dad, I've promised you this several times already."

It was true he had made me promise this in previous years, and not only me but also my brothers, but we had always taken his concern lightly. After all, we believed our parents would still be happily together for many more years.

He was a step ahead of us. Shortly after, when both parents needed hospital treatment at the same time, he agreed to enter a nursing home, knowing he would never leave it, and that we only had the resources to transfer one parent to Europe for better care. This was his response to the certitude of approaching death—get the vital planning done for the survivors. After his death, I did what he had asked and brought my mother to France.

My father was older than the man in the metro was when he faced up to his passing, and my mother was older still. She survived my father by fifteen years. She was different, more religious than my father was. She agreed to leave her spacious Caribbean home, settle in a studio in Paris near my apartment—a radical change of life. She began new occupations: learning French and painting. Between her church and her art, she lived a new life in Paris, and by ninety years of age she had finished some delightful landscapes of her birthplace. All by herself, she would take a twenty-minute bus trip every Sunday to an English-speaking Catholic church, St Joseph's. That is, until she started missing where to get off the bus. There were sectarian turnarounds: she had been brought up as a Catholic, but after marriage spent most of her life as an Anglican, and then in her closing years returned to her first church because it was closest to where she lived. Her faith, her art, and her family (four children, five grandchildren) were her bulwarks. She died peacefully at ninety-four and even though a dementia akin to Alzheimer's rendered her last four years hazy, she never seemed unhappy or fearful.

Thus, I saw two different approaches, responsibility for the future of one's survivors and personal creativity in whatever domain, which seem to be successful in helping the elderly accept their demise. However, after retirement, in that period from age seventy to whenever, there are so many diverse situations there will inevitably be many other responses. One thing seems vital: mortality must be accepted and not remain a cause of despair. Often, this involves reviewing one's past life to find some sort of meaning.

As seen with my mother, religion is a way of appeasing our fears; it has been so since the beginning of human history and language. It is not *my* way, I don't believe in resurrection, but I am happy when it works for others.

Here is another religious instance. Nine months ago, Mylène and I were preparing for a trip to Ireland when we were notified that a good friend of Mylène's family, Sister Agnes, over ninety years old, was seriously ill and might not have much time left.

Sister Agnes was in a nursing home attached to her convent. She had been in hospital on and off for the past year. When we visited her, she was in a wheelchair with a permanent oxygen feed to her failing lungs, but she was as alert as we had ever seen her.

"Mylène and Christopher! How nice of you to come! Sorry I can't offer you anything."

She was hardly able to move, yet her eyes were still bright, her voice clear, and she remembered our names, our move to Avon and much else.

She smiled.

Sister Agnes had joined the order young and never regretted the lack of a husband and children. Her strong faith was enough. She took a keen interest in all her family, near and far. She had served as a missionary in Japan and elsewhere at high cost to her personal health. We knew that in a month's time it would be seventy years since taking her vows and her induction into the religious order. She said she wasn't sure whether she would still be alive for her anniversary ceremony, planned by the order.

"Sure, you will," Mylène said, "and anyway we'll be back in ten days from Ireland to see you again."

Sister Agnes smiled again, gently.

"It doesn't matter. I'll be happy one way or the other. I'll be taken care of, where I'm going. We'll say goodbye now but enjoy your trip and don't on any account disturb it for me."

We said goodbye and she died five days later while we were in Catholic Ireland. Few attended her funeral, but many thought of her. She had no fear and I am certain her passing was gentle.

What happens if we live even longer? How do the centenarians feel about their last decades? Today, the UN says there are more than three hundred thousand people in the world who are one hundred years old and one baby in three born last year in the developed world is expected to reach this age. A small fraction of the current centenarians may even become super-centenarians (110 years).

A month ago, I attended a funeral in Mylène's family where the deceased had attained 101 years of age. Thoughts of finitude in our lifespan call up grey skies, not sunshine, and it was like that on the day of the funeral. The rain fell gently in the early morning. I dressed in a sober suit which brought back memories of my working life, years before. I had no personal ties to the centenarian but I felt strongly about paying my respects.

"Is a black tie all right?" I asked Mylène.

She nodded, and after breakfast, I picked up an umbrella and crossed the road to the underground garage in Avon where my car was parked. To my relief, the pocket transmitter worked the first time I clicked on it and the garage door creaked open. This device has become unreliable, like many other things in damp weather.

Trotting into the garage, which holds about fifty cars, I located my seventeen-year-old Ford Mondeo and opened the door with a key. The car's electronic key fob is also not working. Everything around is ageing, not least myself.

The neon lights in the garage timed out. I started the engine, programmed my GPS for the town of Dourdan, and turned on the headlights. As I started reversing out of my parking space, I noticed a red warning indicator on the dashboard showing a problem on the left side of the car. I checked the doors, but they were all shut. Then I realised the left headlight must be out of order. It worked on full but not on dim mode. Damn! For driving on the motorway, I needed the dim mode, especially on a grey and rainy day. This might be hazardous—should we take the other car, Mylène's Toyota, instead? I decided not to, because it is less comfortable for me to drive, and it was certainly not a good day for Mylène to be at the wheel. After all, we were attending the funeral of her mother-in-law. I drove out of the garage, picked up Mylène, and decided not to mention the faulty headlight until later. It seemed a reasonable risk to take, not like the man in the metro. With luck, we would start back for home before dark and I wouldn't need the lights.

There are two routes to Dourdan, one from Fontainebleau due west on smallish two-lane roads and the other a bit longer via the Paris region but mostly on motorways. We chose the latter and planned to arrive at midday. The weather remained wet and grey but I did not need headlights.

∾

I HAD time to think about the deceased, who Mylène's family called Mamie. She was the mother of Mylène's late husband and two other children. Mylène had known Mamie for more than half a century, but I had only met her four times, twice at receptions in her daughter Danielle's home and twice in a nursing home. One of these receptions a year earlier was a family celebration of Mamie's one hundred years. She was in a wheelchair and could hardly speak—in fact, she croaked and made other noises we tried to ignore. Nevertheless, she seemed happy and smiled at the hundred-year birthday cake while the young blew out the candles. There to celebrate were her surviving child, Danielle, six of seven grandchildren (including Mylène's four children) mostly in their forties, and eight of fifteen great-grandchildren. I wondered how it would be for me at that age—fewer grandchildren and great-grandchildren but more voice, perhaps.

A book of photos and happy family souvenirs had been created for Mamie, but the most important elements of her life were in the background. She had had a difficult childhood, born in a humble family, but by force of character and intelligence became a teacher. She was tough and intransigent, not liked by some, and when her husband died there was never any question of finding a new partner. She was then aged about sixty and would spend the next forty-odd years by herself mostly in retirement and nursing homes. To her great regret she lost both her sons, one of whom was Mylène's husband, to painful illnesses.

What kept Mamie going? I thought of my car with one headlight missing but still capable of a long voyage. Mamie could have worked as a librarian but refused. She would not live with any of her family. She worked by herself on tapestry, but literature was her passion, and she kept on reading until almost one hundred, at which point either her vision or her concentration became too poor.

The last time I saw her alive was with Mylène on All Saints' Day (La Toussaint), a month before her death. Our visit was unannounced but she was sitting near the door of the nursing home in her wheelchair. The nurses explained to us that she stayed there all day long, staring out, as if waiting for something. She said nothing to us so we took some pictures and gave her a bouquet of hyacinths. Those pictures are her last living record. I can't say whether she was happy or unhappy; the word which comes to mind is "determined".

~

Now, we had arrived at the funeral home, my car purring along as if nothing was wrong with it. When most of the family was present, the master of ceremonies proposed that those who so desired could look at the body. Mamie's daughter Danielle said no, children should not look at the dead, but the other family members wanted to pay their last respects. The lighting was dim, but no amount of camouflage could make Mamie's shrunken face recognisable or pleasant. This was death in its most frightening form.

"She looks like a dried prune!" said Mylène, shocking the family.

It should not have been a surprise. Ten days before she passed away, Mamie had stopped eating and drinking and refused all medication. The nursing home consulted Danielle who agreed there should be no "therapeutic insistence". In any case, her veins were too thin for intravenous nourishment. Either Mamie had lost her appetite, or quite possibly she starved herself to death.

The church funeral was colourful, the burial full of flowers, and the reception which followed replete with Champagne. This is tradition— the young saying goodbye and thinking that only the old die and they are far from it themselves.

What impressed me and moved me to sympathy was the crusty, unyielding centenarian who had long ago come to terms with the reality of her death but wanted it in her own way, at her chosen time. No despair or pain here, just a choice arising from diminished physical means for self-expression.

I can find a parallel with my own grandparents. They were very close as a couple all their lives and when my grandfather died in his bed at age ninety, my grandmother simply faded away two days later —same age, same bed—allowing them a joint funeral.

~

AFTER MAMIE'S funeral and the reception, we started back for Fontainebleau. Despite our morning planning, it was late—past seven o'clock in the evening, dark and increasingly rainy. Now I had to use the headlights, and the rain came pelting down. At first our route was empty of oncoming traffic.

"Don't forget to dim your lights when you see a car coming the other way," Mylène said.

I soon had to do this and found I could only see half the road. I remembered the headlight problem detected that morning and slowed down. When the oncoming car passed, I snapped the main headlights back on and breathed easier. I could see ahead again. However, this didn't last. Why were there so many cars all coming at me? First one, then another came around the next curve, and then more. I went back to dim, repeatedly. Mylène was jittery and tended to see traffic before I did. The rain wouldn't stop and my vision was terrible with just one dimmed headlight half the time. Hopefully things would get better when we reached the Paris motorway. I was glad I had drunk only one glass of Champagne. At last, the rain slowed, the windscreen cleared, and we entered a lighted, four-lane section of the main road. Even on one dim light I could now see well and my thoughts went back to the funeral and our awareness of mortality, in particular my own.

I REFLECTED that for us retired seniors, without coming to terms with our proximate passing it is often hard to know how to live. To embrace life, to plan positively, to be truly dynamic, one must get over the notion of impregnability. However, it's difficult to say, "In a few years I'm going to die, and I'd like to be buried here, or cremated there, and by the way this is my last will and testament." When we are young, death seems to be some sort of accident or bad luck. The thought of it, personal extinction, generates fear—a survival instinct but also an impediment to calm thoughts and planning. In my late-thirties I would occasionally wake at night from awful nightmares about dying.

Today, it's not the same for me, but it wasn't easy. Reconstructing, it took close encounters with the death of my loved ones to change my consciousness, to become reconciled to the idea that it would inevitably happen to me. First, there was my father, at whose funeral I cried while reading my eulogy. I had not been there for him the day he died, leaving an eternal regret.

More terrible, and critical to my current equilibrium, was the death of my wife Colette because I *was* there. Holding her hand in the hospital when she stopped breathing, I felt the life force vanishing. Forty years together and two children. For three months, I remained in a daze and in pain. I realised I could and would die too. I didn't much care when. I was living the worst days of my life and my own death held no more terror for me. This awareness and acceptance have persisted. It has evolved and doesn't imply being foolhardy and neither does it exclude creativity in the relatively brief time remaining. I hope, but cannot know, that it will last. Our worst trials may sometimes have positive effects.

The death of a loved one is a terrible turning point, and I don't recommend to others this manner of coming to terms with personal mortality. There are gentler, more philosophical approaches. If one has had agreeable children, written a book, founded a company—things which project into the future—it makes acceptance easier. Otherwise, there remains music, meditation, and meandering to new places. Whatever the manner, there is a reward for passing this barrier of death-anxiety. Happiness studies worldwide indicate that the most despondent period in our lives is between age forty-five and sixty-five. Surprise—barring a variety of health problems, the happiest people are the senior citizens, over sixty-five, provided they have accepted their situation. Many have come to terms with their past lives in a state of "ego integrity". They can then undertake new missions, find new partners in life, write their stories, pursue politics, indulge in the travelling they never had time for before, maintain their health, and help the next generations to find their way. And they plan for their own demise.

MY THOUGHTS on this mechanism of rebirth were interrupted because as we entered the motorway north to Fontainebleau the rain came back vigorously. My front windscreen wipers started scraping and I realised they needed changing. Then there was a cracking noise from the back, and the rear windscreen wiper disconnected and broke. With the heavy rain, I could no longer see anything behind me on the motorway. I didn't mention this to Mylène. She was more concerned with the way I was weaving the car from right to left and back. The road surface was now covered with water and without adequate headlights I couldn't make out the traffic lanes. Even staying on the road was a problem.

"I can't see a damn thing! Where are the lane markers?"

"Forget about them! Don't look at the ground. Just line us up behind the car in front!"

I wasn't the only one in difficulty and the traffic slowed, but still tensed its way forward at ninety kilometres per hour. One slip and we might be competing with Mamie for tomb space. If this is where it stops, so be it, I thought. But it's not going to be today if I can help it. I can't say whether I was more scared or excited at the challenge.

Almost an hour later we took the motorway exit for Fontainebleau and like magic the storm chose that moment to subside. Another fifteen minutes and we had reached our house. I then confessed to Mylène that the rear wiper had not been working and I had been blind behind. She was not impressed. The morning seemed a long way behind us. I looked back on the day's disturbing events as if it had been a lifetime, and felt profoundly glad to be where I was, home. We would sleep soundly that night. My last waking thoughts were a resolution to get the car lights and the windscreen wipers fixed the next day. I wanted to be ready for the next adventure.

The economists teach us that when a resource becomes rare and irreplaceable its value soars dramatically. The remaining years in a senior citizen's life are in this category. Once our fear of passing has gone, we savour every minute that remains, drinking the Champagne to the last drop.

12

THE ROYAL RUN

Look at the joggers in your nearby park. They all look fit and young. Look again. Several are white-haired seniors. How come they are still running? Shouldn't walking be enough for the elderly? Or is this what it means to be savouring life to the last drop?

As I TIED my running shoes, Mylène asked: "Are you sure you have to go?"

"Yes."

"It's not safe!" But I was already at the door.

Have you ever tried to run in a forest at night when you can't see a thing and your feet don't know where to go? This is not a metaphor for confronting life's dark problems. I entered the park at 6:30 p.m. that December evening and within a hundred metres, the street lamps were no longer visible. Winter had come too soon for me. The days were too short, but I had had too little exercise, so on impulse I was trying my jogger's luck. The forest surrounded me with its gnarled and massive trunks. By day, the Fontainebleau Park is impressive—tall trees, thick undergrowth, and an occasional wild boar. By night, it's scary and big

—more than a square kilometre—and it has no lights. It is a near-rectangle, with gates at each corner. I guess the town hall feels that anyone crazy enough to enter when it is dark must know what he or she is doing. Did I know?

Once in the park, I regretted my rashness. There was no moon, no lights, and the trees hid any available stars. I thought I knew the paths through the forest by heart but I couldn't make them out. Starting from the gate I had entered there should have been three routes; a steep path to my left down the east side that would lead me clockwise round the park; a gentler slope to my right leading counter clockwise, on the north side; and one in the middle, rougher, cutting diagonally across to the Fontainebleau Chateau. I had bad memories of that diagonal route. On a rainy night a year earlier, I had taken that way in total darkness and tripped in several pools of water, fortunately without breaking anything. So, I chose what I hoped was the easier north stretch, and—whatever the danger—started a slow jog. After a minute or two, I could detect shadowy walls of trees and I laboured to stay in the middle of the path. The smell of the old trees spiced the cool air. The branches on either side seemed to reach for each other, hiding most of the sombre sky. These paths had once been paved but were now in disrepair and I would jolt onto a stone every few steps. Not seeing the edges of the path, I could have easily banged into a tree. My pulse rate soared, and not because of the exercise.

I continued downhill, straining my senses to the maximum. I was caught between trepidation and excitement in this new and perilous world. After about a kilometre without tripping over anything larger than dead leaves, I saw a faint light ahead. It was a lamp just outside the park at the end of the northern side. I was soon past it and ran by the dim chateau entrance until I reached the canal on the south side. Here the sky was visible and a few stars dared to show their faces, but no moon. Suddenly a new light approached me from ahead, bobbing up and down. It was another crazy runner with a lamp strapped to his head. I hailed him as he went by and asked where he had bought his lamp.

"Sports store!" he said and jogged away.

I walked the rest of the way back to my entry gate and gave up after one lap around the dark park. I would have to get a lamp.

The next day I bought one. Mylène was reassured, but then to my surprise she said: "I want one too!"

A FEW DAYS LATER, I entered the night-time park, again alone, with the intention of doing two complete rounds. The lamp strapped to my head was supposed to change everything, but I hadn't understood the cryptic instructions, and as I fumbled with the mode switch the beam of light swung upwards. It illuminated the massive trees above me, but not the path ahead. I changed the control from bright to dim, to very dim, to blinking, but nothing helped. I would have to bend my neck ninety degrees to see where my feet were going. And there could be all sorts of unwelcome things underfoot. Not to mention having to reduce my speed to almost a walk—which was the most annoying bit. If I, a jogger, couldn't jog why be out there at all?

Indeed, why was I "out there", running in the rugged, unlighted park? The short-term explanation: it was winter, the night came earlier, and exercise was necessary. Necessary for what, I wondered? Well, for my health of course. A race perhaps? But what about all the other things I did: the hiking, the table tennis, the swimming, and the gymnastics? Wasn't that enough? It's not *intense* enough, I thought. Even with hours of weekly activity to keep one supple, the body loses its punch. I remembered the beginning of my runner's dream, a long time ago.

SUDDENLY, I was a ten-year-old again. Gosh! How thrilling it was to have my first annual sports day at my boarding school—British by tradition even if it was on the Caribbean island of Antigua.

The boys—friends and enemies alike—were assembled on the sports field in groups around the race track, the sandpit, and the goal-posts. Competition at every age level was about to begin between the four houses (Red, Blue, Green, and Yellow). Mine was the Blue House and it was my first year in the school. I was ready to prove my merit and earn points for my house. I intended to compete in *everything*: racing, high jump, long jump, and throwing things. In my mind, I was a combatant. In my body, I was a rather plump ten-year-old who spent his time reading and dreaming rather than running and jumping.

Everything turned against me that day. The sporting events for my age were calibrated according to performances by British students of the same age. If I could attain the standard, I'd earn a point for my house. If I exceeded it, I might be classed among the best three performers and win extra points. But why had they set the high jump bar so high, well above my waist? I couldn't clear it, not even after three tries.

"Vanier—eliminated," the sports master said.

And why had they set the standard distance for long jump so far into the sandpit? No success here either; I just made it from the turf onto the sand and landed hard on my bottom. I also failed with the cricket ball throw. However, finally, I succeeded in the shot put. I hefted the two-kilogram metal ball just over the regulation distance: one point for tubby.

Then it was time for the most prestigious event of the day: a race round the 440-yard track, the standard time being two minutes. Before I could move, the other boys in my group exploded into action, legs thumping on the track. Where did they get their energy? I completed the distance huffing and puffing, the last in the group, way over the standard. As I plodded over the finish line there were more than a few laughs from my classmates.

"Christopher Vanier, fat as a tannia!"

I had good marks in school, but here on the track I was humiliated. My Blue House won the sports day, but this didn't cheer me up. Sports were not for me. At least, not this type of sport. During the next four years in that school I would not earn a single further standard point, not even for shot put. In other games like football and wrestling, I barely defended myself. But I made a plan, that day on the race track. So what if all the other boys were faster than me today? Maybe one day I could outdo the sprinters. How about going ten or twenty times round the track at a slower speed? On a longer distance, I might do better.

～

BACK IN THE DARK PARK, I grinned at this memory. As a ten-year-old, I had never heard of jogging and marathons, but I did have ambition. As if out of sympathy, my night lamp began working properly. It took just a little twist; the way things often do. Oh, what comfort to see my feet again and all the obstacles nearby! My pace picked up and having completed a first lap around the park in about twenty-five minutes, I started happily on a second lap. This time I took the rough diagonal route, knowing I would be able see any obstacles. I reflected that the ten-year-old who had been me had not quite pierced the runner's mystique. Yes, long-distance running is more satisfying than short races for most of us, but no, the real adversary is not the other runners, it is ourselves. Can we strain our bodies until it hurts to run any further? It took me another thirty years to understand this. No pain, no gain!

In my twenties at university, I did some track racing over a mile. At Cambridge, I remember running this distance in five minutes and twenty-five seconds, the equivalent of one minute and twenty-two seconds over 440 yards. It would have been a good standard point for my childhood but had little to do with adult long-distance jogging. Subsequently, my sporting life consisted of tennis, swimming, and gymnastics, in moderate doses.

It was at age forty that I began to fulfil my ten-year-old ambition. My engineering career had taken me to work in a twenty-floor tower on the banks of the river Seine. To offset our dry computers and calculations with some greenery, at lunchtime I would cross the river with a few friends for some exercise in the Boulogne woods.

"Why don't we run a bit?" asked another engineer.

"In suit and tie?" I queried.

"There's a tennis club nearby. We can change into running kit. And later, we can get back to work in half an hour. Probably even time for a quick lunch."

It was so much fun we gradually increased our outings to the limit of our two-hour lunch break. We were jogging five kilometres (5K). I learned the first principle of training: most muscle soreness and stiffness develop over the two days following your effort, especially the second day. Then it goes away and the renewed muscle tissue is stronger. Joints are different. For many months, my knees were sore and only gradually did the pain go away.

In my second year of distance running someone suggested doing the Cross du Figaro, a winter race of ten kilometres. That's when I discovered a second principle. My body adapts to running a given distance but each time I increased it by a few kilometres, watch out! My leg muscles would shout and scream for a week. I did the 10K race, calmed down the complaining calves and thighs, and started reading books on running. I learned about interval training and a runner's diet before and after exercise. I ran the Paris 20K, and two years later at the age of forty-five, my first marathon. Even for training, I discovered that running is a very individual sport. No two runners have the same rhythm, and unlike today's forest walking, it's not a place to make friends.

Continuing my solo night-time run, and thinking about my first marathon, I successfully completed the diagonal path, jogged vigorously past the chateau, and headed for the south side canal. The darkness around me was in profound contrast with sunny memories of my 42K initiation.

It had been an early morning in the month of May 1987, the temperature just over fifteen degrees Celsius near the Eiffel Tower, where twelve thousand runners were lined up on the Iéna Bridge. In the middle of the crowd, my first concern was about drinking. I clutched a full plastic bottle, looked at my watch, and waited for the nine o'clock starter's shot. There would be no water available for the first ten kilometres and a runner must keep from dehydrating. However, if you drink too much too soon, you will have to stop and let it out within a kilometre. My objective was to drink just before the start, so my body would keep the liquid and consume it gradually. I drank when my watch showed ten minutes left, and then worried about how to dispose of the bottle. With the others pressing around me, I lowered it gently to the ground, trampled on it, and observed that some who might have drunk too early were regretting it and trying to find a place to pee. Then the starter's pistol went off.

I knew I had to take it easy in the early phases, and this wasn't hard in the crowd, but despite trying to plan, it was all new—I had never jogged more than twenty kilometres. I had done this in one hour and forty-five minutes so I figured the marathon should take me just a little more than three hours and thirty minutes, about five minutes per kilometre on average. It wasn't realistic, I was dreaming, and I suffered. At first, I told myself it was normal, just more pains and stiffness than usual. Then at twenty-five kilometres, after several water-stops, I lost my courage. Why am I doing this? It hurts too much. I considered stopping to escape the self-torment. What was the interest in going on? If I gave up, I might do better next year. I slowed down. My breathing became increasingly laboured. What saved me was a memory from the books I had read. They said the first-time marathoner *always* wants to give up. And that the 25K-30K mark is the worst moment because the body has used up its readily available sugars for energy and then can only consume fats, which are less efficient for absorbing oxygen. Just accept to move more slowly. So, if I wasn't the only one feeling the torture, maybe I could continue a bit? Scanning the crowd I had hitherto ignored, I saw a few others slowing down. Then, I stopped thinking and just slugged forward like an automaton. I finished in over four hours (about six minutes per kilometre) and virtually collapsed. How I got home and how my family reacted is wiped out of my mind now, almost thirty years later. This is comparable to giving birth: the duration though not the intensity of pain is often obliterated from memory, especially with an epidural, so the mother can undertake new childbirths later. Perhaps my marathon effort was all right for a beginner but it took me a month to recover. I might have given up running after that torture, mightn't I?

∽

WELL, no! Still training in the dark, I had now covered another third of my circuit, savouring my memories and the night-time reflexions on the canal next to me. I wasn't jogging at my fastest, but after forty minutes I felt relaxed and under control. And this is the final lesson, the key to the jogger's persistence, the reason I keep on running, something I learned in my first marathon years. The body rewards the runner's efforts, and the name of the recompense that it produces is endorphins (literally, "endogenous morphine"). These are natural pain-killing substances, neurotransmitters in the brain. They produce a "runner's high", a euphoria and resistance to body pains (like the effects produced by smoking and drugs, but without the negative aspects). Running-induced endorphins are natural and have no side effects. The body can also produce endorphins through strenuous cycling but running is the primordial source.

I discovered endorphins while training in Park Monceau thirty years ago. You must be a fit runner, working out two or more times per week. And you must be running for at least twenty minutes, at roughly 75 percent of your highest pulse rate (for me, between 110 and 130 heartbeats per minute). Instead of being sore and tired, these endorphins let me finish my training on a positive note. Your body is simultaneously your partner and your adversary. The high is good while it lasts but it won't stop your stressed muscles from feeling sore later.

In addition, I discovered that the "runner's high" euphoria is also a trance-like state during which the runner is free to meditate or write stories in his head. On several occasions when I had problems with an essay I would run for an hour and juggle the possibilities. I even wrote a sci-fi story about an alien talking to a runner during his endorphin phase.

BY NOW I was jogging alongside the Fontainebleau canal on the south side of the park and dreaming of other past marathons. I ran three further Paris races after that first painful one. My race times improved:

the best was three hours and twenty minutes, placing me in the upper fortieth percentile.

My brother Noel in the USA was a far better runner than I was (at four minutes per kilometre) and for several years we searched for a way to run in the same race. The closest we had gotten was a brotherly jog in Paris along the banks of the Seine, where Noel got so far ahead of the group that he got lost. Finally, an occasion arose for which we were both available: a special Boston centennial marathon in 1996. I was then fifty-four and had not been training. In addition, I had put on six unnecessary kilograms. I entered the race anyway, with thirty-eight thousand other starters, and my time went back up to four hours plus. I discovered new places to get extremely sore. It could have been worse: one of the runners ahead of me died of a heart attack just after the finish line.

We visited my parents in the Caribbean right after the Boston race and amazed my bedridden father with our tales. That was my last marathon. I felt my age was beginning to tell and decided not to race more than twenty kilometres in the future. Worse was to come. In 2003, age sixty-one, shortly after my last Paris–Versailles race, I developed a knee injury from unknown causes (I suspected my running shoes of being, like me, too old). My sports doctor in Paris spared me surgery— on the condition I take anti-inflammatory drugs, and use crutches for the next six months, which I did. Afterwards, I began very light jogging again but suffered one or two asthma attacks. My body had won the battle of inactivity. It looked like the end of my racing career, endorphins or not.

I shook my head stubbornly as I passed the end of the canal and started the last stretch of the night-time park, on the east side. I had begun taking preventive treatment for asthma. Marathons are over, I thought, and it had meant a gloomy end to running. Walking in the forest was jovial during my first years in this forest area, but hardly to be compared with my past dreams.

∾

ON THAT LAST STRETCH, I cheered up, remembering what had happened in my third year in Avon. I had heard about a prestigious local race, the Foulée Impériale de Fontainebleau, what I call the Royal Run. Curiously, my sporting club RSAG does not encourage racing, thinking it too dangerous. I had not competed in any race for the past eleven years, but something in the air made me ambitious. The challenge of a race for a runner is like a book for a writer, it forces discipline. The good walkers and cyclists in my sports club didn't seem interested, which only intrigued me more. The Royal Run would take place in early April, and proposed several events, from three kilometres to twenty-one kilometres. Ten kilometres seemed a good target for me, much less than my former exploits but a lot more effort than my current walking. The question was: could I begin racing again as a senior? I needed a medical certificate to enter the race.

While getting a prescription for anti-asthmatic pills, I said to my doctor: "I want to run the April 10K race and I need your green light."

He duly checked my pulse and blood pressure. "Seems okay, but what's your goal? Why do you want to compete?"

"Isn't it normal to compete? Didn't you tell me last year that *you* ran this race yourself?"

"Not recently! I'm over fifty-five now and *you're* over seventy. Races are risky. Why don't you just walk the 10K with your friends?"

"But I like the challenge! And haven't you read the latest American sports research, doctor? Walking is good for endurance and general health but unless you *stress* your body regularly over age seventy, physical decline is inevitable. Running maintains your fitness level longer."

He handed me the certificate and smiled wryly: "Maybe I'll run it again then!"

～

SINCE I'D STUCK my neck out, I had to deliver. I registered for the 10K race, and I started mild jogging in the cold months of January and February, but only five jogging sessions in March. I began to be afraid and hoped fear would help me to run.

During my last training session, I developed a cramp in my right leg. It took me three days to recover. What if it were to happen again during the real race? The last few days, I took it easy. I just wanted to finish that damned Royal Run, at this point "royal" only in name. I suspected I'd finish in the last 10 percent of the runners.

Race day arrived. While shaving that morning, I looked at myself in the mirror and said, "You old fool! Why take the unnecessary risk of heart failure, asthmatic crisis, and badly strained muscles? Why didn't you listen to your doctor? It's not going to be much fun running ten kilometres this afternoon!"

In the afternoon, I buried myself in the crowd of runners behind the starting line. I looked furtively around but talked to no one. I was hoping to do the race in an hour, but I might be a lot slower. I was surrounded by much younger competitors, svelte females, muscular young males, just a few grey-haired types, and most were smiling as if the race was a joke. I could see no one my age.

There was a digital tag in my shoe which registered my start time. The first kilometre was a traffic jam, too many runners in the narrow streets. The second kilometre was hardly better. We were in central Fontainebleau and didn't enter the park until the third kilometre. At this point, the path cleared and my speed picked up. I overtook some of the slower runners, and my confidence went up a notch. I remember a man with a pink shirt and a woman with a blue top. I tried to pass them repeatedly without success but everything seemed possible, up to the seventh kilometre. Then things collapsed: my legs informed me that the endorphin boost was over, not used to running this distance so fast for so many years. I remembered my past marathons and would have laughed if I'd had the breath to do so. The eighth and ninth kilometres were even more bad news. What a shame if I had to drop out. But it seemed hopeless. I couldn't win the struggle against my body at my age. I couldn't go on. My running ambition was a childhood mirage. Then I noticed a few other runners giving up, all younger than me. Maybe my long-ago marathon years had served some purpose. I slowed down, no longer hoping to pass anyone, but I continued. By the tenth and last kilometre we had left the park and were struggling back to the finish line in central Fontainebleau. I couldn't sprint the last two hundred metres like most of my competitors did. My digital shoe tag was more alive than I was.

Breathing hard, I queued up with the other survivors for a few gulps of water and a souvenir shirt. Then I walked stiffly over to the podium and listened to the organisers congratulating the winners. The mayor of Avon climbed onto the stage in running gear. She was about forty-five and rather pretty: I realised she had run the 10K race with us. Later, I discovered that the mayor had arrived ten minutes after me. The overall race winner, a sleek twenty-five-year-old, had arrived in about thirty-three minutes. The medals were awarded by age category and gender, first the juniors, then the forty-year-old veterans, and so on. I was tired and about to leave when I heard my name.

"And third place for the over-seventies is Christopher Vanier . . ."

In a daze of surprise, I climbed onto the platform to receive a medal and a kiss from the mayor. No one had told me there would be recognition of the oldies category. I had finished in one hour and five minutes and in the eightieth percentile of one thousand runners, with six of us over seventy. I was the only one from our club.

In my mind, I dedicated that race to my father. I had seen his knees failing, partly from lack of exercise in the tropics. At seventy-five, just a little older than my present self, he was chair-ridden, then bedridden when I last saw him. This race was my proof that, with care, seniors can maintain an active place in the world. Two years later, I would be distanced by an eighty-year-old who trained regularly.

I HAD NOW REACHED the end of my night-time run in the Fontainebleau Park and could see street lights just beyond the gate where I had entered. I turned off my headlamp and clicked on my training watch to record the second lap time. It would be better than the first lap, but not a record; memories have their price. It's not easy, this struggle to keep running, but if we push ourselves beyond our comfort zone, if we listen to the body's quirks and give it enough recovery time, then our will can dominate that bag of blood and bones for a while longer. See you soon again, Royal Run!

13

GIVING UP PARIS

What is the point of being in France if you don't live in Paris? When I arrived in 1970, I thought it was the only place for me.

Yet there I was in Avon, enjoying every breath of its fresh air, hiking in the forest, running in the Fontainebleau Park, reluctant to visit Paris except to see family and friends, and wondering what to do with my large apartment in the Seventeenth Arrondissement.

When Mylène and I had left the polluted French capital in 2012, I had lingering notions of being a Parisian on holiday. I tried to maintain my old family home even with no family in it. This, despite the opinion of my French notary, a tall, blond-haired, deep-voiced official always clad in a dark suit, who had advised me to sell it in 2008, after the death of my wife Colette.

"You could get more than the inheritance estimate of seven hundred thousand euros," he said, opening his eyes wide. "We only used that figure to minimise your taxes. But watch out, prices are going to fall! I'll send a reliable estate agency around as soon as possible."

Funny, I thought a notary should be neutral, being a public officer without whom one cannot buy or sell property. It seems his interest can extend significantly into real estate commerce—something suspicious there. The agent's estimate was closer to eight hundred thousand euros, but I resisted, and lived in my flat for a while with Mylène. Then, when we moved to Avon four years later, I decided to rent it out. I had said my goodbyes and knew I would probably never again live there but I couldn't accept letting it go.

First, I renovated the apartment, using a building company. Most expensive, I added double-glazed windows to enclose my two outside balconies (*loggias*). This created about five square metres of extra living space. I also replaced the old carpeting; bought new kitchen equipment; repainted everything; retiled the bathrooms; updated the electricity, lighting, and networks; and bought lots of bright new IKEA furniture. I removed all our family paintings and replaced them with neutral flower scenes. The work took two years, off and on—costly, but emotionally satisfying. It still seemed part of my life, full of memories of Colette. Then I tried to find tenants.

I badly wanted to remain the owner, having regretfully sold my parents' home in St. Kitts overlooking the splendid bay of Basseterre ten years earlier. It had stayed in the family for fifty years. I had the idea that enduring families hand their homes down from generation to generation. Unfortunately, it no longer works like this. Families expand and contract—first babies, then children growing up and leaving, then parents fading away. Few families seem to live for more than ten years in the same place. I had been in that Seventeenth District apartment for twenty-seven years.

"How much do you want to rent out your apartment for?" an estate agent asked me in 2014.

For 140 square metres completely renovated, we agreed on 5,500 euros per month short-term and somewhat less long-term.

"But I don't want short-term," I said. "Nothing less than two months and by September I want long-term."

The agent looked at me quizzically and nodded. I realised later that long-term contracts were much less profitable for him.

Nothing appropriate was proposed to me for several months.

In desperation, I accepted a summer rental to an Algerian wine grower and his family who were buying a new apartment which wasn't yet ready. All went well except for the time-consuming visits I had to make from Avon. Then came frustration, no more rentals.

This made me rethink my original decision. My Paris apartment was still officially my main residence, despite my move to Avon. I discovered that the Paris municipality (mairie) would only allow me four months of short-term renting per year. But if I rented long-term, the apartment would lose the status of my principal residence, and thus incur a high capital gains tax if I decided to sell later. And while empty, the apartment would keep on costing me about fourteen thousand euros per year in property taxes, heating, and building charges. So, like a stubborn engineer, against my desire to keep the apartment, I went to my computer and started doing simulations. Whatever rental scheme I used, my net yield would be less than 2 percent of the apartment's value. With deep regrets, I decided to sell and be damned. I couldn't have it all.

Looking for some positive aspects, I felt I could invest the proceeds with Mylène in Avon and still leave a long-term inheritance for my children. They would get a useful part of the sale money at once. This is part of old age—I was doing what many of my senior friends in Avon had already done, getting rid of a large family home in exchange for something smaller and more appropriate.

Around this time, my brother Noel wrote to me from the USA to say he had just bought a retirement home in Colorado. It took him only two days! Of course, it would take me a bit longer to sell in Paris, but I would get help.

I went back to my notary's plush office in October 2015 and explained I had changed my mind about selling. His handsome face lit up. "Good thing you waited! Prices are up, but they'll surely fall soon. What's your asking figure?"

"Maybe one million fifty thousand euros," I said. It was six years after his previous estimate, and I had checked the Internet figures.

"Ah, no!" he replied. "I recommend at least 1.1 million euros. Always give yourself leg room. I'll introduce you to a dynamic agency on the Champs Elysées."

Okay, I thought, the game is launched. It should be easy to sell.

Maybe my notary would be useful after all. Then I glumly recalled some unfinished administrative business with him from years before.

"And the cellar," I said. "Don't forget the incoherent cellar plans."

"A detail," he hesitated, then shrugged. "Just get it sold."

I had a bad feeling about this but couldn't see a way out.

My notary's suggested agency on the Champs Elysées was indeed dynamic. They accepted my target of 1.1 million euros provided they had three months exclusivity.

I showed their salesman my beloved apartment and gave him the keys. He was corpulent, moustached, and voluble. Then I sat back—it was out of my hands—I could relax. In three months, my apartment would be sold. I could forget the struggle and concentrate on my new life with Mylène in Avon.

The agency bombarded the sales media and hauled in prospective buyers. At the end of each week they reported that people liked the apartment but not the neighbourhood. Too many immigrants. Well, I thought, I was an immigrant, too. Still am, for that matter. No bids went beyond nine hundred thousand euros and the agency turned them all down. The sales campaign began in early November and it took two months to find a serious buyer. I knew the prejudice against the immigrant population was ill-founded. Having lived in the area for thirty years, I had found adequate parks, schools, shops, services, and street markets. How else could I get my daily mangoes?

It turned out the ideal buyers also lived in the area, near Place de Clichy, and were very much at ease in the neighbourhood. They even sent their children to the same school mine had gone to. By Christmas, my broker thought he had the sale under control.

"This is the one!" he said. "I strongly advise accepting this buyer's offer. I've negotiated with dozens of people and this is probably your last chance."

The only little problem was the price.

I suddenly realised that though I had bought four Paris properties for myself and my children, I had negligible experience in selling them.

The buyer refused the figure of 1.1 million euros, as I had antici-pated. But he also refused 1.05 million euros and said he wouldn't even pay a million for a place with defects.

"What defects?" I asked by phone. "Who are these people?"

"They're very slick," the broker said. "She is a legal advisor in a large bank and he is an accountant in a prosperous company. They have two children, aged eight and ten. They don't like the smell of the cellar and distrust your balconies."

"Get the best offer you can," I said. "There's nothing wrong with the cellar."

The Christmas festivities intervened and amidst the Champagne, I did not discuss my apartment problems. The buyers would probably come around, I thought.

Two days later, between Christmas and New Year's, the broker called me and said, "They're ready to sign a preliminary contract but they won't budge from a purchase price of nine hundred ninety thousand, and only if they have certain guarantees."

I didn't feel I could accept this.

"You have to come to an agreement," the broker insisted. "I've done my best for two months and I can assure you no other buyer will pay this amount."

"Let me think about it for a day or two," I said. "Don't reply to the buyer just yet."

That night, around our dinner table, I discussed things with Mylène, who had not been directly involved up to then. "It looks as if I was too optimistic," I said, "but my Internet research of property prices in the Seventeenth District can't be far out. To go from one-point-one million to one million was probably inevitable, since the notary had jacked up the asking price, but what with agency fees I'm losing another sixty thousand!"

"Leave it to me," Mylène said. "You don't know a thing about French negotiations."

I started in surprise: "What negotiations? If the broker is ready to give up, what can I do? I don't know the buyer and normally I shouldn't be talking to him. That's what I pay the darned broker for."

"You engineers! I'll have to teach you." She grimaced.

"Well, what do you suggest to get a better price?"

"You have to realise the buyer is not your friend but your adversary. However, our first attack will not be on the buyer but on our broker. He's energetic, but not effective against a strong buyer. When he says this represents the best opportunity, it's not just for you, the seller, but for him, the intermediary. Let me do this."

So, I let her phone the broker and listened uneasily. Within fifteen minutes, Mylène had secured a reduction in the sales commission and saved me twenty thousand euros, even if the buyer didn't budge. Then she made the broker arrange a phone conversation between the buyer and us. He wasn't too happy to give up his role but set up things for later that evening at 9 p.m. The person who would call us was named Ségolène, the legal advisor. When Mylène heard her name, she told me I would have to do the talking.

"Male to female is better in these circumstances, and she may ask some technical questions. You must listen, not talk, and only reply when necessary. Put the speaker phone on and I'll write suggestions while she talks. And I'll kick you under the table if needed. Don't bring up prices right now."

When Ségolène called, she sounded a little stiff and was full of complaints.

"The floor covering in your apartment is linoleum, whereas the listing implied floorboards," she said.

"Sorry about that—the pattern on the linoleum does look like parquet, but it's easy to keep clean."

"The cellar is very damp. When I opened the door, I smelled it at once. I can't use a place like that. It's unhealthy. I hang up clothes in the cellar, and it just won't work in your place. This definitely decreases the value of your apartment."

Ségolène went on for some time about this odour problem. Mylène kicked my foot under the table—as promised—to stop me intervening. I was annoyed at the buyer's insistence on smells.

Now, that cellar, that infamous cellar, was the only room I hadn't emptied of my junk. After a long pause, I replied.

"Well, I keep wine in my cellar, perhaps three hundred bottles, and no doubt this has created a smell. On the other hand, you may have noticed I have many boxes of papers down there which have not been moisture-damaged. I expect ventilation can remove the odours."

We exchanged email addresses and set up a new telephone meeting in two days' time to discuss other matters, including prices. I asked whether I might reply to Ségolène's emails in English.

"That's fine, I speak English! By the way, I'd like to visit the apartment again with an architect friend."

The next day I told the broker we had made contact with the buyer and he should give them one more visit.

The president of our owners council said *his* cellar was dry and not in need of ventilation.

At our following phone conversation, Ségolène had a lot more complaints. First it was the doors, and then the balconies.

"All the doors inside your apartment are badly fitted. My architect pointed out that they have a five-centimetre gap at the bottom, making it difficult to soundproof one room from another. I'm very sensitive to noise. I'll have to replace all those doors, and that will cost."

I couldn't keep my reply short, but I tried to speak in a measured tone.

"I wouldn't replace them *all*, if I were you. It's part of the healthy ventilation system. The outside windows are airtight except for a small gap to let in fresh air. In the bathrooms and kitchen there is a mechanical ventilation system which sucks in stale air and sends it out via vents up to the rooftop. So, the doors to these ventilated rooms must have an aperture to permit an air current from the rest of the apartment. It's most effective at the bottom. Closed bedroom doors need this bottom opening too. You could always make an exception for one or two bedrooms which need soundproofing, provided you open the windows regularly. This is the building design, and not just in my apartment."

There was silence from Ségolène. Then she talked about the kitchen and laundry equipment, which were almost brand new.

"We have the same machines," she said, "but if you wish to leave yours, we could doubtless sell ours." I agreed a bit too hastily, losing two or three thousand euros in a few seconds.

Going back to the cellar, Ségolène said something that disturbed me a lot: "The location of your cellar is a bit confusing. It doesn't agree with the original floor plan."

"That's my notary's job," I replied. "He guarantees everything will be in order before the sale."

I disguised my growing uncertainty about this problem.

Then the discussion centred on another problem: the balconies on the street side of my apartment. About half the apartments in our building have such balconies and over the years the owners have closed them off, as I had just done. The apartment owners had consulted each other and were careful to choose a style of window in harmony with the building facade. In our annual owners meetings, we had voted acceptance of these balcony closures. The building companies which installed the windows had said nothing about their legality.

However, a bureaucratic city like Paris has administrative traps everywhere. Each apartment owner ought to have applied for a new building permit. The increase in living space requires city hall authorisation, not least because annual property taxes are proportional to the surface area, and a notary must register the updated architect's plans. In addition, the *syndic* (building management company) would have to recalculate the annual maintenance charges for each owner. No current owner would complain about the non-compliance of our hidden balconies, but what about my jurist buyer?

Mylène stamped on my foot to indicate I should listen.

Ségolène was upset about the illegal closed balconies. She postulated that in some undetermined future a new resident of the building might turn in the other owners. This legal imbroglio might make it difficult to resell the apartment. If she took the risk of buying, I should decrease the current price to take this into account.

I disagreed, saying that many buildings in Paris had irregularities of this sort and no one would upset the apple cart. Any objection would not come from a present or future owner, bound by the consensus in the council minutes.

When our price negotiations started, I remained under Mylène's guidance but reverted to my native tongue, English. I declared to the buyers that despite anything the broker might have said, their offer of nine hundred ninety thousand euros would not do and we should approach my initial offer of one million fifty thousand. After long hesitation and consultation with her husband, Ségolène proposed one million ten thousand as their final offer. I lowered my "final offer" to one million forty thousand.

"No!" Ségolène said.

I was tempted to back down but a further kick from Mylène stopped me. Instead, I said: "Look, do you really want this place? We raised two children here just as you might do, but you have to increase your price."

Justin then intervened and said: "OK, we propose one million twenty thousand."

When Mylène nodded, I said: "Done!" and we all relaxed. Between the agent's fees and the buyer's price, Mylène had saved me fifty thousand euros.

Of course, the sale money would not be all mine. My deceased wife Colette had owned 50 percent of the apartment and each of our two children would receive a part of this. Since her death the apartment had remained in a state the French call joint ownership (*indivision*). Our marriage contract conferred to me—the *usufruitier*—the right to rent or to sell. My share of the sale would not be taxed, but my children would each have to pay a modest capital gains tax.

What was their feeling about the sale? Both children owned their own flats and had no need of the old family place. Had it been different, I would not have sold. My son was glad to receive a timely inheritance and immediately made plans to reinvest his future proceeds. My daughter Chloé had less well-defined plans and was sad that her family nest would disappear but realised that one day she might need the money to buy a larger apartment for herself. Letting go of the past is not simple. I had shed my own tears seven years earlier when Colette died. In theory, all I was losing were memories. How much did they weigh?

I breathed easier and slept better when we agreed on the price. However, unknown to me, the legal fun was just about to begin. My sales representative advised the two notaries (representing seller and buyer) of the agreement and they began asking for additional papers. The next step would be to sign a pre-sale contract and for a fairy-tale moment we tried (both seller and buyer) to get this done before the year's end. Our notary said, "Sign before they diddle you!" But it was impossible.

Ségolène and her husband needed to secure their financing. They couldn't find a buyer for their current apartment, so they opted for borrowing temporarily almost the whole purchase price. This implied a high initial monthly payment and for a bank to accept this they needed a good insurance policy on the loan. In France, this means establishing tedious background credentials and medical certification. A simple cholesterol anomaly could block the deal. So, their notary held things back.

As I had feared, my problem was the cellar; not the odour nor the ventilation but something more fundamental. I found out it was not legally mine to sell. It made me furious. This was the result of an error going back twenty-seven years. In 1988, when I bought the apartment, the building was not yet finished and the transaction was based on the architect's plans. The builder was a British company called Wimpey. We purchased the entire second floor of the five-floor building. When Wimpey had finished everything except for last-minute fittings, we requested several changes. Most important, we refused the cellar which Wimpey proposed (No. 124). It had awkward curved walls and a horrid central pillar. I demanded something better and, as we were buying the largest apartment in the building, Wimpey bent over backwards to oblige.

"No problem," they said. "We have a comfortable rectangular cellar which is part of the common building area and is currently unassigned." So, they changed the numbers on the cellar doors and gave me the new key. Cellar No. 124 had magically moved. This might have worked in the UK but not in France where the builder had already filed his plan with the public registry (*cadastre*) and given it to the notary's office. These plans were used to determine property taxes and building charges. My new cellar was larger than the old one by about six square metres, but no account had been taken of this for twenty-seven years. Legally, that new cellar was not mine.

Now, maybe Wimpey had been hasty in reassigning my cellar with just a touch of paint on the door but the responsibility lay with the notary who had supervised the sale of all the apartments in the building and hadn't properly registered the modification. As fate would have it, my elegant notary for the sale in 2015 was the same as the one for the purchase in 1988. And yet—and this made me boil— three times in the past I had pestered him to correct the situation, but on each occasion, he had replied, "When you sell it, we shall sort things out." I had even had the flat owners council vote approval of the new cellar distribution on three occasions and draw up new plans, in which my current cellar was renumbered 133. The old one reverted to its original number, 124, and allocated to another owner. Our notary took no account. Our current building management company refused to deal with my notary on this question.

In January of 2015, with a sale figure agreed and a pre-sale contract to sign, my notary had no time left. When I reminded him of the problem, he said: "It's simple, just give the buyer your original cellar."

"You mean the terrible room with a pillar in the middle? No way! The buyer has already visited my cellar, number 133, the one I've always used. She would refuse the other one. Anyway, the original number 124 is occupied, didn't you know?"

"I'll find a way to solve this," he said.

At this point, I became not only cross but seriously worried.

When she heard this, Mylène got angry and insisted I bypass my notary. I emailed his boss, the head of the notary's office. I emphasised that the cellar arrangement was *their* responsibility and they had to get it fixed. Within twenty-four hours I received a written reply guaranteeing the new cellar arrangement would be legalised in time for the sale. Our notary transmitted this information to the buyer's notary.

The pre-sale signing was then set for January 27. I attended alone, carrying signed authorisations from my children. Those present were my broker, the two notaries, and the husband and wife buyers. Justin was comfortable and quiet. Ségolène was a thin, determined blonde in her forties. My broker and notary sat together companionably on the far side of the table. I was resolutely camped between the buyers and their notary. The pre-sale contract was a complex document of twenty-five-odd pages with provisions for just about everything which might happen up to the closing date (not yet defined): what to do if the seller or the buyer died, what if the buyer's loan was not granted by his bank, if one participant backed out . . . and stipulations about the cellar problem, furniture and machines to be left or removed . . . how to share out the taxes and building charges and utility contracts after the sale . . .

Ségolène had found places in my apartment where there seemed to be water damage to the paintwork and she inserted a clause in the contract that the seller must repair it before the sale. Everything was smiles and cheerful looks up to near the end when Ségolène said she would soon need several further visits to the apartment with building companies.

"No," I said. "I don't want any more visits before the closing day."

I was afraid she would find more defects, and I needed some peace and quiet to take out my furniture. Suppose I broke something or scratched some paint off the walls?

Suddenly furious, Ségolène shouted she must have experts in to get all the work done before next September, when schools reopen. Her husband cringed. My notary went pale and shrunk into his seat. The buyers' notary smiled uncertainly. Hemmed in on all sides, I began to get angry.

"It's still my place and I need to use it without interference! Suppose you backed out of the deal?"

Our broker saved the day. "Why don't we say that the buyers' bank loan must be confirmed in writing so they can't back out without a fifty-thousand-euro penalty, and then they may have access? This will be, at most, a forty-five-day period."

Still furious, Ségolène walked out of the room. Justin tried to reassure us: "She's checking with our workmen whether her renovation can still be done on time."

Ten minutes later she re-joined the meeting, silent and apparently accepting a change in her plans. One last item remained: the closed balconies. I was expecting big trouble, but the buyer and both notaries decided it was best to bury this point. The new surface area would be quoted in any future sale, but the point would not be mentioned either in the contract or at the owners council meeting or to the city registry. One wonders how many apartments in France are assessed for property taxes based on a false surface area.

The crucial problem remaining was the urgent obligation of my notary to solve the cellar problem. Without this, the sale could not go through. They say the devil is in the details, but I was about to discover the detail in the details.

While waiting for my notary, I fixed the water damage problem Ségolène had mentioned by checking the origin with my upstairs neighbour and repainting the wall and ceiling concerned.

Tension built up higher and higher as to whether the notary would come through. It was late February before he became organised and we met in the syndic's offices on March 16. The syndic in France is an outside organisation in charge of managing the common areas of a building, agreed-on works, accounting, and maintenance. Present at this decisive meeting were my notary, the current owners council president Gérard, the syndic manager, and me.

My notary outlined his long-awaited scheme in three acts. First, there would be a legal sale of cellar No. 133, which I would purchase from the owners' building for a symbolic price of one euro. Second, the building would purchase from me the old cellar, No. 124, again for one euro. And third, but not set up for the moment, the same transactions would apply to the owner currently in No. 124 with respect to *his* original cellar. These being legal transactions, there would be a registration fee to change the plans in the city registry. The municipal government has a pre-emptive option in all such property transactions but my notary produced a paper showing they had declined this privilege.

I signed the buy and sell contracts, the notary agreed to pay for the registration, and there was a polite scramble to find one-euro coins.

Then came the insidious details. There remained three further obstacles to completing the procedure.

First, both cellars would have to undergo a complete technical inspection (called a building diagnostic) for the presence of termites and asbestos, and the measurement of their exact surface area. My current cellar (No. 133) had already been inspected but not the old No. 124. And we didn't have access to this cellar. The owner lived in the South of France and had rented out his apartment. Gérard volunteered to find the current renter of No. 124, and the notary said he would pay the cost of the inspection.

Second, our syndic would have to recalculate the building charges and reprint the contract; each of the twelve apartment owners would then have to agree and sign. Never mind that they had already voted twice on this new cellar arrangement in preceding years! The new owners of cellar No. 133 would have to pay a few dozen euros per annum more and the others a few euros less.

Third, there had to be a formal owners meeting to approve all this. The notary turned to me. "The vote must be unanimous. All the owners must be present or represented and all votes must be positive. If not, the transaction is invalid and we will have to start all over again in a few months."

"But I don't know all the owners!" I said in horror. "And one or two are always absent!"

The notary smiled a sarcastic smile: "It's up to you to contact them." He had satisfied his legal responsibility and would not go further.

Hell, I thought, what does it take to sell a Paris apartment?

The syndic manager consulted his planning and said: "We can't have the general assembly before April 20. Four weeks plus a bit—that satisfies the legal deadline."

Ségolène complained about this delay, but her loan authorisation wouldn't be ready before then, so we agreed she could have a further visit to the apartment on the day of the owners meeting if she showed written confirmation from her bank. My notary had advised me to invite Justin and her to this meeting and to give them my voting powers. The reason for this was partly political—people who talk to each other have fewer fights—but also financial. Any budgetary measures voted for the next year with the new owners' agreement would not entail my responsibility. Thus, my notary patted himself on the back for having "solved" the cellar problem and left the rest to me.

But the details had nasty claws for me, first the cellar inspections. Gérard gave me the name and phone number of the tenant who rented cellar No. 124. I had to contact this tenant, collect her key to the cellar, come in from Avon to organise the inspection with a testing company, and make sure they got paid.

Last obstacle—the flat owners meeting. I sent emails to all owners explaining the importance of the cellar transaction and saying goodbye to those whom I had known for so long. I then went fishing for the phone numbers of those owners who might be absent to get their consent by proxy vote. But, I worried, what if someone forgot or changed their mind?

For me, that meeting was impossibly stressful. Normally chatty, I sat frozen amidst my fellow owners, most of them friends, and for the first time in twenty-seven years, I didn't say a word. Justin and Ségolène also avoided any controversial subjects. Not until we had counted all the votes did I begin to breathe freely again. Voting had been unanimous. The cellar imbroglio had been resolved after twenty-seven years. When the meeting was over, I provided Champagne for all present.

One more tiring task remained before the final closing. I had to remove all my furniture and empty the cellar. I got help from my own children and Mylène's. There were many heavy bookcases, cupboards, and beds to go. Mylène's daughter Dorothée advertised my furniture on a web site. It took many visits. I emptied the cellar, making three trips by car. With my children, I worked nonstop on the last day, sorting, packing, and throwing away. Afterwards, we had dinner together and chatted about old times. I had a last look at my old Paris home in its quiet street, and I trembled. Then, I started the drive back to Fontainebleau. I had drunk no wine.

My car was packed all the way up to the roof, and I could only see behind with the side mirrors. My son offered to accompany me, but there was no space. I managed all right for the first half hour, though the Paris ring road is always crowded. It would take just another hour to reach Fontainebleau, and I began thinking it was all over. The closing the next day, Monday, May 11, would bring nothing new. My son would be there and would meet those difficult buyers about to take over our historic home.

The next thing I knew my car was weaving in and out of the traffic lane and I realised I had been asleep. I clenched my hands to concentrate. The sale could not take place if I had an accident. Why was I so tired? What an effort to keep in my lane. Yet I'd done this trip from Paris to Fontainebleau many times. But this was the last time—I no longer had a place in Paris—and twenty-seven years of my life were about to disappear. I thought I had the courage to give up my old home, but it was also the memories which were vanishing. Fighting sleep, I tried to reason it out. Sure, I had done my spreadsheets and strategic planning, and sure, I could recall many snippets of my life in the seventeenth: the first day I entered the place; the story of the memorial plaque; my daughter burying a bird in the garden; my son locking himself in his room when a burglar entered the apartment; Colette writing at her desk, and me giving her injections for her blood ailment. But many of the memories were gone or going, and without the anchor of the apartment others would freewheel into empty space: who was my daughter's classmate from Norway who had spent time with us; where did we go cycling? I tried to swallow these losses and the notion that one day I might not even recognise the neighbourhood where I had lived. Somehow, I came to the motorway exit for Fontainebleau in one piece. It was not just the fading memories. That apartment still symbolised most of my life with Colette and my two children. Having been very logical about selling it I now found the loss like an emotional hammer pounding on me.

After the sale the next day, we had drinks with Ségolène and Justin and wished them good luck. They were in their mid-forties, a family like ours had been when Colette and I had bought the apartment, with the same number of young children. This was comforting. Curiously, Justin's parents lived in Fontainebleau, not far from our new house.

The sale had taken eight months instead of four. I felt empty, something carved out of me, as if I could sleep for a month. I remembered with incredulity my bother Noel's US transaction in two days.

It was just as well I had numerous after-sale things to occupy me in the following days, like banking and investments. Sorting out all my boxes in Fontainebleau would take weeks and the 150 bottles of ten-year-old wine would require a year or two to drink, even with help. Luckily, 2005 was a good year for the French vineyards.

I had closed the Paris chapter, but there was life to come in Avon. Letting go is part of senior living.

14

CRETE

Travel is a step into the unknown. For seniors like ourselves, it means leaving the comfort of home, embarking on an adventure with perilous aspects. But we need change—retirement cannot be burial. Some of my friends unretire after seventy, or don't retire at all. André still does professional accounting; Sishir is still a consultant for his embassy; Jean François does art exhibitions. I had other projects—writing, sports, investing, care of grandchildren—but it was never enough. Mylène and I feel it's our last chance to see faraway places, to find out for ourselves what the world is about, maybe even to extend our stay if it's hospitable enough.

We travel a lot. Before Avon, we used tour operators to visit India, Canada, the Caribbean, and South Africa. Since then, we have tried several formulas. Often, it has been self-organised trips to England and Scotland with French grandchildren, where our goal was to help them learn English, so badly taught in French schools. We've also travelled to visit family, where the goal is to help them with our time and resources.

But mostly we travel with our sporting club, all over France, three weeks or more each year, where the goal is hiking most of the day. Our club organiser gets us good rates, but our rules stipulate there must be lots of physical exercise. The lazy holidays on a beach or in a hammock are over if they ever existed. Sport for seniors is a question not just of fun but of survival, a sort of medical religion. Add to this the "birds of a feather" effect, the presence of friends of our own age and inclinations, and one can see why it's popular. After ten or fifteen kilometres of walking (much further for the cyclists), we meet in the evenings for a jovial dinner, wine unlimited. Talk ranges from who's taken a tumble to what we've seen behind the trees. Sightseeing has a much lower priority than exercise. We've been to Brittany (several times), Alsace, the Alps (both winter and summer), and the South West (near Aubrac), but now it was something special. A September week in Crete was one of our sporting federation's rare international ventures. The premise was to find a good balance between more sightseeing than usual and good physical activity. One unknown—we didn't know if any of our friends would be going. Another, the Cretans were a mystery.

IT WAS A MONDAY MORNING, and we were in a last-minute departure hassle. Two heavy suitcases were not enough, so Mylène added a smaller black carry-on case for her extras. We tend to pack too much stuff: day wear, evening wear, sportswear, equipment, books, medicines, and a laptop—stuff we didn't need for travelling when younger. Tired from checking and packing, we took a taxi from our home in Avon to the airport at Roissy. The driver left us at the Aegean Airlines departure lounge in mid-afternoon and, exceptionally, we were among the first of our fifty-odd Seine-et-Marne club members to arrive for the trip.

Our satisfaction at arriving early at the airport didn't last long. No sooner had we checked in our two heavy suitcases and chosen seats on the plane than we lost concentration.

We strolled through the departure gate and before approaching the coffee stand, I asked Mylène, "Where's your hand luggage?"

"Huh?"

"Yes, the small black suitcase!"

Panic, a feeling easily aroused at airports, growled. We had no idea where we had left this luggage, anywhere between the arrival lounge, the check-in counter, and the departure gate. And now that we had gone through the boarding gate, would they let us back out to hunt? They did, and a hectic period of backtracking and searching ensued. We ran along corridors and took the elevator back down to the ground floor. We had been more than silly. The ticket counter waved us away politely. The lost-and-found counter was of no help. Against the odds, we finally located the suitcase sitting smugly next to a chair where we had sat and paused to check tickets. Then we re-embarked.

Put this fluster down to tiredness and seniors' failing memory. We were still in good time for the take-off but the take-off was not in time for us. A loudspeaker announced a two-hour delay for our flight. We wouldn't get to Heraklion until after midnight. Perhaps this was an early manifestation of Greek mishaps.

We had hoped to catch the end of the summer and steep ourselves in sunshine, scenery, and Cretan mythology. But with all the fuss over Greeks not paying their debt to Europe and a possible Grexit, I wondered what the Greek character was really like. My French friends said: "Poor Greeks, they're suffering", but my English friends said: "They should never have joined the euro. Look at us!" This was not simply philosophical speculation for me. Unlike the French, who distrust stock markets, I hold the un-French viewpoint that it's a duty as well as an opportunity to invest in a country's industry. I had lost money because of the Greek crisis. European values had decreased out of all proportion for problems in a small country. So, who were they, those Greeks, past and present? We weren't sure what to expect.

We landed, bone tired, after midnight, and there was little to see on the bus trip from the airport to our hotel. Fortunately, we had been given a small dinner on the plane. The Marmara Marine Beach resort was twenty kilometres from Heraklion. On the way, I noticed the roads were in good shape and the lighted houses which flashed by appeared modern, not village shacks. The road signs were in unreadable Greek. I smelled the salty nearby sea but could not see it. On arrival at the hotel, we checked in along with our club companions.

Our room was spacious and clean, but less well organised than the equivalent French resort room, missing some final additions. Whoever designed it hadn't realised that cupboard doors shouldn't be able to block narrow corridor space; nor that decent shelves are necessary for week-long stays; that the design of toilets should allow them to be easily cleaned; and above all, that mattresses must be comfortable. It looked like a Greek problem, getting projects 80 percent right and then spoiling the last 20 percent. We unpacked rapidly and slept so late we almost missed breakfast the next morning.

DAWN ON TUESDAY brought deliciously sunny and warm weather, far different from the grey rain we'd left in Fontainebleau—and this warmth would persist during our entire week. We discovered our veranda looking out on a huge garden of brown-and-green palm trees, and not one but three large blue swimming pools. After breakfast, we attended a welcome meeting from the hotel staff to outline activities and events. When looked around, we discovered that there was no one from our Avon sporting club, and we only knew one or two faces from nearby clubs. We had lost our normal community links. That morning we had to reserve our island excursions for the week. My priority was to visit nearby Santorini, the possible site of Atlantis. One excursion to the interior of Crete was included in our travel plan, but the others were optional, with extra cost.

We assembled in a large meeting room. Our regional Seine-et-Marne club president Christiane, a jovial white-haired lady, wanted us all on a bus the next day for the pre-paid excursion to see the west of Crete.

"Is everyone okay for this trip?" she asked.

I raised my hand, "No, I prefer the day trip to Santorini, it's the only one this week."

Lots of eyes focussed on Mylène and me, but no one else voted for Santorini because of the extra cost.

"Why are you so obsessed with that island?" Mylène asked me later. I explained that I had missed it forty-two years earlier and had been dreaming of the place ever since. In the first years of our marriage, before having any children, my late wife Colette and I had been on a boat tour of the Cyclades islands with Club Med when a storm broke out and they cancelled our stop at Santorini, though we did spend a few days in Crete, up the mountains and down the gorges, and then went on to Mykonos. I was a science fiction fan and had read about magical, mythical Atlantis—a superior civilisation wiped out by nature. I had had to give up my chance of visiting the possible site of its destruction in Santorini and swore that one day I would be back. The fulfilment of this oath would not be just for myself, but also for my vanished wife.

NEXT MORNING, Wednesday, we woke early to catch the boat. Santorini is a big tourist destination and we found ourselves on a cruise ship with about one thousand passengers. The voyage takes two-and-a-half hours and we lapped up the sun and flapped our arms in the sea breeze. We disembarked at the port of Athenios, where the enormous red volcanic cliffs overhanging the harbour menaced all comers. As our welcoming bus wound its way up to the top in fearful twists and bends, I wondered how long the cliff had been this way. I knew there had been a terrible explosion, or earthquake, but I didn't know when. Maybe Atlantis had really existed, or maybe, disappointingly, it was just part of Greek myth.

Our guide for the day, just a voice on the bus at first, introduced herself as Irena. "This part of the Mediterranean has been a theatre of volcanic activity for millions of years, islands appearing and disappearing in fire and flame."

Ours was a French-oriented hotel, and all the staff plus the guides spoke French to us. We couldn't see Irena because we were on the upper level of the bus and her microphone was next to the driver on the lower level.

"Don't fear the road. Our driver knows it by heart." As we reached the next vicious bend, several cars approached from the other direction. Our bus made a scary wide manoeuvre which forced the oncoming traffic to stop and wait. There were rules to this game.

Irena gave us the basic timeline: "Through the Neolithic period and into the Bronze Age, Santorini and Crete housed one of the planet's most advanced civilisations, not Atlantis but the Minoans."

No Atlantis for me, then. I was very disappointed.

"The Minoans were at their apogee in painting, sculpture, and technology in 1500 B.C. when the end of their world arrived. The volcanic explosion, called the Thera eruption, which destroyed their culture, had the power of at least three thousand H-bombs."

Okay, I thought, nature can be more destructive than man, but I wondered what she meant by technology so long ago. It would become clear later. Next came Irena's geography: "Today's claw-shaped island was once a circular mass of which only island fragments remain: Santorini itself, Thirassia, and others. You will visit the central island Nea Kamini which harbours the core of the explosion, but for security reasons we will not take you to the unstable lava activity. Instead you can have fun in some thermal hot waters nearby."

Back in my boyhood in the Caribbean, I had visited the crater of Mount Misery (renamed Liamuiga from the Carib language) in St. Kitts on several occasions and gaped at steam rising from vents in the dormant beast's mouth. Security was non-existent. And on those far away, relatively insignificant islands there is no good historical record of the seismic and volcanic activity. The last known eruption of Liamuiga dates from the seventeenth century and historians hypothesise that a prior eruption destroyed all human life. But no relics exist from earlier on, unlike in Santorini. There may have been inhabitants, or not. I said "insignificant islands", yet St. Kitts is almost twice the size of Santorini. I had even heard a wild theory that Atlantis, if it had existed, might have been in the volcanic Caribbean, near Cuba, but Santorini was much more likely.

Irena continued: "Another place we will not visit for lack of time is the prehistoric city of Akrotiri. This is the best preserved of the Minoan palaces."

I asked myself why she was telling us about a place we wouldn't visit, but figured it was bait for a future trip.

"Thanks to Akrotiri we can date the catastrophic explosion. It was buried under many metres of volcanic ash until discovery in the last century. There were no skeletons in Akrotiri." Strange, I thought.

"This showed the Minoans had evacuated the city, probably because of severe earthquakes just before the eruption. But it didn't save them! The tidal wave caused by the eruption had disastrous consequences all the way to Crete and elsewhere in the Aegean Sea."

I listened, but there was no explanation from Irena concerning the reality or not of Atlantis, a hypothetical master civilisation including not just Santorini and Crete, but Egypt, Libya, and others. I would have to make do with the Minoans. Plato, writing in 330 B.C. about Atlantis, had postulated a much older date than the Thera explosion for its disappearance. His vision of Atlantis may simply have been warning us mortals of the fragility of all civilisations. He described the empire of Atlantis as being very clever but evil, eventually losing the battle against the noble Athenians. In other words, it is another legend, like the myth that Greece can repay its debts to the greedy EU.

Our guide continued: "Today we will first visit the countryside, stopping in the town of Oia"—pronounced ee-ya—"to the west of Santorini, and then go for lunch in the capital, Fira."

En route, we passed stretches of black, red, and even white volcanic rock. There were few trees, but Irena told us the ground was very fertile and I could see grape vines all around to prove this. The problem is they have little water. Both Oia and later Fira were towns built on top of spectacular cliffs with a dramatic view of the western sea—a sea which is really a huge caldera, or crater, formed when the mouth of a volcano collapses after eruption, waiting perhaps for rebirth.

The town of Oia, second largest on the island, was colourful and bustled with tourists. Later, I saw a news bulletin saying that tourist money was flowing from the islands to mainland Greece where it fell into bottomless pockets. The narrow streets were thick with boutiques, restaurants, and consumers. We admired the blue-domed architecture of the Orthodox churches. Excepting a few small zones of Catholicism, this is the prevailing religion, inviting comparison with my own Anglican youth. It was strict: a man in a gown stopped me from taking pictures inside the churches in Oia, though not later in Heraklion.

Bussed back to Fira, the capital, we finally met face to face with our guide Irena, who was short and slim, with a smiling face and strands of rebellious brown hair riffled by the wind. During that week, we probably saw more of Irena than any of our group from France. When the Greeks really want something, they can make it happen. We had to leave Fira quickly to catch a small boat to the volcanic sites, so Irena snapped her fingers at a restaurant owner and he served us Greek salad and a palatable roast chicken within five minutes. Then Mylène and I returned to the port of Athenios for a tour of the smaller islands in the caldera.

The boat we then took was a fourteen-metre, well-sculpted wooden vessel with sails and a motor, named *The Santorini*. Since we were not allowed to see any real magma or steam vents, the fun part of this small-boat tour was to jump off the deck into waters warmed by the lurking underground hot sulphur spots into a greenish-brown colour. Fun, at least, for some: near our boat the water was cold, maybe seventeen degrees Celsius, and one had to swim fifty metres before reaching the warm zone. After hesitating for ten minutes, Mylène dived in. More accustomed to the warm Caribbean seas than the chilly Mediterranean, I obstinately stayed on board and took photographs. When I welcomed Mylène back, she reported that once she had swum sufficiently far from our boat, the water really did get comfortably and luxuriously warm, with a slightly rotten-egg smell.

Then it was back to Athenios, back to Heraklion, and back to our Marmara Marine Beach club at Gouves, well after 9 p.m. and scrambling for something to eat. The buffet was still open but the staff had already cleared up most of the dinner tables and were taking away the last scraps of food.

"There's no soup left!" I said to Mylène.

"We'll see about that!"

Dinner is theoretically open until 10 p.m. I didn't see who Mylène growled at or charmed, but five minutes later a smiling waiter served us with bowls of hot soup at our table, something exceptional in a self-service restaurant.

I went to bed, not displeased with the volcanic scenery of Santorini, but still regretting that I could not substantiate my dreams of Atlantis.

～

THE NEXT DAY, we got our first real glimpse of Crete, quite different from Santorini. The things they have in common are: good wine, abundant sunshine, grapes and olives, the Greek language, long-lost Minoan sites, and endless invaders. Crete, however, has water in its mountains, lots of it, and several peaks over two thousand metres. This means a lot more vegetation and a multitude of goats, tame and wild. The food is good, but don't expect any native beef—there are no cows.

Irena was again our guide and fifty of us left in a bus to the east of Heraklion for a tour in the interior Idi mountain region. The countryside was much more varied than Santorini, dominated by olive trees of all sizes.

We wondered how long it took for an olive tree to grow.

Irena explained: "A few olives can be reaped within five years, but real productivity takes twenty years. We say planting an olive tree is an investment for one's children." From our bus window, looking at the endless plantations of young trees, it seemed there must be innumerable Cretan children.

In the little villages, I saw men in coffee shops, seniors like us, not talking but sitting, drinking, and staring quietly into the distance. I imagined them dreaming of family, farms, and frolics of youth, powered by the fine odour of coffee and the dappled sunlight. Each village had its picturesque Orthodox church. The streets were narrow and we gripped our seats as the bus negotiated vertiginous turns between walls and balconies. Many houses had solar panels for heating water, a few for generating electricity. We entered one of the numerous grottos and saw Bronze Age stalactites. At Axos, we had lunch and watched a waitress feeding some goats in the centre of the restaurant with milk from a baby bottle. "I want to do that!" said Mylène. I was surprised, given her trepidation before large animals, but this was a very young goat, almost an infant. I filmed her while the goat sucked on the bottle nipple. Sometimes seniors like myself and Mylène regret being so far beyond childbearing. But later, when we saw feta cheese being made from goat's milk, we couldn't imagine a human parallel (though, who knows?).

The island of Crete radiated peacefulness and charm, but there were some discordant notes. There were cars seemingly abandoned.

Many houses were half-built, with the top floor missing. And there were ungracious piles of roadside garbage near the villages.

We were exploring the village near to the restaurant on foot when Mylène and I found a moment to talk to our guide. "Irena, tell us about those half-built houses. The interior of Crete looks a bit desolate compared with the south. Have the owners of the unfinished homes died or gone bankrupt? Or is it laziness? Or financing—no bank loan so they have to build in stages?"

"A little of all you say, but mostly it's the taxes! If the owner doesn't complete the last floor, the government won't tax the house. It's worthwhile to start a new floor and leave the steel reinforcing rods to stick up in the air. It's not a new practice, there's just more of it today."

"But it looks ugly!"

"It's the Crisis. People have to eat."

I understood an owner's tax avoidance urge, but if too many did this it boded ill for the country's ability to balance its budget.

"And what about the abandoned cars?"

"Again, it's money! Gasoline costs too much and car owners get taxed, too."

"But what transport do they have left in these villages far from cities like Heraklion?"

She pointed to an elderly farmer riding his donkey down the main street.

I didn't feel it was polite to ask about the plastic bottles and other junk thrown by the wayside. Instead, I inquired how she liked her job as a guide.

Irena sighed and looked at us with wide open eyes. Then she smiled. "Do you really want to know?"

"Well, yes."

"I like what I'm doing but I can't make a living out of it. I'm obliged to share with other guides, like our bus driver must share with others, so even in full tourist season, like now, I can't get more than three or four days' work per week. And there's nothing, nothing at all, between November and April. So, over a full year I only earn two hundred euros per month on average. And I have a child and a grand-child to support!"

We guessed she must have been in her mid-fifties. Mylène asked, "What about the father, your husband?"

Irena shrugged, "Gone, departed, ten years ago. I've been working since then."

We didn't ask if "departed" meant dead or vanished.

She continued grimly, "And the worst is still to come. Our pensions are based on salary contributions. Normally, I should have the right to retire at age sixty-seven (it used to be fifty-five), but with the recent changes to the law and just ten years of employment behind me I need a high total of contributions or else I get nothing. I've calculated I'll have to work until ninety-five."

I said nothing, but thought of our own collapsing French pension system, financially planned after the Second World War for retired people who would die before seventy, now catering to my generation, forecast to live beyond ninety, with not enough workers to pay for us. When we seniors retired our pensions were about 65 percent of our last salary; but for our children it will be less than 50 percent, and they will have to work longer. The mechanisms are similar, just a great deal more severe in Greece.

We were at a loss but told Irena we had very much liked her commentaries about the island and hoped things would get better for her.

She smiled at us without replying.

Long forgotten Minoan civilisations suddenly seemed to have less and less importance compared with a suffering modern day country.

The afternoon ended with a vigorous sea bath but as the waves came in and crashed onto the shore I continued to think about Irena. Suddenly, there was a cry, and one of our seniors had to be rescued. Unused to surf, the waves had doubled her up and twisted a leg. Swimmers from our club quickly helped her back to shore. Another call for help, I thought.

"What are we going to do about her?" I asked Mylène that night at dinner.

"Who do you mean?" she said and plunged into her Greek salad.

"Irena, of course: I'd like to make a special effort, like giving her one hundred euros."

"Crazy! That's too much!"

"It's not for services rendered. I detest tips. It's out of sympathy for the Greek people's situation. It's not her fault; the financial press says it's mostly the previous governments' incompetence."

"Well, okay, if you see it that way. Maybe we could also find something for her in France over the winter season."

We put together an envelope with money, email, and physical addresses, and Mylène prepared a letter with advice.

THE NEXT DAY, Friday, we signed up for a hike in the Imbros Gorge. Crete is famous for hiking down the Samaria Gorge—a national park—which I had navigated some forty-two years earlier and eight kilograms lighter. Both gorges are rough and rocky, with canyon walls rising to three hundred metres above the hikers, but whereas Samaria is eighteen kilometres long and takes five to six hours for good hikers, Imbros is only eight kilometres long and can be done in two hours. The hotel decided not take chances and directed us to Imbros. One can't trust those seniors not to break a leg. In addition, those who weren't sufficiently in shape for the rocky hike had the choice of walking just a small part of it, from the bottom, a short way back up and back down. A quarter of our elderly companions chose this option but the rest of us were very happy to get some serious action. Most of our club voyages in France involved much more hiking than this.

Mylène and I completed the descent in about one and a half hours. I am more used to difficult hiking, but near the end Mylène said, "My feet hurt! There are too many loose stones."

Afterwards, another hiker with whom I had played table tennis, claimed to have done the eight kilometres in one hour.

Halfway down I saw, about eighty metres above us, on a narrow ledge, a creature I had been looking out for, featured in my tourist book. It was a large, light-brown goat with long hair and two impressive black, curved horns, and it was my childhood namesake, or rather nick-namesake—a kri-kri. I can't be sure of my sighting since there are few of these creatures (also called agrimi) left in the world, and only found on the highest and most dangerous places in Crete.

Compared with jogging on flat or rising terrains, going downhill uses different leg muscles but there was only one accident. A keen photographer in the group took one step too many while filming and fell, leaving me the dubious pleasure of photographing his bruised leg and forehead. Irena accompanied us during this day, her role being mainly to bring up the rear, a *serre-file*, as we would have called it in Avon. We lunched at a beach restaurant and the glasses of raki partially erased the soreness in our group's muscles. Relaxing in the sea, we hardly noticed nor cared that all the swimmers and sunbathers were tourists, not locals.

On the bus back to our hotel, we realised this would probably be our last contact with Irena. Our club leader passed round an envelope. When I opened it, I saw several coins, a few five-euro notes: perhaps seventy euros in all. We added nothing to the envelope but after the group had presented it Mylène said, "It's our turn," and rushed to give Irena our own contribution, enclosed in our letter of friendship.

Dinner that evening at the hotel restaurant, like the other evenings, was an adventure. The dining hall was immense, and too noisy for comfort. No one we knew was visible in the crowd. We sought refuge at a table on the fringes of the hall, next to the garden, and became a target for the cat population. They crept out of the bushes and tried to guess which guest might give them food. I admire cats, and imprudently I donated some meat to a small miaowling creature which was immediately attacked by a larger feline, with yowls on each side. End of generosity.

Hotel guests had come from all over the world, and we seated ourselves at a table for six. We met a couple from Reunion Island interested in anything to do with tax havens; Crete was not as promising as they had thought, but maybe Cyprus? Then came a surprise this far away from France: we drank Greek wine with another couple, medical personnel who lived near Toulon, only five minutes from the home of Mylène's son. We were unanimous in our excitement about Crete.

~

ON SATURDAY, we headed for the ancient palace of Knossos, close to Heraklion. I remembered visiting this site forty-two years earlier and being impressed by the wall paintings, but by now I had forgotten its significance. After all, graffiti on walls are a dime a dozen in Europe, and I remained very frustrated with having to replace Atlanteans with Minoans. I stared at the ochre-coloured columns, the excavation, and the reconstruction bits. Our new guide, an excellent—if dry—academic explained that Knossos was the equivalent of the Akrotiri on Santorini, with a larger palace but it had been more damaged by various fires, floods, and conquests. A British archaeologist, Evans, had started digging it up a century ago.

Stone is stone and doesn't talk of itself to novices like us, but some details soaked in. When shown, I recognised the technology of Minoan water conduits, the air ventilation and cooling geometry, high crafts-manship with metal, paint, and wood, all appealing to my engineering spirit. Maybe the Minoans were worth something after all.

I tried to grasp the time scale with humans occupying this site since 6000 BC. The flowering of the Minoans was just four hundred years, ending in 1500 B.C., and it was apparently the first successful culture to have existed in Europe. Then, after the Thera eruption, it fell apart. I wonder how many of our present-day world powers will still be there in four hundred years.

Had the Minoans endured, I speculated that we wouldn't have needed Jerusalem, Charlemagne, 1066, the Renaissance and all that, and the Internet might have arrived centuries earlier. But earthquakes and the Santorini explosion put an end to them, and subsequently stronger forces repeatedly overran Crete.

After a short-lived Cretan state between 1898 and 1913, there was unification with Greece. I looked at the ruins of Knossos, a structure with over twelve hundred rooms, and thought, "What a waste of talent."

Was there a special hidey-hole for the Minotaur? About this beast and his supposed labyrinth, I learned something else from our guide. For the Minoans, "labyrinth" did not mean a maze. The word comes from "labrys" in an ancient tongue, and designates a double-edged axe, the emblem of Knossos. Of course, one could get lost in a palace of

twelve hundred rooms, which may have given rise to the maze inter-
pretation. But don't let anyone lead you down a blind alley.

The Minoans have vanished and we can't even decipher their writing, but at least their art remains. Even for someone like me, who feels
that history is often bunk, because it mostly deals with the rulers, not
the common people, this ancient culture was impressive, and
completely at odds with perceived modern-day decrepitude.

I photographed the Heraklion Museum artefacts from Knossos
until my camera became tired, and then we decided to explore the city
on our own and left the group. We lunched near the Morosini fountain
where stone lions gaped at us. We met two children. One was a boy in
the street, near to some sellers of souvenirs, perhaps his family. After a
little haggling, we bought some toys to take back to France, jelly-like
tomatoes which flattened when dropped and then quickly rebuilt their
rounded shape. Could it signify the resilience of the country? Or
perhaps the Greeks would remain forever crushed after their financial
fall. As we walked away, another boy about ten years old stepped in
front of us and held his hand out, aggressively. Annoyed, I said,
"No! *No!*"

The boy grimaced and mockingly replied, "Nyah! Nyah!" He
pursued us for a while and then gave up.

In the restaurant, we saw a girl of about the same age as the beggar
boy at the table next to us, accompanied by her mother. She was
reading a book with her luncheon plate in front of her. The patient
mother kept taking food from the plate and feeding her daughter. The
girl simply opened her mouth and kept on reading. At no point did the
mother become annoyed and ask the girl to feed herself. We were there
for thirty minutes and the girl never stopped reading. When she had
finished the plate, the mother waited a few more minutes, paid the bill,
and escorted the girl outside.

I remembered myself at that age, and how I would take a book
everywhere, even reading in our family car, oblivious to the world
around me. Bookworms of the world, unite!

However they got that way, it seemed to me these Cretan children
symbolised the future. Some of them would beg for a living and others

would apply their minds, but which group would decide the fate of the country? I hoped it would be the readers.

Next, we visited the Holy Church of Titus the Apostle—a beautiful Orthodox structure near the port of Heraklion. What intrigued me was the alcove where the supposed skull of the saint resides in a gold box. Titus was a follower of Paul the Apostle and he subsequently created the Cretan Church, dying at the ripe old age of ninety-four. His skull survived fires and earthquakes, but to escape the Turks in 1669 it was secretly transferred to Venice and only returned to Crete in 1966. Now, though the gold box is real enough, I doubt anyone can prove what's inside it. It may well be another Greek myth to celebrate Titus the senior.

We finished the afternoon by visiting stores in old Heraklion. Now, for foreigners like us, the trouble with the Greeks is that they speak Greek. We wanted to interact with the locals outside of the hotel, and here was a chance to talk to Cretan sales staff. Everywhere they were welcoming. They spoke better English than most French storekeepers. Bargaining was possible and their sales push was not intrusive. We felt positive feelings, neither exploited nor brushed off the way one sometimes is in Paris. Mylène bought postcards and small souvenirs.

That evening, most of our club participated in an elaborate dinner-and-dance evening at a restaurant thirty minutes' drive from our hotel. The food was like that of the hotel: excellent salads and local produce but don't expect good beef or pork. This time it was superb fish. I am not a dancer but I enjoyed the acrobatic jumping and foot-clapping of the Cretan dancers. They wore traditional costumes—tight black trousers for the men down to knee level, then high boots and decorated waistcoat; decorated skirts and loose trousers for the women. One act stayed in my memory. The slimmest and supplest of the dancers was helped onto a table and from there he balanced on one foot on a glass, itself on top of a bottle.

"Makes you think," I said to Mylène.

"You mean equilibrium—fragility—politics—collapse?"

"Nyah! Just how important bottles of wine can be!"

～

SUNDAY, our last day, we stayed in the club, swimming and playing table tennis. After dinner, the Marmara entertainment officer introduced an insignificant balding man dressed in drab, dark clothing and three resplendent dancers—one slim man, one muscled heavier companion, and a very beautiful girl, all in colourful dress. They danced individually and together, under the orders of the small balding man. Little by little he participated until we realised his dancing was at least as good as the others. At the end of the performance, he thanked and named the dancers.

"This powerhouse is Dimitri!" he said and brought the heavier dancer to the front to do a somersault.

"And this is also Dimitri!" he continued as he encouraged the second male dancer to spin and clap his feet in the air.

"And finally, who do you think this is?" he asked, encouraging the girl to do a spin and a curtsy.

"Dimitri!" shouted the audience.

"No, Dimitra!" he replied.

There was loud applause and laughs.

A pirouette, and then: "No, excuse me, just joking, her real name is Mikhaela."

More applause, then the three dancers lifted their impresario onto their shoulders.

"And myself? You've guessed it: I'm Dimitri!!"

THE NEXT DAY at the Heraklion airport, I had never seen such a large selection of wines and spirits available duty-free to passengers before take-off. I settled for the pleasure of a Cretan Syrah labelled "The Last Supper". I told myself that one day soon, I would have to compare wines and hospitality from all the countries I have lived in.

We returned home by plane and train. Late in the evening we reached the station in Avon, and our luggage became a problem. My back hurt—perhaps the awkward bed in the hotel—and I had to carry the two heavy cases one-by-one. Nevertheless, I felt I could do it.

"Get some help!" said Mylène when I dragged our belongings out of the train, ignoring an offer of assistance.

"It's okay."

To exit the station, we had a tunnel to cross: steps down, then a passage under the railway tracks, then twenty steps up. I took the cases one-by-one down the first set of steps, again refusing the help of a polite young man. Going up the second steps was harder, and I paused to catch my breath at the top after heaving the first suitcase up. At the bottom, I saw a large man tapping our second case. With what I took for a friendly gesture, he inquired, "Need help with this?"

Having refused twice, I thought I had shown my mettle, and accepted his offer. Imagine my surprise when the stranger climbed the stairs with our suitcase, opened his hand, and said: "That'll be one euro."

I did not reply. Surprised and much annoyed at his temerity, I searched my coin purse and gave him his reward. I would have brought the case up myself had I suspected the man was making a commercial gesture. Mylène said I should have read it on his face. Welcome to France and our ways of duplicity. The beggar boy in Heraklion had been more honest in his way than his adult French counterpart.

But then, dragging our suitcases the last steps back to our house in Avon, I put this begging aside. I stopped being disappointed by the disappearance of the gifted Minoans. I thought of the charming guides, the exuberant dancers, the friendly storekeepers, the bookworm girl. In the cold air of France, despite the myths, the tax avoidance, and the financial frailty, I warmed to the people of Crete. It was a country I could live in.

Two months later we received a moving letter of thanks from Irena with a sprig of yellow Cretan herbs inside.

15

ODYSSEY OF A MIGRANT

I wonder where my country is? Our visit to Crete started me thinking.

Many of us are born into a family that has lived in a country for generations, with parents and grandparents decorating the landscape. This family is part of a nation and imposes a cultural identity on the child. He or she doesn't have a choice. As he grows, he is schooled in the country of birth and absorbs language, values, history, religion—all the tools of survival plus a host of personal attachments or dislikes. Grown up, he will probably work in that country—his country—and if he travels, he will obtain the country's passport. Normally, he has no dilemma, no serious angst about his country.

But what if something changes, a dislocation? Perhaps he can't find suitable work, or education; or conflicts arise. Then he may become one of the numerous migrants of this planet. The country of his birth may no longer be his home. It may even become a disaster zone. Hopefully, he will find another home, a second country which suits him better. One of the shames of our modern world is the refusal of many countries to accept a migrant, even when he is full of energy to study and work. This is a tragedy born of populist sentiments, and it's not just the would-be migrant's loss. Economies and societies without stimulus from outside tend to stagnate.

It may help to explore the soul of "successful" migrants, like myself, because we are numerous. For those who do change countries once or several times, and contribute each time, where is our national allegiance? The complications begin when you have a choice.

It's not the geography of a country that's problematic for me; it's the nation behind it. Wherever I am, I feel something is out there, nebulous but powerful, in the government, in the news, in people's attitudes. It's all around, enveloping, subtly trying to control me. It wants my adherence, wants me to become part of it, to believe in it. No serious criticism of the nation, please! Jokes about politicians are allowed, but not about the whole culture. In the tricky balance between collective and individual interests I am not opposed to the collective—we need to work together for a common good—but I feel that nations often form rigid frameworks and thereafter their leaders perpetuate inter-country and intra-country barriers in their own interests. Laws and taxes are not in question; a nation must have these to exist and if the migrant can't accept them, he shouldn't make it his home. Against unqualified allegiance, I resist, but what is left if I have no unequivocal national bonds? Now retired, I'm still trying to answer this question. The fate of a migrant is very variable, always dynamic but often quite negative. I know I've been lucky. Here is my trajectory, candidate country by country.

St. Christopher

In my head, I'm gravitating between all the places I've lived, trying to find something solid. There, I've put a pile of old and current passports on the table to get my ideas straight. The first one is from my birthplace, the small island of St. Christopher (St. Kitts) in the Caribbean, where I got my forename. Appropriately for me and many other islanders, St. Christopher was the patron saint of travellers. More Caribbean-born persons live abroad than at their birthplace.

Could this still be my country? I don't live there anymore, but I have an up-to-date passport. A decade ago, I sold the family home overlooking the bay of Basseterre to pay for my mother Elsie's last years of life in France. At the time, neither my brothers Peter and Noel, nor my sister Hazel had the resources to take her in. Thanks to the EU, Elsie's British passport gave her access to the French social system where she was well treated. After her death, we—the family—only returned to the island to bury her ashes.

A St. Christopher passport should make me a citizen with the right to vote, shouldn't it? And I want to vote—the last government has been rotten and managed to stay in power for over fifteen years. But there is no absentee ballot. I would have to fly there from France just to make one small voice heard; about one thousand euros in travel costs. In addition, I don't hear about the elections much in advance; I usually discover them on the Internet when they are over. In other words, despite my passport, in practice I can't vote and have *never* voted in St. Christopher.

Surely, though, passport or not, voting rights or not, the culture and history of the place where I was born should give me a national identity. If, of course, this country was the place where my ancestors lived. Or is identity more complicated than a simple coincidence of places and past generations? In fact, I have *no* ancestors born in St. Christopher. My parents Ralph and Elsie moved there a few months before I was born. And where was their country? My father was born in St. Croix, a Caribbean island then Danish, now American. And his father, my grandfather, was born in Guyana, then a British colony, now independent. My great-grandfather's ancestors came from Surinam (Dutch Guyana), and long before that from France, a persecuted Huguenot family. Which is why, decades later, I joined the Huguenot Society. Looks like a long line of migrants. No country pleased them for more than a generation. On my mother's side, it's not so different. She was born and raised on the island of Dominica, but her mother—who died while giving birth to her—had emigrated from England. Beyond that, in her antecedents there is a German link. Oh, and I forgot to mention my paternal grandmother's ancestors from Denmark. And I should also cite my maternal grandfather's links with both Wales and Africa. Confusing, isn't it? How do I pick a national identity from this spider web of links?

One might ask the questions: don't I *like* my birthplace, don't I have fond memories of my life there, and don't I still have friends there?

Yes, yes, and yes, and this is true of all the countries I have lived in. However, these personal affections are not enough to justify adherence to a nation. The powerful ogre behind a country is impersonal: political, cultural, and historical. It requires you to like and love what the nation is *and has been*.

Let's forget about my lack of previous generations in St. Christopher and just concentrate on the island's history. The past up to early nineteenth century is mostly about sugar and slavery. A while back, a St. Christopher's government wanted to decorate the island's capital town square with paintings and statues of blacks being mistreated. The government dropped the project at the last minute—bad for tourism. But mistreated they certainly had been!

Long before the black slaves, the Amerindians were the target. Sir Thomas Warner, the British coloniser of the seventeenth century, exterminated all the Arawaks who originally lived on the island, many killed in their sleep. Did I mention that one of my great-grandmothers was an Amerindian in Guyana? Her stern picture stares down at me from my wall, passed on by my paternal grandfather, a priest who migrated to the Caribbean islands after her death. Talk about a joyous past! The rest of the time, St. Christopher, like most of the other islands, was a battleground for European (French-English-Spanish) wars. I can't find any pride in this cruel past. It doesn't belong to me. So, no vote, no pride, no belonging, no family: there's no future for me under the coconut trees (though I still find the juice delicious). Like all true migrants I'll have to find my country somewhere else. However, successful migrants must have skills.

USA

I turned the pages of an early St. Christopher passport and came across an old visa for the USA. Surely, coming from an insignificant Caribbean island which hardly merited the label of a "state" I should have adored America, the most powerful nation on the planet. I saw from the passport that I had stayed there for the first time for a month after winning the Lincoln Sesquicentennial Essay Competition for the Caribbean region in 1959, aged seventeen. Another passport, UK this time, indicated a five-year stay, from 1965, for my doctoral engineering programme at Syracuse University. I remember with affection the generosity and openness of university life. Why didn't the USA become my home and my nation after I finished my PhD?

Love was the first culprit, arrogance the second. Near the end of my graduate studies, I fell head-over-heels in love with a French visiting professor, Colette. We got married, despite all obstacles. My university had offered me a teaching post and my wife had an offer for teaching French in a nearby college. However, unlike my relatively unconstrained graduate student visa, my wife had an exchange visa that required a return to France after two years. This would not allow us to stay on. Just before her visa expired, we appealed to the US immigration service without any answer, and then requested the university's intervention. We even paid a New York lawyer for advice; instead he made Colette cry, telling her how silly she was to have asked for that type of visa. Reluctantly, we booked our passage to France by sea. This was the love motive.

Though powerful, the American nation was far from perfect from my outsider's point of view. On the positive side, their first government after independence from the British had included Alexander Hamilton, born on Nevis, sister island of St. Christopher. In addition, for a scientist like me, America had the lure of being the world's centre for technology and research. But America was also a country with a huge racial divide, and undertones of violence. I had been carefully shielded from these problems during my Lincoln Prize visit, even meeting up with Ralph Bunch, a famous black US representative at the UN, but on campus in the late 1960s the civil rights movement influenced foreign students like me. Lincoln's abolition of slavery had not solved everything, far from it. It hadn't even been his main goal when the US civil war started. The assassination of Martin Luther King showed the distance America still had to go. Much of its external power served to wage wars in places like Vietnam and Iraq, for no evidently good result. Leap forward to the present and we find one unfortunate consequence of America's remarkable constitution is the right to possess firearms, and the US-led wars haven't ceased.

I recall in 1965 talking to an engineering friend, Hank, on campus. He came from New York.

"Do you get fed up with all us foreigners here?" I asked.

"Nah! When someone annoys me, I clout them in the face," he said, with a large smile, "especially if they don't like life in America."

When Presidents Johnson, then Nixon, took the US to war in Vietnam, a few of those who protested, like the Kent State students, were shot. I took part in several anti-war marches by night, until I discovered the protestors' tactics were as violent as those of the authorities.

My wife and I tried to look at our residence and nationality in a spirit of adventure. We could live and work anywhere, we figured, and at least in France, reputed country of freedom, I would really learn to speak French.

Then came our arrogance motive: a week before we were due to leave, bags packed and Paris job interview programmed, the US immigration service relented and said we could both stay on with green cards and take the jobs offered.

"Who do they think they are?" I said to Colette. "Let's leave anyway." Therefore, with the pride of youth we refused to change our travel plans, left the USA, and began our French adventure. I didn't care that my French salary would be only half the US equivalent.

"We'll stay for two years in France," I said, "then we'll move on." Anything was possible, but I didn't anticipate the two years of residence would become nearly fifty.

My flirtation with the American nation ended like that. I was the odd one out. My two brothers Peter and Noel followed similar doctoral trajectories, except that they married American girls at the end of their studies and soon became successful Americans themselves. Not only did they never look back, but the US military required cancellation of Peter's St. Kitts passport when he started work on defence projects. This sort of nationality discrimination did not apply to me later in France, when I, too, did research for the military. Leaving the USA, I still had to find my true country.

England

Back to my pile of passports, I noted that the one with the five years of visas to the USA was British, a second nationality. My first UK passport was issued to me when I left the Caribbean to study in England.

I had been lucky in my Higher School Certificate exams and had won the Leeward Island's scholarship to a university of my choice. On my father's advice, I opted for Cambridge University, knowing the UK government would pay the costs, for which I was grateful. My dad, a lawyer, said to me, "Go! Son, go far away and prosper!" He himself had lived on three different islands, plus a four-year spell in the UK to study law, returning to the Caribbean in the middle of World War 2.

At the time of my scholarship (1960), St. Christopher was not independent and one could apply for a British passport or a British Overseas Territory passport (later a St. Christopher passport). It happened that my maternal grandmother was born in London and married in Dominica. Her children and grandchildren were thus eligible for genuine British passports, but not the great-grandchildren to come. So why didn't I return to Britain after the USA and a few years in France and adopt that as my country?

It was because of the challenge of the French language. When we left Syracuse, France shouldered Britain aside in our spirits. Colette had to return home to check on her ageing parents and Shell USA had given me a strong recommendation to their offices in Paris. Young, I had disliked French in my Caribbean schooling and I had had no contacts with the neighbouring French territories of Martinique and Guadeloupe. Later, I was a techie—very scientific and deliberately not foreign language oriented—so I had a long way to go.

While working to complete my doctoral program in America I had to pass a foreign language test—a tool of research. I disagreed about its utility. Nevertheless, I still had to take it. I chose French, and that's how I met my future wife.

Bi-cultural marriages are reputed to work best if each member of the couple integrates the other's culture. My wife was already bilingual, I was not, so France became an objective for me; I assumed that superior French language acquisition would be a cakewalk after an engineering PhD. Far be it from me to realise that a language is also a culture, and behind the culture lurks a nation, perhaps unknowable or unlikeable.

In my early years in Paris I often regretted our choice of residence. I tried to feel in some way British. I had joyful memories of my old university, Cambridge; there were still family cousins living in the UK on my maternal grandmother's side; also, my sister Hazel lived in London, where she worked for the British Council. Society in Britain seemed more sympathetic to a handicapped person like her than in most other countries. At first, I had no friends in France. The French looked down their noses at me whenever I mispronounced a word. They were prickly: evidently for them, Paris was better than London or New York, more fashionable, more intellectual. I had to keep some distance. Whenever I visited London my lungs filled with the life-giving English words and accents all around me as if I had been asphyxiated in France. Those French—they didn't like the Eurostar terminal in Waterloo station because of Napoleon's defeat in the place of that name; now the terminal is politely relocated to St. Pancras. It doesn't get much publicity but there are half a million French expats in England, mostly in the London area. Seen from France, their caricature is of low-paid jobs in pubs and despicable fat cats in banks.

However, a critique of France comes later, after my traumatic arrival. The question is why Britain wasn't and isn't my country though my passport is British. As my language skills improved and my IT job moved upwards, I put Britain on a back burner and became resident in Paris, not London. Five years later, I started fathering children, and since they were born in France, they became French. The British embassy registered the births but refused to grant them a British passport because I wasn't living in Britain and the link to their English great-grandmother (UK patriality law) was too weak.

Now, I was trapped. How could I have a nationality different from my children? Later, I encouraged them to attend UK universities and this did them a lot of good on the job market—they became perfect bilinguals. But none of us wanted to live in Britain. A migrant wants above all to succeed in his career, and I became increasingly tied to France economically—house, job, and investments, though I usually took the British side of arguments with the French. London was a very theoretical anchorage point competing with my very real apartment in Paris. A turning point came after nearly two decades, in the mid-1980s. At a conference by a visiting British politician which I attended, I asked: "How do I vote in British elections from France?"

"Well, how long since you were resident in the UK?"

"More than fifteen years."

"Sorry, in that case you *can't* vote until and unless you take up residence in England again."

So, I was not eligible to vote there in *any* election. This hadn't bothered me too much in Margaret Thatcher's time—she seemed to be muscling up the country—but with her successors I would have liked to have my say. I suddenly felt rejected and irritated. Could I call Britain my country if they wouldn't let me vote? Even an American expat in France can register to vote in the USA. They couldn't organise a vote for UK expats anyway; the British consulate in Paris doesn't even know where and how many we are.

I began to be more critical of the "rosbifs" as the "frogs" call them. Like all the arrogant nation-states Britain has a bloody past. At least they won some of their important battles with their Nelsons, Wellingtons, and Churchills, but I find it hard to form a strong positive moral judgement. War, for me, is at best unavoidable.

The death penalty was abolished in 1965 while I was a student in the UK and in 1981 in France, eleven years after my arrival; it remains in force in America, China, and Saudi Arabia, to name a few. I feel that adopting a nation means not only accepting its present but its past. Many migrants may not bother about the past, but I prefer the long view. When I visit London these days with grandchildren, I take them to Marble Arch, because we need to remember its dark past. There's a place on the north side where death is written underfoot. A worn metal plate set in the pavement reads THE SITE OF TYBURN TREE. Compare it with the French guillotine site which existed on Place de la Concorde in the eighteenth century. The Tyburn Tree was a three-posted hangman's cross for executions.

Has anything changed in the world? If we look at the French and the English "final solutions" of yesterday, the guillotine was mercifully more rapid than hanging. But there was something positive on the English side! Before ascending the Tyburn Tree ladder, the condemned were taken to a nearby pub in shackles and allowed to drink a last pint of beer, free of charge.

Britain is an island, giving it some affinity for me with my birthplace in the Caribbean. Not worth much though, that island comparison. From St. Christopher, I could see the sun and sea from almost every high point; in Britain, it's mostly fogs and rain.

Still on the positive side, Britain was the first nation to abolish slavery. Let's give the British nation credit for being one of the most racially neutral European countries. Where else in Europe do you find so many black and brown skins on TV and in politics? But this doesn't mean that today they fully accept migrants, especially outside of London. The recent Windrush scandal concerning the rejection of Caribbean immigrants even after years of living in Britain was shocking. Together with my brothers, we went to the UK to study on that tide and at that time, but because of our English grandmother we were never bothered.

Is all this enough for me to adhere to the nation behind my UK passport? When I visit the UK, I obey its laws, but I don't live there. The English language is a major part of me, but it doesn't belong solely to England! It escapes national boundaries—it's the heritage of all UK ex-colonies, including America. As a nation, I would prefer the European Union, just when Britain wants to leave it. I am deeply annoyed that on a vital question like this, Europe in or out, Britain wouldn't allow expats like me to vote. Sorry, no UK vote, no nation!

France

I have no more passports in the pile, only a plastic French residence card. It says, in translation, "Citizen of an EU state, issued in September 1970, valid for permanent residence anywhere in France, any professional activity allowed." It's almost a passport, except that if Britain leaves the EU the whole thing may become invalid. Moreover, it doesn't confer significant voting rights on me: only minor affairs like EU parliamentary elections (for French delegates) and municipal elections; no French regional, parliamentary, or presidential elections. Should I have adopted France as my country, bearing in mind the Huguenot linkage? This is more complicated than my three previous nationality options.

To begin with, going back to my departure from America, I never worked for Shell in Paris. My interview with this company gave me a first taste of the touchy French. They liked my research credentials and the recommendations from Shell USA, but after several strenuous hours in English (with no coffee) the HR recruiter said: "Sorry, you lack the basic French necessary for the job."

"But I came to learn!" I protested.

"Many Americans say that," he said, "but a year later we still can't communicate properly with them."

I may have looked surprised, but I didn't insist that I wasn't American.

"Would you like the original copies of your recommendation back for further job hunting?"

"You can keep them," I snorted.

After three months, I found work with a French engineering company, SPIE Batignolles. They weren't so fussy about my language skills and mostly wanted me to design heat exchangers and distillation columns on the computer. I stayed with them for seventeen years. I couldn't learn French from my wife, though she was a qualified teacher—it caused too many problems for our relationship. She wanted me to be perfect, and I wasn't! Instead, I took a year of evening classes at the Alliance Française and attained a survival level in the language, enough for my job and enough to be an English-accented foreigner in daily life.

On rare occasions, I even promoted the French language as part of my integration into French society. When my company upgraded their IT facilities in the 1980s from a terminal to a mini-computer, as it was known in those days, some senior structural engineers asked me in French: "Can you program our calculations on your new 'computer'?"

I advised them in their language: "It's not a 'computer'; it's an 'ordinateur'."

It wouldn't have been difficult to become part of the French nation since my wife was French and I had gainful employment. Moreover, at some point after Britain joined the EU it became possible to have both a British and French passport. However, I was never tempted, not even when my engineering group had to work on research for French military projects and I was subject to security screening. Charlemagne—Bonaparte—De Gaulle: it all made a dramatic story, but I felt no affinity at all; these were not my heroes, if I ever had any.

There were occasional advantages to being a native English speaker in a French company. It took my managers a decade to figure it out, but eventually they began sending me on missions to England, Algeria, and Peru. My French engineering colleagues were not at ease in a foreign language environment.

Finally, I left SPIE and went to work for a sugar manufacturer, CFS, in charge of its computer network. It was bitter-sweet to be implicitly in competition with my birth country: Caribbean cane sugar producers against subsidised French beet sugar producers. Remorse, remorse, which country was I backing?

The last part of my career in France was chaotic, beginning with IT counselling for a large banking conglomerate, CNM. This was a high-risk position: I was laid off just before the conglomerate president was; the group splintered into fragments. I survived by teaching IT skills.

My final years of employment were with a French company in the London Docklands producing e-learning material. There I was again in the UK! The work was fun, but produced in English, no one wished to translate it for the French market, so my job ended. I might have stayed in London, having acquired an apartment, but—critically—pension arrangements for my wife and I were not complete, so I returned to Paris to wait out a few years of French unemployment, in limbo, until my official retirement in 2006.

Abruptly I found myself in my early 60s with a full French pension, a permanent residence permit, a Paris apartment, but no French citizenship.

Part of my non-absorption by the French state was the language I had tried so hard to acquire. I have become even more language-sensitive in the latter part of my life. Even after forty-five years in France, I do not feel completely at home in French conversations. It's not that I don't understand or can't communicate in French—in fact I am quite good at it (with a slight Caribbean-English accent). I've spent years in industry correcting technical reports by French engineers and have made many public presentations in French. But I feel happier in English and at my age I'm tired of making an effort. When I visit my bilingual children, I insist they speak English. Otherwise, I feel left out and lapse into silence. I speak as much English as I can to my companion, Mylène, but this has its limits as she's not bilingual. I have given creative writing classes in French to seniors in my club, but for my own writing I only work with English speakers. I read one French newspaper, *Les Echos*, for its financial information, but rely on *The Economist* and the *Financial Times* for the real news. I read English novels, not French ones. I have delved into modern French literature but find it unsatisfying, and ever since I started writing I have preferred fidelity to my linguistic origins.

My deep roots in English usage have increasingly made me feel alienated by the structure of the French language. It can be initially fascinating to observe the teeth and claws of certain animals but you don't want to get too close to them. Why attach a gender to each noun? What a useless complication, having to make the gender agreements! And why are so many letters not pronounced? And when are they going to kill the circumflex? In fact—why isn't it more like English!

Before I start getting too critical, there are many good things to note about the French nation and France as a country. They finally got rid of the guillotine and the French Revolution made France one of the most democratic countries in the world. Everything can be contested and unfortunately it is. It's also one of the few countries where being called an intellectual is not an insult. If you like history, French cities are magnificent, and the country has a very favourable geography from the snow-covered Alps to the warm Mediterranean coast. And the French do have a fine sense of humour, though it's very language-oriented and often doesn't translate into English. And vice-versa for British puns.

French social welfare and medical care is also very protective. We didn't anticipate this aspect, but only in France could we have cared for the last years of my mother Elsie under good conditions. Neither the Caribbean, America, nor the UK would have been possible.

However, like many nations, France has an inflated notion of its importance on the world scene and the significance of its history and culture. I don't feel I need this. France persecuted and ejected my Huguenot ancestors in the Vanier branch (remember the St Bartholomew's Day massacre?) and—just like America and Britain—it keeps wanting to send its troops right and left in favour of some "cause". Look closely, and the causes may often have to do with post-colonisation or other French interests abroad.

Then there are the racist and anti-immigrant issues in France. It's curious how apparently ethical and protective laws can have a nega-tive effect. No survey or census can be carried out by race or religion, so France officially doesn't know how many North African or African-origin citizens it has. Thus, discrimination is difficult to identify in the statistics. It is clear, however, that there is hardly a coloured face in the French political spectrum or on TV. A President Obama would be impossible here. If your first name is Mohammed or Hassan, better not put it on your curriculum vitae. When I compare the passengers in the Paris metro with those in the London tube the superior wellbeing of coloured UK migrants is evident.

French society seems unstable to me—ready to protest for almost anything—and careers for our children and grandchildren in France are difficult and getting more so. It may be a coincidence, but many friends of my age—seniors—have encouraged their offspring to find work abroad, of which more below.

My criticisms may seem like nit-picking. I'm simply saying I don't feel part of the history of the French nation, nor the way this nation currently behaves. What about civic duty and gratitude? Despite my dislikes, shouldn't that encourage me to ask for a French passport? Gratitude is a loaded term. Should one be grateful to one's parents for being born? No, you didn't ask for existence, it all depends on how your parents treat you for future survival. Does a handshake imply gratitude? No, it is usually a simple agreement, a sign of politeness and mutual respect. No gratitude needed. A migrant comes to a new country with his talents and his energy for work. If he stays, his honest labour benefits equally himself and the country where he is. *No grati-tude needed.* A deal is a deal and no more. Civic duties and good behaviour are necessary but no attachment is implied.

LET'S try a trick question to find a hidden nation for me: which sporting teams do I support? Unfortunately, I am a contrarian. When in the Caribbean I supported the English cricket team against the West Indies. When in England I changed my support to the West Indies team. I've never supported any American teams. When in France, I support the English football and rugby teams, and this can cause problems. I suspect that if I moved to England the French teams would suddenly find favour in my eyes! I just don't want the crowd to dictate my allegiances.

Here in Fontainebleau, there are echoes of my migrant trajectory among my retired friends. My sporting companions are Emilio, an elegant Italian; Carlos, born in sunny Spain but arrived in France with a Greek passport; and Friedhelm, a genial German, to name but a few. These have changed countries as I did and usually don't have French passports. Perhaps 170,000 British expats or more live in France; the British embassy doesn't keep track. Also striking is the French expatri-ation of the next generation. About forty years ago it used to be said that the French always returned home from abroad. Today, I can't count the number of seniors here and in Paris whose children and grandchildren are in America, Britain, Canada, Dubai, Germany, Hong Kong, Vietnam, or Singapore, settled in for the very long term by their careers and their spouses. Migrants all.

There was a recruiting slogan in the USA in JFK's time, "Don't ask what your country can do for you, but what you can do for your coun-try." It was catchy but is now out of date. It's normal to work, behave, and contribute in a new country, but what counts are the opportunities offered. Otherwise, we migrants move on, if we can: no blind alle-giance to any nation.

Having made the rounds of my passports, visas, and residence permits, do I care that I have no chosen nation? I respect all the countries I have lived in; I obey their laws when on their territory. But it's just respect. I do not necessarily treasure their history or their racial type or their religion. I will neither sing the *Marseillaise* nor *God Save the Queen* (I'm a terrible singer, anyway). My only long-term link with any place is my parents' grave in St. Christopher and my own family cemetery plot at Montmartre, Paris, where I buried my wife Colette and where my children will bury me and Mylène one day. I must feel free to criticise all nations, free to think. I am a citizen of Europe and the world. Who needs a country? Maybe I should travel some more.

16

VIETNAM

A year after Crete, we travelled to a very different country—non-European, non-democratic, mysterious—Vietnam. The three-week voyage was suggested by a friend in our sporting club, Yvonne. She was born in Saigon and had migrated to France in her childhood. She had organised club voyages to her old home several times in the past, but I had uncertain feelings about the country and its liberator, Ho Chi Minh. To understand this ambiguity, I had to go back into the past, a surprising 135 years.

On one side of the planet, in the Caribbean, my grandfather John George William Vanier was born in 1881. His mother was an Amerindian in Guyana, then British Guyana, and his father John Henry Vanier was a flamboyant estate owner, who would later beget twenty-two other children by various mothers, though only fifteen reached adulthood. That native Amerindian mother was not a legal spouse, and consequently twenty-odd years later my grandfather was disinherited and could not marry the well-to-do girl of his choice. He left home by boat and became an Anglican priest after years of study in Barbados. He lived in a gentle British colonial atmosphere, which he may have disapproved of, but his real regret was the extinction, two centuries earlier, by the colonisers (British and French) of the native

Arawak Indians in most of the Caribbean. As for me, growing up on the island of St. Kitts, despite the long-awaited independence of the island, I carried a grudge against all colonisation.

On the other side of the planet, Ho Chi Minh (not his birth name) came into the world in 1890, the son of a minor mandarin in French Indochina, as Vietnam was then called. The mandarin father was involved in a regrettable killing, which made it impossible for his son to succeed him. Same problem, same solution: in his twenties, young Ho left his colonised country by boat to explore the world. One big difference, whereas the Caribbean became more of a burden to the British than anything else, Vietnam was a country rich in natural resources, and the French colonisers had no intention of giving it up. Thus, Ho Chi Minh did not become a priest, but an ambitious revolutionary. When I heard of the overthrow of the French by Ho and the arrival of new American conquerors, my natural sympathy was with the Viets. How could anyone in the late twentieth century defend colonisation of the oppressed?

I first heard Ho's name mentioned in 1969 when I was finishing my graduate studies at Syracuse, in the USA. The Americans were in the middle of a full-scale (but undeclared) war against North Vietnam. I was slow to form an opinion. The US had a vastly superior military force, so despite my anticolonial feelings at first it seemed the Yanks would win. I was there to study differential equations, not to have political opinions. However, the Vietnamese people had been colonised for an eternity and were just seeking freedom from oppressors. The name of the Vietnamese revolutionary leader began to intrude in the news. He attracted my attention and respect, until I realised he was a scheming communist.

If there was one political credo I had learned while studying in England and America for nine years, it was that Communism is evil. The Russians invented it and became the enemy of America. It was the reverse of democracy—an ideology of dictatorship with no free elections, no choice by the people, and no freedom of information. Naïve perhaps, but this is what most of my American friends thought.

And there is the origin of my ambiguity. I wanted to praise the revolutionary Ho for trying to free his country from colonial rule, but I couldn't accept his use of Communism to power his revolution.

The American effort began to weaken when the US public realised how long the war would last, that Nixon was no improvement over Johnson, and that US troops were committing atrocities (e.g. the My Lai massacre). Nineteen sixty-nine was an eventful year: I got married and Ho Chi Minh died. My grandfather died two years later. I continued to think of Ho as the Vietnamese revolutionary symbol. He had used General Giap to vanquish the French and ceded control to Le Duan against the Americans, but it was Ho's name which stuck in my mind.

With my newly-found wife Colette, I joined demonstrations against the Vietnam war. It was unforgettable to see the huge parade of students around us carrying candles and softly chanting, "Stop the war, Nixon." Maybe my participation in the war protest would have a tiny effect? But the communist element in the Vietnam revolution still bothered me.

Months later, in May 1970, came the Kent State police violence (four students killed, nine wounded). Soon after, I finished my thesis, and because of my wife's visa problems, we left for France in August of that year.

Having to learn French and starting my engineering career in Paris should have wiped the whole Asian political slate clean for me. The Americans could do what they wanted, though by then it seemed probable they would lose. The French had had their own painful defeat years before in Indochina, and the colonial era would soon end. I had one disturbing new element to think about. The Communist party was legal in France. Did this mean Ho's followers could usefully rule Vietnam, or was it all a big mistake? Then I forgot about Vietnam for the next eighteen years. Mere history, so I thought. I didn't have to decide between justifiable revolution and dangerous Communism. But as some say, those who forget history are doomed to repeat it, and this includes ambiguous feelings.

~

THE NEXT TIME Vietnam and Ho Chi Minh came to my attention was in 1988, while buying an apartment in Paris, the one which I sold twenty-seven years later.

We bought at the same time as some Americans, in a five-story building under construction in a quiet cul-de-sac later called Villa Compoint. The builder was an English construction company, Wimpey (builders, not burgers!), and we bought "off plan" before the building was finished. When everyone moved in, December 1988, the Americans made an unpleasant discovery.

Wimpey had not disclosed that the site was "protected". It had historical significance and the building permit was conditional on approval by the Paris Mayor's Office and the French Communist Party. A large commemorative plaque had to be fixed to the building front, naming the VIP who had lived on the site long before. This person, a foreigner, had occupied a garden shed from 1920 to 1923 while being an active member of the French Communist Party. Then he left for Russia and much later returned to his home country where he eventually became president of North Vietnam. What bugged the Americans, and surprised me, was the identity of the person: he was Ho Chi Minh, the revolutionary I had learned to admire in the USA.

It might seem exaggerated for my American friends to have made a fuss about Ho Chi Minh thirteen years after the end of the conflict, but the Vietnam War had been terrible, leaving many hundreds of thousands of dead, especially after the passing of Ho. Was Ho's legacy responsible, or was it Communism? My ambiguity was still there.

When the commemorative plaque went up, my wife and I even began thinking it added value to the building, despite Ho's fearsome image.

I talked to several groups of Vietnamese tourists over the next few years and showed them the back garden where Ho Chi Minh had lived. At first, I found the Viet pilgrims belief in Ho to be uplifting. However, a decade later, the groups got larger, led by an official Viet guide, perhaps a French communist, and I no longer took them into the building. I never imagined I would one day visit their poverty-stricken, war-torn country.

~

HOWEVER, almost thirty years later, I woke up to the reality of a voyage to Vietnam sponsored by my club in Avon, after Mylène had accepted Yvonne's invitation.

I remembered my feelings about empires and colonisation. Eventually, a colonised people want their own rulers, and they rebel. Thus, the Viets had successively kicked the Chinese, the French, the Japanese, and the Americans out of their country.

However, we can't easily categorise a people as good natives or evil colonisers. Things change, and they can be both. The Viets, mostly colonised, were brutal colonisers themselves when, in the nineteenth century, they subjugated the Cham in the southern part of Vietnam.

Of course, there *is* one way for an empire to make sure its colony never rebels: exterminate all the "barbarians" (or at least the males). This is what happened in the Caribbean islands in the seventeenth century. It was also the case in the Canaries, where the Spanish got rid of the Guanche locals. Impossible in Vietnam, where the French settlers never exceeded a few tens of thousands, compared with almost ten million native Viets.

At seventy-four, I was going to Ho Chi Minh's country. Though I couldn't like the man's communist methods, I was curious as to how his achievement of getting rid of the colonisers and uniting Vietnam had worked out. I knew Vietnam had had a bad time during the twenty years following reunification, perhaps worse than when it was colonised. Blame revolutionary excesses, and the reticence of America to forgive and forget. But what next?

We were going to a place ravaged by war four decades earlier. Going to a frightening communist regime, inherited from Russia's dark days, with no democratic elections, and where people couldn't say what they thought.

~

"ARE YOU READY?" I asked Mylène. "The taxi will be here in ten minutes."

"Take the cases out and I'll meet you!"

All ten of us going to Vietnam were silver-haired seniors from our sporting club: among them Yvonne Yan Susu and Claude, Nicole and Roger, Huguette and Jean-Marie, Mylène and me, Evelyne, Michèle; ranging in age from sixty-five to eighty. Not that there would be much vigorous sport, considering the heavy programme of travelling: Hanoi, Tam Coc, Halong, Hoi An, Dak Lak, Buon Me Thuot, Ho Chi Minh City, Can Tho, Siem Reap. I recognised *none* of the names except Hanoi and HCM City.

Since signing up, Mylène had discovered that the temperature might go up to forty degrees Celsius in the south and was horrified, almost ready to back out. I had found out from reading that modern Vietnam was an interesting place, increasingly tech-savvy, though I disliked the communist aspects. Recently, the country had evolved from the dreary image of poverty projected after the end of the US war. With some trepidation, I thought it worth a visit: stuff to see, and the mystery of the first Vietnamese president, Ho Chi Minh. His forces had used brutality, cunning, and courage to win the war but the follow-up was uncertain. I didn't yet know about the Vietnamese dragon, a powerful symbol of the country's strength and magic.

Then, there we were, tired from twelve hours of flying from Paris to Hanoi by Vietnam Airlines. Yvonne welcomed us all to her birthplace, which she had left at the age of seven, and helped us make our way through the airport procedures. She was a swimming instructor in Avon and we all knew her well and liked her. One thing we didn't know was her state of health—she had developed Parkinson's, but she and her husband had decided to keep this to themselves for the time being. It was a brave decision to organise this trip, maybe her last opportunity to show friends her Vietnam.

Yvonne had negotiated in advance for a series of contacts, one in each city. Early in the morning of March 26, 2016, we boarded our first tour bus at the airport and met our first polite and smiling Vietnamese tour guide who would travel with us for four days around the capital, Hanoi, and nearby.

"My name is Hanh Tho Phon," our guide said. At least, that's what I thought I heard. After a couple of bungled efforts by our group at pronouncing it, he suggested: "It will be easier for you to call me Antoine." And so, we did. Short, thin, prematurely balding, with an open face and careful French pronunciation, Antoine was easy to like.

As the bus proceeded to the centre of the city, I asked, "Can we question you about your Communist government? Would it be indiscreet?"

Antoine laughed, as indeed he did to almost every question, "Yes, you can! At least inside this bus!"

"We hear there will be a new president and vice president of Vietnam next week. Were they elected?"

"No, they will be appointed by the head of the Communist party. We do get to vote, but only for regional and local officials. Things are much more efficient when there are no multiple conflicting political parties. Think of your home country! Do *you* have peaceful elections?"

I was surprised we could have such a frank exchange. We discovered Antoine was in his early thirties and had two children, and then we arrived at our hotel, the Skylark, deposited our bags in our rooms, and tried to banish our flight fatigue with a breakfast rich in mango and papaya.

As we left the hotel for our first walk into the unknown, led by our guide, the Vietnamese capital exploded with noise and colour. Communist or not, what vibrant life! So vibrant, indeed, that we couldn't cross the street. There are very few traffic lights in Hanoi, a city of some eight million Vietnamese, most of them buzzing around on scooters and motorcycles plus a few cars.

"All together!" Antoine said. "And don't retreat!"

The courageous ones in our group moved forwards, whereupon the scooters began zooming by, in front of and behind them.

"No!" Mylène said and refused to leave the sidewalk.

"Yes!" I replied, trying, and failing, to pull her into the traffic. Eventually, Antoine had to escort the first group across and return for us. It took several hours to become confident enough to throw oneself into the flow of vehicles and not turn back.

After navigating a few dangerous-looking streets in this manner, Antoine took us into a huge marketplace. "You can buy almost anything here," he said.

Fatigue vanished, and I was overwhelmed by the multitude of goods on three levels: dresses, silks, shoes, gadgets, clothes, and more clothes in hundreds of compact stalls, mostly run by slim, smiling, attractive young women. My camera went wild trying to capture the diversity. It was the bright colours of strange food which soon dominated: spices of all sorts, black mushrooms, green mangoes, yellow papaya, red tomatoes and cherries, objects I couldn't recognise, dried fish, live fish, swimming turtles, caged birds—and dogs. Food? "Yes," Antoine said, "we eat dogs and cats." Vietnamese were cutting red meat and fish into portions, peeling fruit; cooking smells were everywhere, and every few stalls a seller was eating a meal with chopsticks from a bowl—all so different from what I knew. Not Paris, not London, not even my old home in the Caribbean—something else.

We escaped with difficulty from the maze and Antoine announced a city tour on "cyclo-pousse", meaning that each couple sat on a two-place reclining chair pushed by a sturdy Vietnamese on a bicycle. After five minutes, and despite the zooming traffic submerging us, the fatigue of our night flight overcame me, and I fell asleep. Mylène had to hold my head up, worried I might fall off the seat.

I survived and learned from the others that there were more skyscrapers in central Hanoi than in Paris. How could this be? It was a big leap from "less poverty" to "more skyscrapers". Once we had been re-invigorated by a spicy spring-roll lunch, Antoine took us over the red-coloured Sunbeam Bridge to the Jade Temple.

"This is the Lake of the Restored Sword," he said.

The title didn't make sense at first. Why should a sword be restored? Did he mean 'repaired' or 'returned'? Antoine led us by foot to the temple on the island and pointed to a large golden-carved turtle, one of the four animal emblems of Vietnam, almost as famous as the dragon.

As we gathered around Antoine, I looked curiously for a sword, but saw none.

"The sword has gone," our guide explained. "You know the Chinese Han occupied Vietnam for one thousand years, long ago? And we threw them out. Well, there was a second Chinese occupation of Vietnam, some centuries after the millennium. The Ming overran the north and stayed in power until 1427. A brave Viet prince called Lé Loi decided to revolt but he had far too few weapons and soldiers. One day, while he was rowing on this very lake, a large turtle swam up to him with a sword in its mouth. 'Take this,' the turtle said, 'and you will reconquer your country.'

"Surprised, Prince Lé accepted the sword, which glowed with a magic power. Afterwards, he never lost a battle, and increasing numbers of Vietnamese soldiers flocked to his banner. He understood his army was still too small, so he waged a guerrilla war which lasted ten years. Finally, his forces destroyed the Chinese Ming and he became the first true Vietnamese king, ruling over the north and centre."

I noticed the reference to guerrilla warfare but said nothing. It wouldn't be the last time the Viets used this strategy.

Antoine continued: "Peace returned, and the people were well fed and happy. One day after his victory, King Lé again crossed this lake by boat. Once more, the turtle appeared from the depths and addressed King Lé: 'Well done, King! You have saved the country for your people. Now you have no more need of your sword.'

"To King Lé's surprise, before he could make a move, the magic sword jumped out of its sheath at his side and flew to the turtle's mouth. The creature then dived into the depths and was never seen again. King Lé and his followers then built the Temple of the Restored Sword, right here.

"When a war is over, weapons must be put away, and this is still true."

This bit of philosophy impressed me, though I learned later that when King Lé died his descendants fought brutally over his succession. I wondered if "putting away your weapons" still applied to more recent post-conflict situations. Reflecting on this magical tale, I realised that at the same time it was a paradigm for Ho's liberation of the country, but also a deliberate political linkage of the present communist rule with a royal past.

Not far from the Jade Temple in Hanoi was a mausoleum, the last resting place of Ho Chi Minh, deceased in 1969. I wanted to visit it but this was not on our tourist program. I was eager to see everything and my thoughts went back to the puzzle of Ho Chi Minh: after the bloodshed, had his ideas been able to create a true nation?

I FELT IMMEDIATELY at home in Vietnam, communist or not. The temperature, for a start. It was never less than twenty-five degrees, even in the highlands, and it went up to thirty-five degrees in the south. Despite the sun having to fight its way through an Asian mist most days, it felt like my youth in the Caribbean. Before we left France, Mylène had been complaining of inexplicable body pains, the sort of fibromyalgia attack which often happens in the winter. Here, in Vietnam, it all vanished. Either magic, or the warm and stimulating climate.

Although there were no black skins, the yellow and brown of the population reminded me of the Caribbean and South America. To crown things, I could forget talking French for three weeks, except to my fellow club members. The Vietnamese speak mostly English to foreigners and I was appointed a translator for our group.

Once we could face the intense traffic of downtown Hanoi and had tasted the diversity of the street markets, we started looking at the Vietnamese. Two things stood out: their youth and their energy. How was it all the women were so young and pretty—hardly any grey hair or wrinkles—and the males lithe and muscular. Where were the elderly? We saw a few, of course, but far less than we would have in Paris or London. We asked our guide about this.

"A high birth rate, for sure. After the Second World War our population was half that of France. Now we are much more, ninety-four million, and lately the government even discourages women from having more than two children. So, lots of young people. But also, we work hard and age very suddenly in our fifties. Insufficient medical services mean life expectancy is lower than in France, ten years less. The very old have indeed disappeared."

This didn't sound very positive, but no worse than under colonial rule.

"Another question, Antoine. Why do almost all the female motorcyclists wear masks? Is it because of pollution?"

Antoine laughed, "No, no, it's for beauty reasons—there's very little pollution in our cities—women believe a mask preserves their skin. And judging by the number of Chinese who come here to marry Vietnamese, it seems to work.

"And some Europeans," he added.

"And you haven't asked me about education," Antoine chuckled. "We have a ninety-six percent literacy rate among the young, and most go on to university."

I had also read that a Vietnamese IT professional costs less than his equivalent in India, which is one reason Samsung's biggest factory is here.

Everywhere, the Vietnamese were working at something. In the towns, they were selling, at their computers, serving meals; in the suburbs, they were repairing, building; in the fields, they were farming; in the factories, they were producing, painting, making things; never idle, no lounging. Everywhere, they welcomed tourists like us.

There must be some problems, I thought. Nothing's perfect.

I saw no beggars. In Avon, I can't visit the nearby supermarket without someone stretching a hand out. The nearest to mendicity that I encountered in Vietnam were the young who would ask to take pictures of us outside temples and visitor sites. At first, we refused, but eventually we let them try their luck. After the visit, they would present us with excellent souvenir photos for a fraction of a euro, sometimes in a wooden frame, which we could accept or reject. Mostly, I bought.

We travelled everywhere by chartered bus and the traffic on the highways was as turbulent as that in the city. The ten of us could sit back and relax but the driver's job was—let's say—a bit stressful. When we passed an overturned car, I asked our guide: "What is the accident rate in Vietnam?"

"Quite high," he replied, without further detail.

"Could we hire a car and drive ourselves?"

"No, no! Vietnam does not allow tourists to drive, for everyone's safety. Transport for you must be by bus or taxi."

Authoritarianism or just good prevention?

On our third day in the country we left the vibrant city of Hanoi for a visit to the Tam Coc grottos by row-boat. Two-by-two we were helped into seats with our backs to the oarsman or, in our case, oarswoman. It took a few minutes to realise by looking at the other boats that there was something unusual about the propulsion. The rowers weren't using their hands; instead they entwined their feet around the oars and pushed rhythmically. They had very supple toes and adjusted their sitting position so as never to lose contact; an adaptable work force.

All ten of us slept that night on a chartered boat in the Bay of Halong, a place of legend, surrounded by dozens of green islands with misty peaks, islands which seemed to have been wrenched out of the ocean by some mysterious force. The next morning our mission was to visit the Cavern of Surprises.

"What surprises?" we asked, but our guide just laughed.

Our Fontainebleau trip organiser, Yvonne, had never been to these islands and was keen to be surprised. Her husband, Claude, was less keen: he had a quick wit but was a slow walker and mistrustful of the whole expedition because of his wife's health. Our tour boat snaked through a village of fishermen, each with his floating house. I snapped my camera many times, wondering whether the drums on which the houses floated—some metal, some wooden—would withstand even a small hurricane.

Finally, we docked at a small harbour near Tuan Chau and gazed up five hundred metres at the steep, rocky mountains surrounding us. A rough walkway wound its way up one cliff, and high above us I could see a platform with a few tiny visitors on it.

"Is that where we're going?" I asked the guide.

"No," he said, "that's just a lookout, the cave's above," and he pointed to a black opening in the uppermost rocks.

It took twenty minutes of hard stair-climbing for our group to reach the first platform. Mylène and I took it slowly, but not so slowly as Yvonne and her husband. Up in front were our club's good walkers, Jean-Marie and Roger. I snapped the bay, far below, from the platform and we continued up to the cave entrance.

At this point our anticipations rose. What was the surprise going to be? Cave wall hieroglyphs? Skeletons? Souvenirs of past battles? The artificial lighting cast colours and strange shadows all around us. The ceiling of the cavern must have been thirty metres above us. There was a rough path paved in places, about a metre wide, with a deep ditch on each side. We made our way round a huge central pillar and suddenly there it was: red-lighted, a jagged fiery cylinder with a rounded tip pointing upwards at forty-five degrees, the cave's manhood exposed. The shock was unavoidable and then we laughed in embarrassment. Was this a communist joke on libidinous tourists? Or was it just an accidental rock formation, fully four metres long? Impressive, none-theless, the cavern fertility symbol. Not that the Vietnamese need any encouragement—their birth rate is high enough.

With grins on our faces, we continued down the path into a darker area, confident we had understood the surprise. Suddenly there was a scream of pain, and we stopped in confusion. Someone had fallen into the ditch. It was Yvonne, and she lay writhing and moaning below us. First to help was Mylène who held Yvonne's injured head and tried to calm her. We gathered round, and two others with first-aid knowledge turned Yvonne on her side and checked her breathing. Her husband arrived belatedly from behind and seemed to scold her for falling. Tumult for several minutes—we couldn't see the bottom of the ditch, didn't know how badly she was injured, until the Vietnamese security team came running incredibly quickly to the rescue with a stretcher. After ten minutes' rest and some water to drink, Yvonne refused the stretcher and continued walking unsteadily between her husband and a security person. We had only covered half of the cavern but the rest seemed to go by in a flash. I was thankful for the security team though it underlined the ever-present government surveillance.

"Did you know she's ill?" someone asked on the way down. No, we didn't, and considered her courageous to have organised the trip with her ailment. Apart from a few facial cuts, we didn't find out the extent of Yvonne's injuries until our return to France—she moved slowly afterwards but never complained, neither that day nor on the following days. She had hurt herself in the cavern but continued the voyage under the dragon's protection. Despite having lived for so many years in France, Yvonne still displayed a great deal of the Viet-namese spirit, especially its resilience.

∼

WE RETURNED TO THE BOOMING, bustling capital Hanoi by bus from the Bay of Halong and after saying goodbye to our guide Antoine, we flew down south to the middle of Vietnam, the city of Da Nang, on the coast. The city is big and touristy so our group transferred to the smaller town of Hoi An, where our female seniors, including Mylène, could run riot in the local stores—silk production, carving, clothes, pearls—it was all there. There were impressive metal plaques and carvings in one of the temples and I remember discreetly running my hand over a large S-shape which designated a dragon. It seemed to commemorate glorious past adventures. And perhaps the future?

I was not immune to the shopping and snapped up three Ralph Lauren shirts which Mylène spotted at one euro each (paid for in Vietnamese dong). Much later, when I got back to France, I noticed my polo shirts were labelled RALP LAUREN. Bravo to the Vietnamese manufacturers for avoiding customs queries, but since Ralph is my middle name, I feel I've been renamed.

The next day the temperature rose to thirty-five degrees. We slowed down to a laborious walk, and some, like Mylène, became red in the face and melted into any shade available. Yvonne had difficulty moving and didn't visit most of the temples; we thought the heat was responsible but realised afterwards it was more serious.

We explored My Son, an ancient archaeological site of the Champa dating from the twelfth century. At this point the different ethnic groups in the country were unknown to us; our limit was being able to distinguish "Vietnamese" from "Chinese"; we didn't yet know what "Kinh" meant, much less "Cham".

Our new guide (younger, browner, and less fluent than Antoine) led us gently through the heat. One of the first things we saw was a deep grass hollow next to an ancient temple. A sign in the middle was so small that to read it I had to get close with my camera; it said HERE FELL A HUGE US BOMB.

"Was this a war zone?" I asked the guide.

"By mistake," he replied, "the Americans thought rebel Viet Cong were hiding in the temples. Much of the destruction you see is due to those attacks and not the age of the buildings."

True enough, in most of the damaged temples we saw shell holes and even two souvenir bombs.

However, the beauty of the remaining sculptures soon eclipsed these brutal images of war. Impossible not to recognise the Hindu gods, Vishnu and company, and the female dancers. I have a photo of Mylène inside a temple, patting a hefty black stone pillar with a rounded top.

"Ah," the guide said, "that's a *linga*, a much-used carving dedicated to Shiva."

It immediately reminded me of the stone surprise in the Bay of Halong, but that had been natural, this was sculpture.

"Yes," remarked the guide as if reading my mind, "these *lingas* depict male and female sexual interaction, the essence of life."

I took several more pictures.

"But who were these Cham?" we wanted to know. "Where did they come from?"

It appeared the Cham have Indian Hindu origins going back to the second century, though they also turned to Buddhism for a while and some were Muslims. They were a seafaring and trading nation which finally settled in South Vietnam and fought against all comers over many centuries.

"And where are they now?" we insisted.

"Well, the last Champa kingdom was crushed in 1832, and their king fled to Cambodia," our guide said. "Today, there are about 160,000 Cham left in Vietnam. They have their own language and write in Sanskrit."

These remaining Cham have been much persecuted. Their kingdom was colonised by the Viets, much like the Viets were by the Han, the Ming, and later by the French. The Viets have tried in vain to assimilate them.

From Hoi An, via Da Nang, we left by plane for the highland area, the city of Buon Me Thuot. Despite a language pronunciation sheet given to us in Hanoi, I never could pronounce this place name and several others. We spent the night near a village of Mnong and explored the environment the next day with our newest guide. Whereas the Cham had been invisible, the Mnong village was a culture shock: no paved roads, just wooden thatched houses on stilts, pigs, buffaloes, cows, poultry everywhere, men wearing loincloths, rice paddies surrounding the village, nothing modern save for a few TV antennas. We learned from the official guidebook, *The Great Family of Ethnic Groups in Vietnam*, that the country has fifty-four different ethnicities, of which we would only have time to see a handful. The Mnong are brown-faced and cheerful; I remember children climbing trees to bring us fruit.

The biggest racial group are the Kinh, another name for the Viets, about 75 million of them, mostly ancestor worshippers. Every citizen must have an identification card stating his race and religion. Imagine the furore about privacy and prejudice this sort of law would cause in France, or even Britain!

We slept in a hotel in the Mnong village. It was on stilts like most village houses and climbing the entry ladder required a serious balancing act. I stepped carefully down the next morning and after breakfast came face to face with an enormous python in a cage, winding and unwinding his coils. This, however, was not the most impressive beast of the day. Our guide (a new one) called out to us: "Hurry up! The elephants are waiting!"

Mylène and I climbed up a four-metre ladder to a platform while a huge grey beast approached, steered by a handler sitting on its neck. A few shaky movements later and we had strapped ourselves onto the passenger chair. Then off went our elephant with lurching steps while the next couple climbed onto the platform. I had thought it would be a smooth ride but we swayed from side to side and clutched the bar for safety.

"Don't worry, your cornac is an expert," our guide said, walking beside us.

"What's a cornac?" I asked Mylène.

"It's French for 'elephant handler'," she informed me.

Our cornac certainly seemed in control, tickling or prodding the elephant's ear from one side or the other as it lumbered down the slope towards a nearby lake, in a sort of symbiosis. When our group had mobilised five elephants, the cornacs took us for a walk in the lake. Movement in two metres of water was gentler than on land and I was able to assuage my mania for pictures. We returned to the shore after an excursion of twenty minutes and dismounted on the same platform we had started from. Yvonne had more than a little trouble dismounting. Somewhat shaky ourselves after the expedition, we asked our guide about the cornacs.

"Do they do this for a living?"

"It's much more than a part-time job in this village! Each handler is dedicated to *his* elephant for a lifetime. They are chosen at age six and never leave the beast; food, water, and rest for the elephant is all their responsibility. It goes to school with them when they are young. If they die before the elephant, a brother or a cousin inherits it. If they marry, their wife is often very jealous of the beast."

I thought of some of my French friends washing and maintaining their fancy cars and wondered whether there might be a bit of cornac in them.

The Mnong are animists and spirit worshipers; we were told they sacrifice buffalos in rituals to give thanks for heaven, earth, forests, fields, and crops. Their matriarchal family organisation was evident when we attended a night-time ceremony of welcome to their village.

Several elderly Mnong women swayed and sang soulful songs while the males beat drums. The rhythm was most unlike my Caribbean calypso memories. Then our guide invited us to drink ceremoniously with the singers. Each of the males in our group (and some of the females, but not Mylène) agreed to drink with a long, thick straw from the same bowl as a female Mnong. When my turn came, I glanced at the mysterious partner next to me, brown and wrinkled but probably a lot younger than me. I was simultaneously nervous and fascinated, and the drink I sucked tasted warm, sweetish, and alcoholic. I suddenly felt a strong rapport for the Mnong next to me, a lot like my Amerindian great-grandmother, whose brown, lined face stares sternly down at me every day in Avon over my work desk. Thereafter, for the rest of the trip, I could only drink Vietnamese beer, no more wine until returning to France. Was it the low price of beer, the taste, the heat, or simply respect and affinity for the Mnong?

"Why doesn't this tribe get more help to modernise?" I asked.

"It's a big problem for our Communist regime," our guide said. "We force them to better educate their children, hoping they will join our evolving economy, but the young people, once educated, simply leave the villages to work in the cities."

Back came memories of my grandfather who confessed never returning to see his family in Guyana after his college studies and went on to his destiny as a priest far away from his birthplace.

The highlands impressed us with cocoa and coffee plantations, rubber production and a large war museum, showing the exploits of the Viet Cong and the North Vietnamese army.

On one occasion, our guide organised a visit to the home of a middle-class family to see their farm and have a foot massage. Their house was surrounded by long rows of vegetable crops of all sorts tended in late afternoon by a stooped elderly lady. As we relaxed in chairs for the massage given by several energetic daughters, the aged gardener crept into the house and collapsed into a chair in a bedroom, barely visible.

"That's grandmother," said the woman massaging my feet. "She doesn't talk much."

A TV set made noises in the bedroom, but the grandmother was not looking at it.

"She doesn't follow the TV either," continued my masseuse. "Alzheimer's, I think you call it."

I inquired as to her age, and the masseuse said she was very, very old, almost sixty. I felt embarrassed and said nothing. What were we doing in our seventies gallivanting around a world where sixty was the last stop?

After three days, we flew to Saigon, or rather Ho Chi Minh City. A new guide, Phuong, welcomed us and lodged us in a luxury hotel in the centre of town.

The next day at lunchtime, I discussed food with Phuong.

"I hope it was a good meal," he said, gazing at our empty plates.

I hesitated, not wanting to give offence, and congratulated him on the fried rolls, the soups, and the salads, but not the beef.

This led us to discussing the role of the cow—beast of burden in the fields, or source of meat and milk? In Vietnam, milk is mainly for tourists.

Impossible not be impressed by Ho Chi Minh City. It has 12 million residents compared with 8 million in Hanoi, and the city traffic reflects this. The downtown areas, the fifty-story skyscrapers, the cascade of night lighting, the French architecture, comparable to the world's other great cities. And it all seems orderly—intensely busy, but orderly—no police cars, no visible policemen, just the chaos of horns honking, everyone going about their business. I asked Phuong how much a square meter of living space cost. A lot, but Vietnam does not allow foreigners to buy property.

Like our previous guides, Phuong's skills were in languages, not in economics or politics. He was a handsome, dark-haired, brown-skinned Viet who had earned a university degree in French, and some of our questions troubled him. Via some local English language news-papers, I read that unemployment in Vietnam is almost unmeasurably low, less than 2 percent. To my surprise, the annual GDP growth is 7 percent, comparable with China's better years. It makes tourists like us from the EU gape.

We left by bus with our guide Phuong, going south-east to Can Tho, deep into rice and river country.

The Mekong River was to be our companion for the next few days as we wound our way down the enormous delta, and several of its nine branches. All around us were green rice paddies, sucking up the precious water.

Sailing down a tributary of the Mekong to the Cai Rang floating market in a sampan, we found the same complexity of river traffic as in the streets of Ho Chi Minh. The boats were packed with goods: vegeta-bles, fruit of all kinds, and the sides of the river were lined with floating or semi-fixed houses. The density of commerce was stunning.

∾

TWO DAYS LATER, en route in our bus from Can Tho back to HCM city, Phuong explained how Vietnam had become one of the world's largest rice producers.

"We are the third, or maybe the second, biggest rice producer in the world!" he said proudly.

Researched later, the facts are a little more complicated. In terms of *production*, Vietnam would be ranked fourth, after China, India, and Indonesia. But the Vietnamese don't eat all they produce. In terms of *exports* of rice, they are indeed second, just after Thailand.

"Farmers used to be contented with one yearly crop," Phuong continued, "but the yield depended on the rains.

"Then our agricultural researchers developed rice grains which can produce two or more crops per year—some ecologists don't like it but it's much more efficient! The Mekong Delta is a huge producer, the Red River region somewhat less."

So, is rice the gold of the Vietnamese economy? It helps, but—surprise, surprise—this is not why Vietnam is getting richer. Rice is a basic food and not expensive; it's industry that does the trick. And everyone wants to build factories in this country—Samsung is far from being the only investor. The country's main exports in value are electronic equipment and machinery, followed by crude oil, and then by clothing and leather shoes. Interestingly, the most recent enemy, America, is now the biggest export market.

Phuong continued: "Provided the Chinese don't obstruct the Mekong, our people are productive and happy on their farms. In fact, the whole country works and is happy."

This sounded a bit optimistic to me. And suddenly, I became very confused. All the vitality and good economic performance of the Vietnamese people had blinded me to my previous dislike and distrust of the Communist regime. Where was the truth? Was this the way the world should be, or was it all a grandiose lie?

"But all of this is recent, isn't it?" I said. "After the American War, when your government nationalised all the farms and agriculture, you had a terrible time of it, when the boat people tried to escape, and so many were drowned."

What did Ho Chi Minh dream for his country's future? It took almost twenty years before Vietnam copied China and injected a capitalist economy into the Communist womb. And was it worth it?

"Ah! The boat people!" said Phuong. "And the depression! You are not the first one to ask me about them, but it was before I was born. Details of what happened were hidden. I know about the *doi moi* policy, when the land was handed back to the people, but not about the period before when it was confiscated. When I first heard of that difficult time, I went to libraries to research it, but found nothing. The Internet wasn't much help either—parts of our access are filtered. I asked a tourist friend returning to France to send me documentation on the post-war period, a book if possible. He agreed, and I waited two months, then phoned him. 'I sent it,' he said, 'it's on its way.' "

Phuong's face darkened as he continued: "Well, a few days later my wife got a call from a nearby post office. They said I had a forbidden parcel from France. The content, a book, was an illegal import. I was invited to present myself at the post office to officially refuse delivery!"

I almost laughed.

Phuong jerked his head and continued: "I was so cross they had scanned my parcel, I never went there. No one insisted, and I'm still an accredited guide.

"Some weeks later, I asked another tourist friend who visits Vietnam regularly to buy the same book about the boat people and bring it back for me in his valise. He returned after six months and I learned all about the horrors of that period. As you can see, the only thing we miss is a little more freedom of information, especially about delicate past events."

Phuong smiled wistfully, "But how much is freedom worth? I love our country's success and stability and wouldn't change our regime lightly."

I wondered if Phuong would ever be allowed to visit France. I felt deep sympathy both for him and our first guide Antoine and I grasped at last the strength of their political compromise: yes, I could accept their mix of communism and capitalism, even with some loss of freedom. May Ho Chi Minh sleep in peace!

"Before you leave," Phuong said, "have you understood the significance of the Vietnamese dragon?"

"He's in your carvings, paintings, and metal plaques. What more?" I replied.

"Our old legends say the Viet people were created by the union between a dragon and a fairy. Our dragon is creative, the meeting of heaven and earth, not fiery and terrifying like the Chinese version, and *he has been following you everywhere!*"

"How do you mean?"

"The Vietnamese word for dragon is 'long'. You came into the country thinking you were in Hanoi. But Hanoi stands on the ancient dragon city of Thang Long—ascending dragon. Then you went to the Bay of Ha Long, where long ago our dragon emerged from the sea to create all the islands. And just yesterday you travelled down the Mekong River of many branches, which—though you didn't know it—is also called Cuu Long—nine dragons. Finally, you are soon going to leave by Vietnam Airlines, so you must not forget Van Long, Dragon of the Clouds. Let him keep you safe!"

Indeed, the Vietnamese dragon worked for us. After a few hot days in Cambodia, we returned safely home to France, all ten of us, and Mylène's fibromyalgia pains did not return that winter. Yvonne had broken a rib in the cavern but recovered from her fall after a month of convalescence in France and the loving care of Claude. She gave me one of her striking paintings of Vietnam as a birthday present for Mylène.

Today, I remember the vivacity of Vietnam with admiration.

But what have I forgotten elsewhere?

17

MEMORY BLIPS

Forgotten things? Yes, as I have aged from my fifties into my seventies, I have felt the embarrassing tickles of forgetfulness. The disappearance of the weeping willow in our garden was the start of my introspection on failing memory. Giving up my Paris apartment after twenty-seven years was surprising in its lost memory threads. And I quickly record the details of every exciting voyage else the essentials may vanish. My everyday life over the last four months in Avon shows an accumulation of my cognitive losses. I recorded each incident on the day it occurred—any delay risked losing the story. In my forties, I could remember the details of office meetings for at least six months; I could cite all the films I'd seen, books I'd read during the previous year. Now, names and faces have become slippery, harder to fix and to recall. What was the last film I saw? What's the name of the wake-up hormone? Who was the publisher of my last book in 2010? What was the date of my father's death? Of course, I can find some answers by looking them up, but why do they get lost in the first place?

I'd seen my mother develop frontal-lobe dementia (which is different from Alzheimer's) and I was her caregiver during seven years of her life until she entered a nursing home. I watched her change from an elderly person who wrote emails on her PC to someone who confused the microwave and the TV and couldn't recall the husband she had lived with for fifty years. Could this happen to me? Are my current memory losses a normal part of ageing or a precursor of more serious things (like cognitive impairment)?

"MEMORY," I thought, and stared in disgust at my desktop computer. A writer friend had just sent me a document attached to an email. Alas! My computer couldn't read the document type ".*pages*" from a Mac system. I leaned back in my chair and tapped my feet while thinking. Then I prepared to email my correspondent to say that the only document file types I could deal with were from Microsoft Word, ".doc" or ".docx". Just before sending my reply, I thought again. I looked at the piles of printed computer output on my desk, stuff which Mylène wanted me to sort and file. Much of it was not Word but reports, articles, and legal documents running under Adobe Reader software. So, I could accept Adobe's format on my PC and maybe my correspondent's Mac had Adobe. The third possible file type would thus be "???". Suddenly, I hit a blank. I couldn't remember the three-letter code for the Adobe format. Yet I had hundreds of these documents on my computer and as an IT specialist, I'd dealt with them for years and years! I'd even recently translated a few into Word format. What was going on? The Adobe file symbol on my file Explorer—that might help. I knew it was a small red square with a three-pronged sort of white boomerang in the middle, which changed to a white square with a red boomerang when you opened the document with Adobe. All this I remembered, but WHAT WAS THE FILE TYPE? Years of usage and now I had no recall. In desperation, I abandoned my email reply and used my file Explorer until I hit on a random Adobe document. Click! And there it was; the file type ".pdf". How could I lose this bit of information after so many years of use? It's called dysnomia.

Two days later, while having breakfast, I thought about this memory blip. Some neurons must have disconnected and lost the information.

"Mylène, do you remember the Adobe file type?"

She shook her head.

"Well, I forgot it, but now I've remembered and it is . . ." I hesitated.

Well? I now knew it again, didn't I? It was . . . perhaps ".pfg" or maybe ".pfd"? Dammit! I had lost it again!

"Sorry, I need to check!"

Apparently, I couldn't repair the failed memory connection simply by repeating it aloud or even by writing it down. So, I tried another technique, create a *new* memory path to the information. What did the file type mean anyway? I left the table, went back to my computer and the Internet, and found the definition in a web dictionary: ".pdf" comes from "portable document format", launched by Adobe in 2008 (formerly "Camelot"). This should fix my memory, shouldn't it? And it's all in the web dictionary, whose name is . . . Ah, ah, Wikipedia!

"MEMORY," Mylène said. "I need you to guide me when I reverse my car into a narrow space. Suppose, for example, I'm near to a post in a garage. Which way do I turn the wheel to avoid the post?"

"But surely," I said, "you've been parking all your life, probably quicker and better than I can. What's new?"

"It's a blockage, I don't know why. Everything else is automatic in my control of the vehicle. I don't have to think of gear shifts, breaking, or acceleration, nor how to keep a correct distance between cars in traffic. But when sometimes I must reverse into a parking space, I find I've lost my intuitive reflexes. It happened recently, maybe from a year or so back. And that's why I need your help. Especially in our dimly-lighted underground parking."

"Well, it depends where you are relative to the post," I said, making a hand gesture.

"Suppose, while reversing, the post is on my left and the rear of my car is about to ram it? Should I move my shoulders right or left on the steering wheel?"

"Left!" I said, trying to visualise the scene. "Then, as you reverse, the back of the car will move diagonally away from the post."

"But then, if I'm reversing past the post and the *front* of my car is about to scrape the post, what then?"

"Right!" I said, "in order not to hit it!" For me this was clear, but difficult to explain.

"Sorry, I don't get it. I'll never remember that. You say, 'Turn the wheel left' or 'Turn it right', but I'm no longer even sure how to go straight back. Is there a special position on the steering wheel for this? I'm afraid you'll just have to guide me with hand motions."

"How about just letting me park your car?"

Mostly, we remember procedures which have become entrenched and instinctive, our "motor memory", but sometimes a change in parameters can completely upset us. When Mylène and I hired a car in the UK with right-hand drive, which I had used in my youth, I managed. Mylène, on the contrary, was never able to change gears with her left hand.

"Memory," we thought. It was a grey winter morning and we were both dressed in bright yellow colours as if to conjure away the fog outside. Our kitchen is one of our cheeriest rooms, looking out onto the garden. Often, the birds outside sing during our breakfast. Halfway through eating, we take our daily medicines. I have only one green pill to swallow, morning and evening, to keep my prostate healthy. It comes in a plastic packet of fourteen pills, a week's supply. Each morning I should have a pill with an even number, and each evening an odd number. Anything else disturbs me.

Recently, Mylène has been taking a potent medicine by drops. Every morning she needs twelve drops in a glass of water mixed with other ingredients. It's an important and expensive medicine, and an overdose or an under-dose is not a good idea. She is standing in front of me with the glass in one hand and the bottle of drops in the other. The birds start chirping more loudly. They are bursting with morning energy. Suddenly, she says "Oh!" and frowns.

I look up from my egg.

She says, "I don't know whether I've put my drops in or not! I listened to the birds."

According to me, there's only one sure way out, no matter the cost. "Throw it away and start again," I say.

She does it: empties the glass, adds fresh water and other stuff, and then, fully alert, counts out twelve drops. This is not quite a memory problem—it's divided attention. I'm less susceptible to this, perhaps because I do things like working out in front of the TV and often shift my focus from the screen to my exercise.

"That's new," Mylène says. "I can usually keep track, but I was distracted. Thanks for suggesting I start again. What would you do if, instead of a blank moment, I had an outright heart attack? Shouldn't we have a defibrillator in the house?"

"Perhaps, but I've forgotten my first-aid training. I don't remember how to use one."

"I MUST PUT this on my shopping list," I thought, "or else I'll forget." I had just cut a soft mango open for breakfast and found it brown and unappetising inside. I remembered that the supermarket would refund me for any spoiled fruit or vegetable I discovered after purchase if I returned it to the store.

"Do you have the receipt for it?" Mylène asked me.

"Yes, I think so," I hesitated.

Later, after breakfast, I spent fifteen minutes searching until I found the bill for the purchase two days earlier.

"Yippee! Found it, and I've made my shopping list. Now I'm off to the store."

"I'll follow you in a few minutes," Mylène said.

But inside the supermarket I suddenly realised that whereas I had the receipt for the mango and my list, I had forgotten the rotten mango itself.

A phone call to Mylène to bring the mango with her and things were settled. She arrived a few minutes later with the offending fruit.

And then she said: "Zut! I've got your mango but I've forgotten my own list!"

We shopped as well as we could and prepared to leave the store. Then Mylène put her hand in her pocket and found the shopping list she thought she had forgotten.

"Fine pair of memories we have!" I said. "And all that for a one-euro-fifty-cents refund!"

"Memory," I thought, as she struggled with a bottle of dish-washing liquid.

"Umm! It won't pour!" she said. "And I used it just yesterday."

I got up from the breakfast table to help. The bottle was filled with a pink liquid soap and had a green top with a small funnel.

"Have you opened the top?" I asked.

I didn't have to touch anything. She pulled up on the green funnel and immediately some liquid came out. "And I do this every day!" she complained.

We spared a thought for those casual habits which disappear for no good reason, and then I left to do the morning's shopping, my day's list in hand: mangoes, bananas, bread, and cheese.

I found what I wanted at Carrefour Market except for the mangoes, and instead I selected four bananas and wrapped them in a plastic bag. As I put them on a scale, a Japanese salesman hailed me: "Hello sir, look at this fresh sushi we have today. Would you like to taste?" I know the salesman and his product well and accepted with a smile. The sample of rice, algae and salmon was spicy and quite delicious.

A few minutes later, after buying a postcard, I was at the checkout belt and transferred my purchases from my cart to the moving belt and placed a NEXT CLIENT sign at the end. Another customer followed me into the queue.

My turn came up and I glanced at my purchases. Something was missing. Where were my bananas? In a flash, I remembered putting them on the scale near the Japanese counter and then turning away.

"Sorry, I've forgotten something," I said, and reloaded everything back into my cart.

The bananas were still there, waiting sadly next to the scale. At least I had had a good reason for forgetting them. The sushi was delicious. I hardly cared that my active memory was less efficient than in the past. More sushi, please.

"MEMORY," I thought. "Did I lock my car?" I was walking away from the vehicle in the dark underground garage opposite our home in Avon. I had left the car less than thirty seconds earlier, yet I couldn't recall if I had turned the key in the driver's door. I turned around and went back to the old Ford Mondeo. Sure enough, the door was locked. This was the first time in two months I'd forgotten my car-locking action, but there had been several such memory failures over the last three years, ever since I turned seventy. In most cases, my security impulse was unnecessary. The car had been well and truly locked. But just once or twice . . .

Lately, the car has seemed to echo my memory failure. When I turn the key in the driver's door, all four doors are supposed to unlock. They don't. I fiddle with the system by re-locking and re-opening the driver's door two or three times until the other doors respond. Sometimes I have to open them from the inside. The car seems to have forgotten what it's supposed to do. Nonsense, of course! The car is just a machine and has no memory. Or does it? Maybe I'm a bio-machine and just as memory-fallible as the car's ageing hard-wired circuits.

I went to a seminar on memory problems like this, and now I know what to do. Since my head is full of heaps of other junk, it doesn't want to keep track of locking cars and doors. So, whenever I lock something important, I have to say aloud, "I've just locked it." This helps to keep the memory thread.

"MEMORY," I thought, scratching my head. "Don't I have an appointment today?" It was after breakfast and a look at my January planning sheet showed that, yes, I should be in Paris at 2 p.m. to see my dentist, Jean. Almost forgot. I would have to take the 12:30 train from Avon. I ate a quick lunch and prepared my teeth for the ordeal. My gums were sore on the upper left side where a wisdom tooth had been removed and a nearby tooth was wobbly. Hopefully, Jean would help and I could leave without problems for a snowshoeing trip two days later.

All went well until my train reached the Gare de Lyon. Suddenly, perplexity. "Which metro do I take?" I asked myself. "Where is his office anyway?" A great blankness descended on me. Surely, he was in the centre of Paris? Could it be near Opéra, or Concorde perhaps? No, no! Near to a big church. Not Notre Dame, possibly Madeleine. I looked at a map and found the Madeleine station on line 14. I still wasn't sure, but I took the next train anyway. When I got to Madeleine no exit looked familiar. I remembered one exit led to a sporting goods store, Decathlon, but instead I found myself next to the Fauchon food shop, on the opposite side of the church to my dentist's street. It's weird and a little scary to forget my Paris geography after living there for forty years. What comes next?

As I walked to my dentist's office, the streets around me replaced my faded memories. I knew where I was, where Jean's office was, and even where he had been. When I first came to Paris in 1970, Jean had a dental office in the building where we lived, rue de Levis. He was about our age, near thirty, and had done some training in America, where we came from, so we immediately adopted him. Fifteen years later, when he moved his practice to Boulevard Malsherbes (there, I've just remembered his address), we naturally followed him. I have a complicated mouth and I reckon he must have treated twenty of my twenty-eight teeth. But after not visiting him for just a year, I had forgotten the way to his office.

My next surprise came when he greeted me. He looked hesitant, wrinkled and much older than I remembered; still the same smile though. His female assistant was younger but smiled less.

"You look fit!" he said. "How long since you left Paris? Two years?"

"It's the Fontainebleau air, and it's been four years. How about you? Any retirement plans?" I calculated he must be at least seventy-six, two years older than me.

"It all depends on my children: my daughter now lives in Vietnam, and my son has just taken a job in Dubai. If they don't need help, I'll probably stop working next year."

I described my tooth problems and he tried to take an X-ray of the tooth near the gum irritation—number twenty-seven, he said. It took several tries before he got a good image. The problem appeared to be just a temporary swelling.

Then, with a jerk of his fingers he plucked out the wobbly tooth. Or rather the capping structure.

"Strange!" he said. "It was anchored at two points. Did you chew hard on something?"

"Can't remember," I said.

"Nurse!" Jean called to his assistant. "Check the records please for number twenty-seven in Christopher's mouth. I can't recall when I did this implant."

"The capping you just removed was not number twenty-seven but number twenty-five!" the nurse said. "Records indicate you operated on it about ten years ago."

So, he's getting his tooth geography mixed up? I thought.

Jean cleaned the anchorage points with a drill while I cringed a little at the lack of anaesthetic, but there was no pain.

"Some cement, please!" he asked the nurse.

"Which one?"

"Doesn't matter, whatever you find."

A little surprised, I seemed to recall that Jean always prescribed his specific tooth cement, but then I had to bite down on the tooth for several minutes while the product hardened so I couldn't talk.

When it was all over, I said: "Jean, my mouth is very grateful for all you have done for it over the last forty-five years. Now that I'm settled in Avon, I may have to find a local dentist. Can I ask him to phone you for my records?"

"Of course, he can call, though there's no real dossier to transfer."

"Anyway, how much do I owe you?"

"Nothing. It's been a pleasure!"

The nurse scowled, but Jean smiled and I felt a pang as we shook hands for the last time.

"MEMORY," I thought, panting as I ran. I was pulling a heavy suitcase behind me, hurrying towards the Avon/Fontainebleau railway station. Mylène was ahead, dragging her own lighter case. We had only six minutes to catch the train to Paris, and if we didn't catch it, we would probably miss the Eurostar connection at Gare du Nord.

Normally, we should have been all right. I was already three hundred metres away from our front door and we should get to the station with a minute or two to spare. A minute or two! But I had just remembered my pills, left on the kitchen table. Important pills—I need two per day—that I had meant to put in my backpack but hadn't. Permixon, I needed that damned stuff for my prostate! But if I turned back now and tried to run twice three hundred metres, plus unlocking and relocking the front doors, we would surely miss the train. Why had I forgotten something so important at the last minute? Idiot! Well, I would have to suffer. Maybe in London I could find a Boots pharmacy with the same pills. It was a prescription drug in France, but in London, who knows?

I said nothing to Mylène for an hour or two, but when we were safely on the Eurostar and rocketing towards the channel tunnel, I sombrely confessed my forgetfulness, and explained I would need to visit a pharmacy soon after arrival.

She turned to me with a smile. "I've got your pills! I picked them up when I left the kitchen just in case."

I smiled. How incredibly thoughtful of her!

On the last day of our trip, we had another blip, this time accompanied by panic. We were preparing to leave our hotel after three days spent helping my sister Hazel in Bayswater. I had renovated her computer installation as I had done several times in the past. Her athetoid spastic handicap keeps her at home these days, reliant on the Internet, and her companion is not computer literate. It was near the end of the morning, time to quit our room. After packing our cases we would travel to St. Pancras station by taxi or bus and catch our return Eurostar an hour or two later. Tension always rises when we pack suitcases. What have we forgotten? Is the bathroom clear?

Suddenly, Mylène cried out, "Where's my ID card?"

"In your handbag, surely."

"No, no I've just looked. It should be in my red purse but it isn't! You must have it. Didn't you pick it up and put it in your passport when we went through immigration three days ago?"

"I didn't touch it, but I'll check." I check things even when I'm pretty sure; memory is a strange thing. However, there was nothing of Mylène's in my passport.

"Then your suitcase!"

"Let me check your handbag first."

"It's not there!"

I checked it, however, opening the red purse and its' several pockets. Nothing.

Panic increased. We began moving rapidly from corner to corner of the room.

"Where has it gone, how are we going to pass immigration without any ID?"

"I told you to travel with your passport as well as the ID card, remember?"

"Then I might have lost them both!"

We checked our two suitcases, nearly full, and backpacks, repeatedly.

It was time to leave the hotel and the missing bit of plastic was nowhere.

On the floor? Under the bed? In the bathroom? Nowhere!

"We won't be able to take the train!"

"It's here somewhere. Try your purse again."

A moment of hesitation, then she said, "Aha! It's here in a side pocket."

In addition to its four main compartments, her red folding purse had a discrete side pocket which neither of us had opened. And there it was, waiting to be discovered.

The cause of my blip when I lose something important is that I've not put the object away properly, just left it on a table, say, until I have time. Then it may get covered up or pushed away somewhere, and I won't find it. Mylène's dangerous habit is that she will put an important object, not to be forgotten, in a "special" place, somewhere different each time, somewhere unusual. Then when the time comes, she can't remember why it's not in its "usual" place.

During my seminar on memory problems, we were advised to choose a special place, once and for all, for important objects like smartphones, keys, or wallets.

In the train, remembering the things we had nearly forgotten, a comforting thought came to me. Two people have twice as many memory blips as one, but if they form a cooperating couple, each may be able to decipher the other's blip, or at least calm things down. A memorable partnership!

"FORGOT AGAIN!" I said under my breath, as I searched my backpack for water. For the first sunny day after several weeks of winter weather, Mylène and I were out on a forest hike with our fellow club members. We had been late on arrival at the meeting place, almost missing the group. I had been driving, and as we got out of the car, I told Mylène to run ahead and catch up with them while I took out the backpack and locked the vehicle.

An hour later the group paused—it was time to rehydrate. I carry Mylène's water supply because of her painful shoulder, so I opened the backpack to give it to her. There was no bottle there—no wonder the pack had seemed so light! But I knew I had prepared her bottle! Okay, I must have left it in the kitchen in the hurry to leave. Chalk up one negative point for me. As luck would have it, I did have a small bottle of a chocolate drink in the pack, so Mylène was not without sustenance. I abstained.

Returning to our car after almost three hours of walking and getting slightly wet, I saw several fellow walkers gesticulating around my car.

A friend shouted: "There's a door left open! Maybe a theft!"

Hurrying to the car, I discovered Mylène's front door unlocked. Now, my car, like most, has automatic door locking. Remember? The doors lock when I turn the key in the driver's door, provided they are properly closed. Apparently, in her hurry to join the group Mylène had not shut her door properly. The other three doors were locked but not that one.

Happily, there was nothing of value in the car, not even a GPS.

"Why didn't you check the doors?" she said.

"Well, I was in a hurry too and didn't see what was happening on your side of the car." I usually do check, so chalk a second negative point for me. And on this occasion, under time stress, the couple-correcting mechanism didn't work.

∾

"Memory," she said by phone to me. "Help! I can't find the doctor's office. I forgot my map—please check in the living room."

Mylène had been to see this doctor, in fact a physiotherapist, just two days earlier where she was being treated for back pains. Today, she was late for her appointment and, in her panic, she had forgotten which way to go. It was less than ten minutes from our home by car and she knew the street address—34 rue Jeanne d'Arc—but where was that? I talked to her on the phone and tried to figure out where *she* was from the map but nothing was clear. Finally, the second passer-by she questioned was able to direct her. And then on reaching the medical facility, her vehicle broke down, as if in sympathy. The car battery wouldn't start. I told her to call me when her appointment was over and I'd come with my car and a starter cable.

An hour later, her car started by itself—sort of—and she was able to drive home. "This has never happened before," she said. "If I go somewhere by car or on foot, I always remember my route."

"It's because you panicked," I surmised. "But as for your car, the battery must be too low."

I parked her car in our garden and got out my battery charger. I connected the cable to a house socket and prepared to open the bonnet of her Nissan. This was a procedure I'd had to carry out several times before: connect the charger, open the car bonnet, attach the red and the black clips, and let it charge for an hour or so.

But where was the catch to open the bonnet? I searched with my hands under the steering wheel. Nothing. I knew it must be close by. I had done this before, but all I could recall was that the catch was not easy to find. I couldn't give up. I got out of the car, went down on my knees, and scanned everything under the dashboard. At last I found it, on the left, a smooth, difficult-to-detect catch.

The rest of the charging procedure went normally. When I compared my memory loss with Mylène's earlier on, I realised I hadn't been at all stressed. So, any half-cooked procedure can vanish from our memory, stress or not, if it's poorly digested. But at least I can still solve problems.

"MEMORY," she said. "I forgot to take out the garbage yesterday so it wasn't collected."

"Memory," I replied. "I forgot my appointment with the hair-dresser. I'm not even sure which day it was. I'll have to call her."

"MEMORY," she said. "I never know where I've left my phone."

"I'd be the same if I didn't keep mine in my trouser pocket!"

"But I don't have pockets in my dresses!"

"MEMORY," I said to my doctor. "I've forgotten which of my vaccinations are up to date, and I've lost my records. I'm going abroad in three weeks. Can you help?"

"Sorry, my records are incomplete, and I can't remember either, but let's protect you against typhoid and malaria, just in case. And I'll give you a fresh vaccination certificate to lose again."

WHEN SEVERAL PARTIES ARE INVOLVED, it's sometimes not clear whose memory is at fault.

I was playing table tennis at my club in the late evening and my adversary was a friend, Sishir. He is a strong player and was the winner of our last regional tournament. He is seventy-six, three years older than me. He thinks he is getting too slow to be a champion and wants me to succeed him. At that point in the evening we were equal, two sets each, and had begun the deciding set for the match. I had been vaccinated three hours earlier and my left shoulder was hurting. I couldn't decide whether the pain was a spur to my attacking game or a handicap to my concentration. We had finished two services each and the score I had noted was a tie, two-two. I announced the score and passed the ball to Sishir to serve.

"No," he said, "we are eight-eight."

I thought I had misheard and repeated, "No, two-two."

"Eight-eight," said Sishir. "Have you been dreaming?"

I didn't want to call my friend a liar, but I was certain we had only played four points, not sixteen; and I had once been a high-ranking umpire.

It's only a friendly game, I thought, let's not fight. "Okay, have it your way, Sishir. Serve!" I said.

I put his service into the net, losing the point, and three points later he won eleven-nine, set and match. I tried to improve my tactics, but I was disturbed and Sishir won the second match three sets to one, and the third, three to zero; an unflattering descent!

One of us had had a memory blip, but who? I don't think Sishir would cheat; he really thought we had played the missing twelve points. Could he have gone to sleep? Or was it me?

On occasion, time does seem to shoot past. Driving my car the next day from Paris to home, I looked at the GPS distance about halfway and it registered thirty-two kilometres before the Fontainebleau exit. Still a bit far, I thought. I kept on looking but it seemed to take ages for the distance to decrease by a kilometre. Ah, I thought and began studying the traffic. Maybe I could do a spell in the fast lane? I looked back at the distance to cover and suddenly it was only twenty-one kilo-metres. It meant ten kilometres had passed while I was glancing at traffic; seven minutes evaporated from my train of thought.

I'll never know whether Sishir or I had the blip.

I DO KNOW that at my age I've probably lost about 6 percent of the brain weight I had at age thirty and maybe 5 percent of my twenty billion neocortical neurons, plus shrinkage of some remaining neurons and loss of some synaptic junctions and dopamine. But it seems we can compensate and resist. Gradual cognitive losses will happen, but dementia is far from inevitable: we can continue to learn. Some call it a biological process of neuroplasticity and neurogenesis (new growth). I prefer to think of normal ageing being tempered by our capacity for self-repair and the redundancy of our mental systems and strategies.

I have visions of my disappearing memories.

First, the military outlook: I am a general commanding an army fighting against the hordes of forgetfulness. I have troops controlling the vast hinterland of my past, especially the faraway past, known as "crystallised intelligence", though the enemy sometimes infiltrates the more up-to-date regions. My front-line troops are subjected to daily attacks on fresh experiences. I try to build defences around new and vulnerable mental constructs, my "fluid intelligence", if I have time. But the enemy is invisible and very rapid; I am only aware of an attack when I find something missing.

Next, I am an information technology specialist. My data system has enormous neuronal disks with fabulous stores of old information; only occasionally do the access mechanisms go astray. I have back-ground tasks running which easily find major childhood data. But bugs have developed in the foreground programs, those which store data input (dates, names, places) in new files. The information is not being maintained properly! My only solution is to use unconventional storage supports, outside of the rapid disk system, like notes on paper, reminders, names, lists, phones, and calendars. Granted, it's not organically connected with the rest of the data system, but it can't be erased by a blip.

Lastly, I am a philosopher, thinking of my place in the universe. The past is me, and so if it dribbles away bit by bit, how much of me still exists? Apparently, I can still learn, but will the new me be different from the old? Perhaps I should accept that not remembering, not knowing how to do something, does not stop me looking for new solutions?

Dysnomia, the difficulty in remembering names or recalling words, is not necessarily pathology, and some ageing decline in "fluid intelligence" is normal, not to be confused with wisdom and good judgement that can remain strong in healthy seniors.

Lastly, there is the idea of the story saving the storyteller. To distinguish between benign senescence and MCI (mild cognitive impairment) it seems that those of us seniors who confess our memory blips are in better shape than those who say nothing and whose family, friends, or neighbours complain about the senior's forgetfulness. Anyone for more blip stories?

18

THE GRASS KEEPS ON GROWING

When illness threatens to stunt our existence, or that of our loved ones, we need a vision of growth. Through my bedroom window I admired the thick green lawn we had planted in our back garden; no vegetables, no fruit, just grass bordered by white gravel. I missed the weeping willow we had been forced to cut down, its heart rotten, but the soft carpet of grass which replaced it was a compensation. If one waters it, grass keeps on growing.

Some parts of our new lawn grow faster than others and I take pleasure in mowing them to create new harmony. Curious—when younger I had never much cared for gardens and the idea of buying an electric mower and investing time in lawn upkeep was new. Soon after my mower arrived, early in the month of May 2016, spring flower time, my sister Hazel Skyped me about her health.

"I'm getting strange pains in my leg and the doctors don't know what the cause is," she said. Or at least that's what I thought I understood after two or three tries. My sister has been handicapped from birth with athetoid cerebral palsy, an inability to control muscle tone, and her strangled pronunciation is difficult to follow, even for her close family, especially over the phone. The handicap affects all her movements, making handwriting near impossible. It was an uphill battle to complete her schooling and gain a university degree, dictating all her exams to an amanuensis. She then worked for thirty years with the British Council, and found a congenial if eccentric lifetime companion, Peter C. Those who know her learn to interpret her speech, and computer technology has solved her difficulty with handwriting.

She has lived a courageous intellectual life. We were both originally from St. Kitts in the Caribbean; now Hazel has settled in Bayswater, London, and I live in Avon, sixty kilometres south of Paris. We see each other once or twice a year. Recently, Hazel's mobility has been destroyed, the legacy of past surgical operations and the constant need of strong medicines. Able to walk, fall, and pick herself up in her early years, since retirement she has been using a wheelchair. I tried to get the social care services to provide some physiotherapy, but it didn't work; at the first session Hazel sprained her ankle. It doesn't help that her companion has also become frail and can no longer wheel her around; he himself fell one night in their apartment and had to wait until morning to be picked up by the emergency services. Nevertheless, two years ago our family celebrated her seventieth birthday with pride.

But what were these strange new pains? She described a swelling under her left thigh, between buttocks and knee, which hurt when sitting in her wheelchair.

"What does your doctor say?" I asked, thinking it might be a tumour, but hoping for something less serious.

"He's not sure," she said. "He sent me to St. Mary's hospital for a scan two weeks ago, but there's been no result yet."

She grimaced, and I could see her hunching her shoulders on my Skype computer screen. "It's very painful sitting down on the swelling, and every little movement provokes the beast. I have to go back to St. Mary's next week for a follow-up. Oh, and my TV has stopped working and Peter can't fix it!"

Peter is older than Hazel, charming, likes music and literature, but is no handyman; his balance is poor and when he travels around London, he must use a three-wheel walker.

The days went by, with more phone calls, emails, and Skypes tracing the laborious National Health Service mechanisms to which

Hazel was relying on. The verdict came in late May: Hazel had a soft-tissue sarcoma.

"How big is it?" I asked by phone.

"Big, the size of a coconut," she said.

She was summoned to the Royal Marsden Hospital for a biopsy, with treatment to be decided on in the following weeks. I read up on sarcomas: whereas tumours can be benign, a sarcoma in connective tissue is always malignant. Only 3 percent of cancers are of this type, and they can propagate; the prognosis depends on circumstances, from short term to several years. Treatment is by radiotherapy (RT) and/or chemotherapy combined with surgery.

After her first visit to Marsden, the doctors gave Hazel a printed programme: six weeks of radiotherapy as an outpatient, starting in mid-June; next, a pause of a month to allow shrinkage of the sarcoma; finally, admission for possible surgery in September. The sarcoma should have been classified as stage 3 or 4 by the hospital, because of the lung nodules found, but we were never informed of this.

"Marsden is supposed to be the best cancer hospital in Britain," Hazel said, "but the preparation is taking such a long time, and I have nothing to occupy me in my flat."

I took a break from a busy schedule in Avon and went to London two days later, on June 4. Over the weekend, I replaced her failed TV set, something which had long-lasting benefits not only for my sister but for her companion in the months ahead. My sister asked me to photograph the large sarcoma swelling, but I didn't have the stomach for it.

Nevertheless, I slipped into a new role of family coordinator on behalf of my sister; the rest of the family was too far away. Hazel was now so immobile she could no longer phone or email or Skype. The radiotherapy swallowed up all her energy. I began phoning Peter every two or three days and then relaying the information to my brothers by email. Soon, I added Hazel's Caribbean friends to the mailing list, then the English side of the family, and later, her work friends from the British Council. Peter doesn't use a computer and can neither send nor receive messages. In time, my "family & friends" letters, spaced about ten days apart, covered two dozen correspondents, each proposing to visit Hazel when appropriate.

"How are the Marsden radiotherapy treatments going?" I asked Hazel in late June.

"Going there by ambulance every day is *very* tiring," Hazel replied, "and the radiotherapy tickles, but in July there'll be a pause."

As Burns reminds us, the best-laid plans of mice and men often go awry.

I felt the need to reassure my sister face-to-face during her radiotherapy. In addition, July–August was the time of year when Mylène and I often took grandchildren to Britain to improve their English. So, we booked four weeks in an apartment in Hatfield, a medium-sized town thirty miles north of London, arriving July 18. We were focussed on showing Mylène's grandchildren another side of England, the family town. Hazel's eventual surgery was supposed to be two months away, so I only anticipated weekly visits to my sister in Bayswater.

Before departure, I had stared for a long time at our green lawn. It was warm weather and the grass was growing rapidly; there would certainly be a lot to cut after a month of absence. However, the automatic watering system would be adequate to keep it from drying out. If only my sister's problems were as simple as that.

Immediately after our arrival in London, there was a drastic change of plan. Peter signalled that the radiotherapy had failed and surgery would probably take place within the next three days. Hazel had already been admitted to the Royal Marsden. We hardly had time to put down our bags in Hatfield, and we stopped using the word "holiday".

My brothers started making plans to travel from the USA for what might be a last visit to our sister. It was hard to judge: if they came too soon after the surgery Hazel might not be able to communicate, if they came too late, it might be too late. We decided not to change the arrangements for the grandchildren, but to keep them completely away from Hazel's hospital, though both had previously met her. We found them a summer school in English at the Hertfordshire University campus, close to our rented apartment. I slowly realised we would be making the one-hour-and-a-half train journey from Hatfield to the London hospital, not once a week, but daily.

The day after arrival, we struggled with the transport system, train plus underground, and eventually found the Royal Marsden hospital in South Kensington, a plush neighbourhood. The reception service guided us to Hazel's ward, where the protocol required us to wash hands and wear protective aprons before we could enter.

The hospital room was well-equipped with displays on several bright screens zigzagging up and down, plastic IV feeder tubes winding their way around and into my sister, a mobile TV set above her head which she would later learn to use, an emergency button, multiple plugs for equipment, and nurses who seemed to come and go every ten minutes. Slouched in an armchair between my sister's bed and his three-wheel walker was Peter, Hazel's bearded companion of forty years. His welcoming smile hid his contrarian nature, that of a man who refused to contemplate marriage, death, capitalism, religion or any such nonsense. But what dedication! Not being able to use the underground, it took him two hours to get to the hospital, which he did seven days a week.

My sister gave a squeal of pleasure as Mylène and I entered. It had been six weeks since I had last seen her, a tense time of waiting. She thanked me again for the TV set, which her companion now found indispensable. The doctors were still considering how to treat her sarcoma. They wanted to operate because the radiotherapy had failed, its stimulus only making the beast inside Hazel grow bigger and more hostile. But was she strong enough to stand up to a lengthy anaesthesia? The specialists would decide.

That day Mylène and I had come from Paris to surround her with our love. The next day, July 20, the surgeons would go into combat with their cutting weapons. The anaesthesia risk was accepted.

As her elder brother and next of kin, I had tried to digest this situation soberly and not give in to emotions. In this way, I could be more useful; any crying would come later. In my club of sporting seniors at Fontainebleau, several have stabilised cancers, some for five years or more. My friend André had a similar though much smaller soft tissue sarcoma removed from his upper arm. Today, two years later, he continues to play vigorous table tennis with me and he organises nature walks in the forest; but he returns to the hospital for yearly check-ups. Another friend, Gerard, has bone marrow cancer and after a terrible first six months he is surviving with chemotherapy and has resumed some of his sporting life, including swimming and cycling, weaker but still smiling. Hazel was in theory more fragile, but each cancer is different, and my sister is a fighter. I have not forgotten my late wife Colette's leukaemia and her sudden, tragic departure. We seniors see a lot of cancer. It's like a dark cavern, with long corridors and short ones, but most leading to oblivion.

The day before surgery, a member of the surgical team came to explain things to the family: Hazel, Peter C, Mylène, and me. This was my first contact with the Marsden hierarchy. Naïvely, I had thought surgery meant getting rid of Hazel's sarcoma, curing the patient, with just a little cleaning up to do afterwards, perhaps chemotherapy. The cancer specialist explained something different. There were already cancer nodules in Hazel's lungs, so there was no question of eliminating the disease. The objective was to relieve Hazel's pain, not to cure her; it's called palliative care.

From then on, I stepped up the frequency of my phone calls to Peter C; not every three days but every night to share the latest news, initially from Hatfield and later from Avon after our return to France. He saw Hazel every day, usually from lunchtime to dinner. My initial motivation was to exchange information I could pass on, but I realised Peter was rendering indispensable support to his companion Hazel that no one else could, and he, too, needed support and guidance. I had learned years earlier from my mother's descent into dementia that carers under stress also need much care.

The day after surgery, I understood by phoning the hospital that a family visit would not be productive, so Peter stayed home in Bayswater and we at Hatfield. The next day, medical security in the postoperative ward was the tightest I have ever seen. There was a nurse at Hazel's bedside every minute, monitoring vital signs. Family visitors like us were covered in protective plastic and advised not to touch the patient. A few kisses got through security! Apparently, the operation had gone well—the surgeons had removed 3.5 kilograms of sarcoma, the weight of a large baby. Now for the complications: infections, blood imbalance, fever, swellings. Hazel could neither talk nor move but we imagined she recognised and took comfort in her visitors. She was in post-op for five days, and on the weekend my children, Cyril and Chloé, came to London for a one-day visit. Hazel was in considerable pain and the effect of the powerful morphine painkillers was to make her sleep much of the day and also to hallucinate. Later, she hardly remembered anything of her first postoperative month at Marsden.

Back in her convalescence ward on the eight floor a week later, we visited Marsden most days, and Peter C went every day. Mylène took pictures of me with Hazel, and we took Peter to the pub afterwards. In early August, about two weeks after the operation, there was a formal meeting with the surgical team, the palliative team, the oncologists, and the family. The chief surgeon gave a positive view of the operation, given the exceptional size of the sarcoma. It was gone, and with it the hamstring muscles and tendons. No life-threatening infections had been detected, and no metastasis to internal organs, excepting the lung nodules detected early on. When asked about Hazel's swollen arm, he claimed this was due to a temporary blood problem. The palliative team reminded us that the immediate objective was pain relief, not cure, and any further treatment depended on the oncologists. More radiotherapy could be ruled out, immunotherapy was useless for this type of cancer, and Hazel was probably too weak for chemotherapy. When we asked for a prognosis, the palliative team replied that if the lung nodules did not grow and the cancer stabilised, a year or so of life was possible. A lot would depend on the body's recovery during the three months following the operation. It seemed like a long time.

In mid-August, Mylène and I returned to Avon and reunited the grandchildren with their parents. Our lawn in Avon had grown like a jungle and I mowed it twice. After the second mowing, the grass tops looked pale yellow in places and Mylène complained that I had cut too deep.

"Just wait," I said, "it'll grow back." And sure enough, a week later it was green again. Grass is so resilient—with humans it can take a lot longer.

The second month did not go very well. Hazel had infection after infection, some linked to her blood, some to urinary problems. Her left arm remained swollen to twice its normal size for weeks and she suffered fevers and tachycardia regularly. Sometimes she would sleep for the entire day and eat very little, until the nurses forced energy drinks on her. Her head remained frozen in a left-leaning position; her hands immobile. During all this time, Hazel never voluntarily complained of pain; the nurses had to drag it out of her each day: "How badly does it hurt, out of ten?"

"Oh, eight now, this morning nine."

Near the end of August my brother Peter (not to be confused with Hazel's companion Peter C) came from the USA to visit Hazel and I crossed the channel to meet him for a day, a happy if sombre reunion. To his disappointment, it was not until the third day of his visit when Hazel seemed to recognise him. Her speech was incomprehensible most of the time.

During my brother's stay, there was a second round-table meeting with the Marsden doctors, minus the surgeons. The subject was under what conditions Hazel could be discharged. Visitors like us have only to take in the panoramic view of London from the visitors' day room to understand that care at Marsden costs the NHS perhaps ten thousand pounds per day. Once the current infections and low blood protein were cured the palliative team were prepared to work towards refitting Hazel's flat with an appropriate hospital bed and to request round-the-clock nursing care at home. Looking at Hazel, asleep and unresponsive during this meeting, my brother, a research physicist, questioned the practicality of our sister's return to her flat soon.

"Will she ever be able to stand up again?" we asked the palliative team.

"Well, her right leg has not been altered, and the affected leg has only lost the kicking muscles. She won't walk, but with enough physio she *might* eventually be able to stand up and grip onto something."

I remembered Hazel's past trials: as a baby, some doctors said she would never walk, but she did so at age four. After a complex cervical replacement operation at age sixty, it was again forecast she'd never walk again, but she did so six months later. Would it now be a case of three times lucky, or three strikes and you're out?

Hazel's companion was more optimistic and agreed to have a Marsden equipment specialist look at their Bayswater flat. The Marsden strategy was that NHS financing, if possible, had to be arranged a long way in advance. An hour after the meeting on August 23 we were given a well-written, typed summary. My brother returned to the USA the next day, and I returned to France, tired, in the early hours of the morning.

My thoughts were in turmoil while travelling in the Eurostar. I knew what would happen to my sister, but not when—a few weeks, a month, at most a year. I would save my regrets for later. I tried to stop thinking of my sister and to make sense of cancer's effects in my seniors' universe in Fontainebleau. We are all in our last decades of life. I suddenly saw us like fruit on a tree, ripening at different speeds. Every so often, the deathly farmer would come by and pluck whoever was ripe. The frequency of loss of our contemporaries has become existentially disturbing, with cancer a leading cause. About thirty or forty years ago, our grandparents departed. Today they seem mythical, an adventure story to tell the next generation, upbeat or downbeat depending on our memories. Not so with our parents' death: it's still too fresh at a mere five or ten years of distance. We remember the farewells, the sadness, the void they left. My wife Colette's departure from leukaemia was the biggest shock of my life. Now it is the turn of our friends and siblings. My sister, to start with. Despite good sporting activity, in our club of four hundred we have two or three funerals per year. Counting family and other friends, every few months we lose someone. Those of us who reach our nineties will lose nearly all their contemporaries—if we can still count! Why them and not us?

What will we leave behind? Our financial legacy will disperse quickly and be forgotten; our writings and images may last a little longer. Mostly, I like to think about what we have planted.

I got back home very late, but the next day I looked out of my bedroom window again. Many of our senior friends in Avon seem to have well-tended gardens, ours being one of the more modest. I again found reassurance in the deep green grass. But this is not my only emotional investment in growing things.

I had my six-year-old grandson to stay for a weekend in late August. I loved the way he took to the lawn: the mower, the weed-cutter, the leaf blower, the weed burner. He was amazed by the forest around Avon, full of curiosity about the plants, the seeds, and he brought a chemistry set to challenge me. Both Mylène and I have planted two generations of vigorous descendants, and like the grass, these new generations keep on growing. Mylène already has ten grandchildren. My vision of the ripening fruit and the deathly farmer is perhaps misleading—an elderly or "ripe" human fruit may still have some strength to resist, taking force from the new growths. But what about those, like my sister, who have no children? Can't they take comfort in a wider field of grass than their own patch?

In early September Peter advised me that Hazel's speech had not returned to normal, and when she did talk it was often incoherent. "Gaga!" was Peter's word. Nevertheless, the most dangerous infections seemed to be over, and so Marsden, thinking Hazel strong enough, transferred her to the Alexandra Rehabilitation Home, in north Kensington, where she could get more intensive physio care. This was in line with Hazel's request and Marsden's ambition that one day she might return to her rehabilitated flat in Bayswater.

The illusion of recovery didn't last long. She had been in the Alexandra Home only three days when Peter phoned me. Normally, I phone him and not the other way around. Something was wrong. It was late evening and I was driving so I couldn't take the call at once.

"What's up, Peter?" I asked when I could call back.

"Hazel had a respiratory crisis. She's been taken to the emergency room at St. Mary's Hospital. I'm there now. I'll stay all night if necessary."

I volunteered to call back at midnight and advised him to find a seat where he could sleep, or else go home and return next morning. At midnight, Peter was still waiting. St. Mary's is a large, general-purpose hospital and the accident and emergency room is always full. St. Mary's doctors were the ones who first diagnosed Hazel's cancer but didn't have the surgical expertise to remove it. Later the same night, they decided the crackling sounds in Hazel's chest indicated an infection and admitted her as a patient. Peter returned to Bayswater the next morning, exhausted. Then, St. Mary's advised that Hazel showed signs of fever and tachycardia. No return to the Alexandra Home would be possible for some time until her problems were cleared up.

Marsden had been too optimistic. My other brother Noel came from the USA to visit Hazel near the end of September, and I booked myself into his hotel for two days. With all the other negative events happening, one positive was to be able to meet with my brothers; we hadn't seen each other for years. I had lunch with Noel, and we exchanged news of our children, and wondered what arrangements to make if Hazel died. St. Mary's hospital is near Paddington, and within walking distance of our hotel. On arrival at the twelfth floor, I found Hazel in a distracted state, wide-eyed and breathing heavily.

"When is Mum coming to visit me?" she asked.

"Sister dear, our mother died four years ago. Remember? You wanted to attend her funeral in the Caribbean but it wasn't possible. However, the tombstone you bought for her is well in place. You've been dreaming, but don't worry, your brothers are here to see you."

She relaxed and we were able to talk in bits and pieces, Hazel's speech being particularly difficult to grasp. I left the room to request a meeting with the palliative staff of St. Mary's. An hour later, a female palliative doctor took Noel and me into a small conference room to explain things.

"How much have you been told?" she asked.

"Not much—what is the state of Hazel's lungs and where do we go from here?" I said.

"She has had pneumonia, partly because of her weakness. She has partially lost control of several body functions, including speech and swallowing. Some solid food particles got into her lungs instead of her stomach. This irritation caused a rattling cough and then pneumonia; her asthmatic tendency doesn't help. She was weak to start with, you see, and every day in bed costs up to 5 percent of her remaining muscle strength. She's been lying in bed for two months and her rigidity is getting worse; she's lost a lot of weight. She also has a new urinary infection."

Our faces must have shown some dismay because the palliative specialist paused and looked at Noel and myself soberly before continuing.

"However, after a week of antibiotics here your sister no longer needs emergency treatment. The tachycardia and pneumonia symptoms have gone and with an all-liquid food diet she won't choke again. We've prepared a further antibiotic treatment for two weeks and with this she can leave this hospital and go back to a nursing home."

"Is that meant to be positive?"

"Well, it's not all. We've done a new CT scan of her lungs and the cancer nodules we first detected in May are still there, maybe more developed."

"Maybe?"

"Progressing."

"What is your prognosis? Marsden talked about a year, maybe longer."

"Sorry, we think that given her current state and the sequence of postoperative complications, survival is a matter of weeks, three or four months at most."

"What's to be done if she leaves the hospital?"

"In our opinion, there's no way she can return to her flat as Marsden recommended, not ever. She's going to need continual nursing—too expensive, impossible, in a cluttered flat."

"Back to the Alexandra home, then?"

"No, we don't think rehab stands much of a chance either. But the Princess Louise Nursing Home next door has palliative facilities for the last stages of life. On our recommendation, they have a room for her."

"And what about the 'Do Not Resuscitate' business?"

"All parties have agreed that, no, we won't resuscitate if her heart stops."

"Not me! I said yes, please resuscitate, and I'm next of kin."

"I respect your point of view, but Hazel herself understood the question and replied no. Please understand, the doctor in charge has the last word, anyway. You wouldn't want a long-term vegetative sister, would you?"

In view of the divergent prognoses between hospitals, my brother Noel, a research chemist, asked a last question: "But why is Hazel going downhill like this, so fast? It's now two months since the surgery in July. Could the infections, pneumonia, and so on be simply her body's weakness caused by such a massive shock, or is it a new aggression from the sarcoma cancer?"

"There's no answer to that."

"And when will she be moved to Princess Louise?"

"Tomorrow."

Noel looked at me with the hint of a smile but I didn't react at the time. Afterwards, thinking of the next phase in Hazel's adventures, I recalled our childhood thrills in the Caribbean: Hazel, Peter, Noel, and myself—all the crazy things we had done together or alone; my sister getting injured by my missiles and explosives; Noel almost getting drowned in the channel between St. Kitts and Nevis; my brother Peter and I escaping broken bones from night-time cycling crashes. But there had always been a new chapter, something to joke about later. And now?

The next day, an ambulance took Hazel and her bedside belongings from St. Mary's to the Princess Louise Nursing Home in North Kensington. Noel and I followed by taxi, and Peter C arrived later.

Princess Louise was a breath of fresh air. Wooden floors, walls with pictures, a pleasant day room with dining tables, no more plastic gloves and aprons, no more frenzied white-gowned personnel. The sedate nursing staff was mostly from the Caribbean, and when I told the senior nurse, Rachel, that Hazel had studied in Jamaica, it turned out she had been born there. We introduced ourselves, Noel and Christopher, and Rachel laughed.

"Why, I have a son called Noel and a nephew called Christopher! Please feel right at home!"

Noel returned to the USA, and I to France, but we weren't Hazel's only visitors. Our English relatives, Jan and Stephen, John and Christine, and Elizabeth went to Princess Louise, and friends Felix and Jenny, care-giver Phoebe, and my son Cyril. Caribbean friends like

Rosemary, Jean and Carolyn kept up to date. Those who cared for Hazel naturally preferred the nursing home environment, but what did Hazel think?

I made a new one-day visit to London in mid-October—very tiring —from dawn till midnight. If my sister was going to spend whatever time remained for her in the Princess Louise Nursing Home and never return to her flat, what could I do to make things easier? If her intelligence resurfaced, she would surely want to communicate with the outside world at some point. Her time in Bayswater had been divided between her PC and her TV set. Princess Louise provided a TV set, but perhaps I could provide her with an Internet linkage? Trying to install her PC in the nursing home would be a last resort. For the moment, she was spending most of the time in bed with an hour or two per day in her wheelchair. I investigated tablets for her, but since her fingers weren't capable of any very precise movements, a Windows interface with a keyboard seemed best. After much research, I bought a Chinese model for her. Next, I had to find out whether Princess Louise offered a WIFI linkage; Peter took five days to confirm this possibility. I was then ready to experiment.

I arrived before Peter, who had a morning medical appointment, signed the visitor book, and went to Hazel's room. Along her corridor, all the doors were open and all the residents were immobile in their beds; few lights were on. Hazel was in an armchair on wheels. Expecting a welcome, I got shouted at.

"Chris! I'm so bored! When am I going to go home?"

Taken aback by her anger, I nevertheless noticed how much better her elocution was compared with her torpor in St. Mary's or Marsden, about as good as it had ever been.

"Sorry, sister, but you can't go back to Bayswater. It takes two nurses and a hoist to get you into that chair or into the bathroom. The NHS won't provide this, and your apartment can't be easily renovated —it's impossible for you."

"I'll pay for all the nurses necessary!"

"Take it from me, your brother, it won't work. I'm here to help you to make the best of this place. It's surely more pleasant than a hospital room."

"No! I preferred the hospital!"

"Here, I've brought something for you. You once said you'd like to try a tablet."

This calmed her down and I realised her combativeness had returned but not yet her memory and practical sense. There was no way she could pay for full-time nursing in her flat.

Step by step. Peter had told me now she could hold a cup and drink from it. If we have the will, things mental and physical can grow back. Like the grass.

We spent the afternoon working on her tablet. She couldn't use the touch controls—her fingers wouldn't obey—but she reacquainted herself with Windows 10. We connected to the WIFI server of the nursing home, and then downloaded her Amazon Kindle books. She has over three hundred of them! We also downloaded Skype but it seemed blocked. Peter C had arrived by this time and we tried to open Hazel's Gmail. However, the password was irrecoverable, so we created a new Gmail account. Problems can be fun, and by the time I left, Hazel had forgotten her gripes.

Following my visit, I continued to phone Peter every evening, and he reported that control of her finger movements had improved. He set up a lectern so she could use a tablet or Kindle more easily in bed or in her chair. She began eating with a spoon or fork, though Peter still had to cut up the food, and she no longer complained of boredom. The nursing home provided food for Hazel's companion at lunchtime, and Hazel spurned her nursing home purées and instead stole Peter's fish and chips; soon, thereafter, she would have her own solid food. For my next visit, I got her a larger tablet, a wireless mouse with a trackball, and a wireless keyboard, as she had in her flat. She could already use a phone again. We badgered the nursing home for her to get physiotherapy training twice a week; the therapist tried to include Peter C in the group. The objective was to revitalise Hazel's leg muscles so that—one day—she might stand again, even for a few seconds. Hazel practiced the exercises by herself each morning. I thought of her when I did my own pre-breakfast gymnastics in Avon. Growth means moving forwards, whatever the handicap or menace, and my sister showed how a handicapped over-seventy, still with cancer nodules in her lungs, could believe in the future.

One thing continued to bother me. When the pessimists from St. Mary's sent Hazel to Princess Louise, they chose the ward for last-gasp patients, those who only have a short time left to live, many with dementia. It seemed justified at the time. But now, given her improvements, Hazel might be there for longer than forecast, perhaps a lot longer. There was no one else lucid in her ward, and no conversation was possible with neighbours. I told Peter C this regretfully, and he laughed.

"Yes, it's true, all the others are gaga. This means Hazel is the only resident to whom the nurses can talk. She's become their darling!"

Hazel's determination returned, full force, and she wanted out. She wrote to me in January of 2017 saying, "I don't feel old: I care about having no mental variety, challenge, society, work, action."

∽

IT WAS HER LAST LETTER. On March 7, her lungs suddenly gave way, and on March 16 fifteen of her family and friends who loved her dearly gathered in a quiet room in the Kensal Green cemetery to pay homage to her. Present were her companion Peter Cator; her English family—the Garretts; my daughter Chloé and I; friends from the Caribbean; and several managers from the British Council Association where she had worked.

It was a civil ceremony. We read eulogies to her, and both my daughter Chloé and I could not stop the current of tears trying to punctuate our words. Most of us were older than Hazel—a young seventy-two—and had hoped to love her for many more years. But we would make her example live on in our minds and the minds of all her nephews and nieces.

Then Hazel was cremated.

∽

HEALING CANNOT BE INSTANTANEOUS, and it took me three months.

During that time, I settled all of Hazel's affairs, then took a fortnight off at Tenerife to help to calm the gloom. Returning to London, I cleared out her apartment, helped her companion move to his own place, and finally, at the start of June, went to Belle Ile in Brittany with Mylène to begin my seventy-fifth year of life. On the last day of a week of intensive hiking along the sunny coast, uphill and downhill, after fifteen tough kilometres, suddenly I felt renewed, as if I could continue for many more hours, days, and years.

When Hazel's ashes were buried in August, it was a moment of family fraternity rather than sadness. Thank you, Hazel, for having set us an example, to accept oneself, and to keep learning up to the end.

ABOUT CHRISTOPHER VANIER

Born on the island of St. Kitts, at the age of seventeen Christopher Vanier won a Caribbean-wide literary prize organised by the USA to commemorate Abraham Lincoln's 150th anniversary. He thought himself destined to be a writer, but a scholarship from Cambridge University made him opt instead for science. Ten years later, he began an engineering and information technology career in France, lasting until his retirement thirty-five years later. Returning to writing, he published his first memoir book in 2009, *Caribbean Chemistry*, on the identity problems of youth. He left Paris for Fontainebleau after the death of his wife, and dedicated this second memoir, *On the Run in Fontainebleau*, to navigating the perils of retirement.

Made in the USA
Middletown, DE
27 August 2019